Economic Discrimination and Political Exchange

WORLD POLITICAL ECONOMY IN THE 1930s AND 1980s

Kenneth A. Oye

PRINCETON UNIVERSITY PRESS

PRINCETON, NEW JERSEY

Library of Congress Cataloging-in-Publication Data

Oye, Kenneth A., 1949–
Economic discrimination and political exchange : world political
economy in the 1930s and 1980s / Kenneth A. Oye.
p.   cm.—(Princeton studies in international history and politics)
Includes bibliographical references (p.   ) and index.
1. Tariff preferences.   2. Commercial policy.
3. Depressions—1929.   4. International economic relations.
5. Economic history—1918–1945.   6. Economic history—1945–1971.
I. Title.   II. Series.
HF1721.O96   1992   382′.3—dc20   91-41019

ISBN: 0-691-07849-1

This book has been composed in Linotron Baskerville

Economic Discrimination and Political Exchange

_____

CONTENTS

PART V: *Conclusion*

LIST OF FIGURES AND TABLES

PREFACE

A SENIOR political economist once offered me a bit of advice: "Never qualify any position.[1] Any properly qualified position is an uncontroversial position. Academics love controversy." I am ignoring his suggestion. Because this book has policy implications, the caveats should be considered as carefully as the main line of argument.

This study suggests that unrestricted bargaining and economic openness are far more complementary than conventional wisdom implies. It offers a general defense of bilateralism and regionalism and presents specific illustrations of liberalizing economic discrimination. It offers a general defense of the practice of coupling commercial, financial, and monetary issues and provides examples of liberalizing applications of linkage strategies. However, my position is qualified.

Economic discrimination and political exchange are a management mode of last resort. If institutionalized rules succeed in expanding openness, stabilizing multilateral international financial orders, and maintaining fresh lending, then unrestricted bargaining has little to offer. If a benign hegemon stands ready to serve as a lender of last resort, a market for distress goods, and a stabilizer of international monetary order, then bilateral and regional discrimination will obstruct international flows of goods and capital and may well reduce overall levels of economic growth.

Unfortunately, both of these conventional modes of management are prone to failure. During the 1930s, the collapse of international commercial and financial affairs was catastrophic. Explicitly discriminatory bilateral and regional bargaining was pervasive. During the 1980s, institutionalized multilateral negotiations have succeeded in some areas and failed in others. Tariffs on manufactured goods remain at historical lows and major financial centers were insulated from the debt crisis in the periphery. However, nontariff barriers are rising, barriers to agricultural imports remain substantial, and debt/export ratios of Third World states have continued to increase. Economic discrimination has played and will play a significant role in addressing these unresolved problems. Unrestricted bargaining is a natural response to the failures of regimes and hegemonic leadership. No more. And no less.

[1] . . . except in qualifying footnotes.

I acknowledge with gratitude the advice of an extraordinary group of colleagues, graduate students, and undergraduate students who have commented on portions of this book. Two anonymous readers for Princeton University Press offered extremely useful suggestions on both presentation and substance. Diane Kunz, Brad Lee, Stephen Schuker, and Mark Trachtenberg scrutinized the historical chapters for a May 1989 American Academy of Arts and Sciences interdisciplinary workshop. Robert Gilpin, Robert Jervis, and Robert Keohane read the penultimate version of the manuscript in its entirety. I appreciate the time and the attention that these nine scholars devoted to this study. Of course, any historical errors or theoretical flaws that remain are the responsibility of the author.

This book was made possible by the financial support of a Pew Trust grant for research on economics and security, by the institutional support of the Center of International Studies at Princeton University and its director, Henry Bienen, and by the hospitality of the Departments of Political Science at the University of Pennsylvania and Swarthmore College. Karen Alter, Barry Cohen, and Byoung-Joo Kim served as cite checkers and indexers. Finally, Malcolm DeBevoise, Walter Lippincott, Sandy Thatcher, and Gail Ullman of Princeton University Press shepherded this project through the transition from manuscript to book with their customary professionalism.

PART I

Introduction

Chapter One

THE ECONOMIC STATE OF NATURE REVISITED

UNRESTRICTED BARGAINING AND

ECONOMIC ORDER

THIS BOOK offers a qualified defense of unrestricted bargaining as a form of international economic management. To write of ad hoc bargaining as a mode of management may seem oxymoronic. Unrestricted bargaining is inextricably associated with practices that are commonly viewed as pernicious. It engenders economic discrimination as nations turn toward bilateralism and regionalism to extract concessions from negotiating partners. It breaks down orderly distinctions between issues as nations couple unrelated problems to increase leverage. In fact, ad hoc bargaining erodes respect for nondiscriminatory rules and undermines functionally defined international regimes. Yet, at times, these seemingly destructive practices can promote rather than preclude realization of mutual economic interests.

At an abstract level, this book is an inquiry into the economic state of nature. Unrestricted bargaining is a reference point defined by the absence of order. Like their namesakes, modern Grotians and Hobbesians imagine a world without rules or rulers to legitimate their conceptions of governance. Proponents of economic regimes and of hegemonic order use the economic state of nature as a common benchmark.[1] This study resurveys the reference point. It uses elementary microeconomic methods to identify conditions under which ad hoc bargaining can and cannot perform as a reasonably efficient mode of political management. It also offers a revisionist interpretation of the most recent period of unrestricted bargaining—the 1930s. Conventional wisdom holds that decentralized bargaining was the principal cause of global economic disaster during the interwar years. By contrast, this study suggests that ad hoc bargaining slowed and ultimately reversed movement toward economic closure.

[1] Although their conceptions of appropriate management differ, Robert Keohane and Charles Kindleberger concur on the deficiencies of unrestricted bargaining. See Robert O. Keohane, *After Hegemony: Cooperation and Discord in the World Political Economy* (Princeton, N.J.: Princeton University Press, 1984), cited hereafter as *After Hegemony*; and Charles P. Kindleberger, *The World in Depression, 1929–1939*, rev. ed. (Berkeley: University of California Press, 1986).

At a more pragmatic level, this book evaluates the potential role of economic discrimination and political exchange in contemporary foreign economic policy. With few exceptions, political economists contend that discriminatory foreign economic policies yield outcomes that are inefficient at best and catastrophic at worst.[2] Political economists divide over whether the practice of joining substantively unrelated issues impedes or facilitates economic diplomacy.[3] This study suggests that ad hoc bargaining has played a pivotal role in lowering barriers to trade and in drawing third parties into trade negotiations, and may come to play a significant role in restoring international lending in the aftermath of the Third World debt crisis. In fact, the most significant examples of commercial liberalization in the past decade have been achieved through bilateral and regional bargaining. Although unrestricted bargaining and economic closure are commonly equated, this study proposes that economic discrimination and political exchange can promote economic openness.

THEORY AND RESEARCH DESIGN

An elemental tension between rule-based and bargaining-based modes of economic management is at the core of these abstract and pragmatic controversies. Political bargaining generally entails economic discrimination. To confer benefits or impose costs on negotiating partners, nations offer access to markets, repayment of loans, access to credits, and conversion of currencies to some nations at the expense of others. By contrast, management by rules entails impartiality and generality. Nations cannot selectively comply with a rule while fostering respect for a rule by other nations. Substantive rules limit the scope of bargaining, while bargaining erodes compliance with substantive rules. The content of most international economic

[2] For works against discrimination, see William R. Cline, *Reciprocity: A New Approach to World Trade Policy* (Washington, D.C.: Institute of International Economics, 1982); and Richard Pomfret, *Unequal Trade: The Economics of Discriminatory International Trade Policies* (London: Basil Blackwell, 1988). For a work defending discrimination, see Carolyn Rhodes, "Reciprocity in Trade: The Utility of a Bargaining Strategy," *International Organization* 43, no. 2 (Spring 1989).

[3] See Robert D. Tollison and Thomas D. Willett, "An Economic Theory of Mutually Advantageous Issue Linkages in International Negotiations," *International Organization* 33 (Autumn 1979); James Sebenius, "Negotiation Arithmetic," *International Organization* (Spring 1983); McGinnis, "Issue Linkage and the Evolution of International Cooperation," *Journal of Conflict Resolution* (March 1986); and James Alt and Barry Eichengreen, "Simultaneous and Overlapping Games" (Paper delivered at NBER Conference on Political Economy of International Macroeconomic Coordination, Andover, Mass., November 6–7, 1987).

regimes is shaped by this fundamental tension. Regimes typically consist of primary rules proscribing impediments to economic exchange and secondary rules limiting political exchange. This tension is accentuated by a second attribute of unrestricted bargaining. Ad hoc bargaining often spans issues as nations couple commercial, financial, and monetary problems or join economic and security concerns to confer benefits or impose costs on negotiating partners. International regimes are typically organized along functional lines. Regimes may facilitate side payments *within* issue areas,[4] but discourage linkages *between* issue areas. For these reasons, rule-based and bargaining-based modes of international economic management cannot readily coexist. This tension defines pragmatic debates over the effects of economic discrimination and political exchange on economic openness as well as abstract scholarly controversies over the quality of life in the economic state of nature.

The principal purpose of this study is to probe the strengths and weaknesses of rule-based and bargaining-based modes of management. How do economic discrimination and political exchange affect the openness of immediate parties to negotiation and of the international economic system taken as a whole? Stripped of most caveats and qualifications, the central line of argument reduces to the following points.

First, economic discrimination generally has liberalizing effects on the *immediate* parties to a preferential commercial or financial agreement. By facilitating political exchange, economic discrimination may facilitate the negotiation of bilateral and regional zones of openness. By intent and in effect, discriminatory international bargaining strategies may promote international economic liberalization by offsetting, at least in part, domestic biases toward closure. In the absence of economic discrimination, import competing sectors have a clear particularistic interest in lobbying for protection, while export-oriented sectors have a more diffuse interest in lobbying against protection. Conventional Olsonian biases toward overrepresentation of concentrated interests and underrepresentation of diffuse interests are manifested in a tilt toward protection. If market access is explicitly tied to market access, export-oriented interests develop a narrow interest in lobbying against protection. For these reasons, discrimination may increase economic openness between bilateral or regional negotiating partners. The liberalizing effects of discrimination on the

[4] For discussion of how regimes encourage side payments within issue areas, see Vinod K. Aggarwal on "nesting" in his *Liberal Protectionism: The International Politics of Organized Textile Trade* (Berkeley: University of California Press, 1985).

principals to negotiations are strongest when domestic biases toward closure are significant. However, the effects of economic discrimination extend well beyond immediate parties to negotiations. Conclusions on whether discrimination will increase or decrease systemic openness hinge on the direct and indirect effects of discrimination on others.

Second, economic discrimination in favor of the principal parties to an agreement is generally at the expense of third parties. An importer may favor one exporter at the expense of other exporters and a debtor may favor one creditor at the expense of other creditors. In fact, Most Favored Nation (MFN) clauses in trade agreements and cross default clauses in lending agreements exist precisely to minimize such negative third-party externalities by proscribing discrimination. Yet, as the historical and contemporary chapters of this book suggest, negotiators rely on a remarkable array of techniques to exclude third parties from the effective benefits of concessions granted to parties to agreements. Where effective discrimination exists, liberalization between the parties to a bilateral or regional agreement generally comes at the expense of others. The gains from liberalization between the principals are offset, in whole or in part, by losses imposed on others. As a consequence, conventional wisdom holds that effects of economic discrimination on global openness are at best indeterminant and at worst negative. However, the effects of economic discrimination and political exchange on levels of openness are not confined to immediate costs and benefits to principal parties and third parties.

Third, discrimination can have *inadvertent* liberalizing consequences on global movements of goods and capital by creating a strong incentive for third parties to enter into discriminatory negotiations. As noted previously, preferential bilateral or regional agreements come at the expense of third parties. Third parties do not sit idly and accept the loss of markets for goods or capital. They turn to economic discrimination and political exchange to defend their economic position. The effects of economic discrimination on systemic openness will hinge on the extent of openness or closure of the international economic system prior to the proliferation of discriminatory practices. As discriminatory practices spread through an international economic environment, nations pursuing nondiscriminatory economic strategies—whether liberal or illiberal—operate at an increasing disadvantage. If an international economic order is open, then the spread of discriminatory economic practices will impede movements of goods and capital. However, if substantial barriers to the movement of goods and capital exist, then economic discrimination and political exchange may generate self-sustaining movement toward systemic openness by encouraging all parties to negotiate. These indirect and long-term effects of discriminatory economic practices on global openness are a focus of my studies on the 1930s and the 1980s.

The general argument on the merits of economic discrimination and political exchange presented earlier must be qualified. Although the benefits of unrestricted bargaining are underrecognized by academic political economists, if not by practicing commercial and financial negotiators, this book places explicit limitations on the case for ad hoc bargaining. The qualifications are as important as the central argument. The theoretical chapters in this volume identify the conditions under which economic discrimination and political exchange will and will not function as an effective mode of management. The merits of unrestricted bargaining relative to institutionalized systems of rules are not constant.

To evaluate bargaining-based and rule-based modes of management, I begin by defining the problem of management in terms of the internalization of policy externalities. Because the effects of commercial, financial, fiscal, and monetary policies extend beyond national boundaries, nations struggle to induce others to take account of policy externalities. Coasians contend that unrestricted bargaining will generate politically (if not economically) efficient outcomes.[5] By contrast, international regimes theorists reason that public goods problems, transaction costs, and imperfect information degrade the efficiency of unrestrained bargaining.[6] In their view, international regimes facilitate realization of mutual interests by mitigating these sources of political market failure. This study suggests that the efficiency of unrestricted bargaining will hinge on the following factors.

First, the public, private, or divertable character of policy externalities affects the efficiency of unrestricted bargaining. After reviewing more or less standard points on the distinction between externalities with the properties of public and private goods, the study presents a third class of externality. It examines the effects of privatizable or divertable externalities on the efficiency of political exchange and on the nature and pace of discriminatory bargaining. These issues are

[5] See Ronald Coase, "The Problem of Social Cost," *Journal of Law and Economics* 3 (Autumn 1960). For an application of Coase to international relations, see John A. C. Conybeare, "International Organization and the Theory of Property Rights," *International Organization* 34 (Summer 1980).

[6] See Keohane, *After Hegemony*; and Stephen D. Krasner, ed., *International Regimes* (Ithaca, N.Y.: Cornell University Press, 1983).

discussed in Chapter Two, "The Management of Spillover Effects: Public, Private, and Divertable Externalities."

Second, unrestricted bargaining encompasses more political exchange. Nations may extort, exchange, or explain within single issue areas and across issues. Because the welfare implications of these forms of contingent action vary substantially, one cannot analyze the efficiency of *ad hoc* bargaining without accounting for their incidence. The study analyzes the incidence of these forms of contingent action under complete and incomplete information conditions, and suggests that actors are likely to rely far more heavily on exchange and explanation than on extortion. These issues are discussed in Chapter Three, "The Logic of Contingent Action: Exchange, Extortion, and Explanation."

Third, conventional Olsonian biases in the representation of diffuse and concentrated domestic interests tilt nations toward undervaluing both economic openness and reputations for making good on commitments, whereas shifts in economic beliefs can produce radical changes in policy preferences. When domestic biases exist, external bargaining processes may influence internal preference formation. Specifically, bilateral discrimination may concentrate formerly diffuse interests within negotiating partners and thereby partially offset biases toward protection.[7] These issues are discussed in Chapter Four, "The Concept of Preference: Bias and Instability in the Valuation of Outcomes."

The logic behind my selection of the 1930s and the 1980s as the subject of empirical studies is straightforward. The two periods differ markedly in terms of the distribution of international power and the content of international regimes. The three basic elements of the theory of unrestricted bargaining previously sketched are not driven by these variables, whereas competing theories of hegemonic stability and regimes hold that these variables are central. The dissimilarity of the periods permits me to set up something approaching a critical test.

The public, private, or privatizable character of international policy externalities are intrinsic attributes of issues. If the efficiency of unrestricted bargaining is in fact influenced by the characteristics of policy

---

[7] The literature on "endogenous protection" establishes the existence of substantial domestic biases toward protection. See Stephen P. Magee and Leslie Young, "Endogenous Protection in the United States, 1900–1984," in *U.S. Trade Policies in a Changing World Economy*, ed., Robert M. Stern (Cambridge: MIT Press, 1987), 146–47. For an explanation of biases toward protection drawing on both economic and institutionalist perspectives, see Robert E. Baldwin, *The Political Economy of U.S. Import Policy* (Cambridge: MIT Press, 1985).

externalities, then regularities in the management of public macroeconomic externalities and in the management of divertable commercial and financial externalities should carry across both periods.

The tendency of actors to favor exchange and explanation and shy away from extortion follows from conventional assumptions of rational choice theory. The argument hinges on attributes of actors and the quality of information on adversarial intentions. If the argument is valid, then extortion should be uncommon in both periods.

The effects of discriminatory international bargaining on domestic preference formation follow from conventional Olsonian analysis as extended by theorists of endogenous protection. If the argument is correct, then bilateralism and regionalism should have liberalizing effects in situations where domestic biases toward protection are strong during both periods.

In truth, this logic is something of a post hoc rationalization. Because the theories and case studies developed together, the evidence presented on the 1930s and 1980s cannot be said to comprise an independent test of the theory. Every original element of the theory was spurred by an observation at variance with an earlier version of the theory while the evolving theory structured my search for evidence on these periods. A truly independent test must wait until the 1990s.

Depression and Discrimination: Evidence from the 1930s

Charles Kindleberger and others hold that decentralized bargaining was an important cause of global economic disaster. By contrast, this study submits that unrestricted bargaining slowed and ultimately reversed movement toward economic closure. During the early 1930s, bilateralism and regionalism preserved zones of openness. During the middle and late 1930s, discriminatory bargaining was an important force for liberalization. These significant interpretative differences turn on an inferential issue. To isolate the effects of unrestricted bargaining on outcomes, the historical chapters take account of the effects of biased and unstable national preferences before examining international interaction.

To account for economic calamity during the 1930s, Kindleberger assigns a central role to inherent deficiencies of decentralized international political processes. In his view, the major industrial nations recognized, but could not realize, mutual economic interests in the absence of international leadership. Nations turned to myopic policies of commercial protection, financial closure, and competitive devaluation. In his words, "In advancing its own economic good by a tariff, currency depreciation, or foreign exchange control, a country may worsen the welfare of its partners by more than its own gain. Beggar-thy-neighbor tactics may lead to retaliation, so that each country ends up in a worse position from having pursued its own gain."[8] By contrast, this study finds that nations were able to realize mutual interests where mutual interests were recognized through ad hoc bargaining. Three basic findings emerge from the study of the depression.

First, commercial closure and monetary instability followed from dysfunctional economic beliefs rather than dysfunctions of international bargaining processes. For example, the First New Deal was premised on the belief that raising domestic prices through production restraints and gold purchasing would promote recovery. These assumptions effectively precluded trade liberalization and exchange rate stabilization. Changes in macroeconomic beliefs and in associated domestic recovery programs were a precondition for international liberalization.

Second, unrestricted bargaining rediverted commerce and finance along bilateral, regional, and imperial lines without accelerating movement toward closure. All major industrial powers except for the United States exchanged market access for market access and bartered preferential debt servicing for preferential access to fresh credits. Inherently discriminatory single issue and cross issue bargaining preserved a degree of commercial and financial openness—albeit along bilateral, regional, and imperial lines.

Third, unrestricted bargaining ultimately encouraged movement toward liberalization. The spread of discriminatory financial practices, including preferential debt servicing, encouraged modest fresh lending after the multilateral financial system had collapsed. The compartmentalization of world trade increased the export shares of other major industrial powers at the expense of the United States. Their bilateral, regional, and imperial policies inadvertently mobilized American export-oriented interests. The American shift from the relatively nondiscriminatory protectionism of Smoot Hawley to the discriminatory liberalization of the Reciprocal Trade Agreements Act was an inadvertent consequence of the discriminations of other nations.

The organization of the study of the depression is a compromise between functional and chronological order. Chapter Five examines "The Politics of Trade Diversion: Commercial Relations in the

---

[8] See Kindleberger, *The World in Depression*, 10.

1930s," while Chapter Six analyzes "The Politics of Default and Depreciation: Financial and Monetary Relations in the 1930s." This division is imperfect. The economic effects of currency depreciation on trade, of export performance on capital movements, and of capital movements on currency depreciation cut across the lines of these chapters. Nations commonly constructed tactical linkages between market access and debt servicing, debt servicing and exchange rate policy, and exchange rate policy and market access. During the 1930s, commercial, financial, and monetary issues were joined by politics as well as economics.

PROSPERITY AND HYPOCRISY: EVIDENCE FROM THE 1980s

Fifty years ago, nations relied on overtly discriminatory practices to manage or mismanage international economic affairs. Today, nations profess respect for nondiscriminatory norms even as they engage in discriminatory practices. During the 1930s, discrimination was pervasive. Commercial, financial, and monetary relations were organized along bilateral, regional, and imperial lines. Today, the incidence of discrimination varies markedly across issues. Discriminatory practices are common in contemporary trade negotiations, uncommon in financial bargaining, and rare in macroeconomic discussions. If the 1930s were an economic state of nature, the 1980s may be characterized as a faintly corrupt civil society. De facto discrimination and de jure nondiscrimination coexist uneasily in a political economy of hypocrisy.

By historical standards, the contemporary international political economy is also relatively open. Restrictions on movements of goods and capital are low and falling and cross-national differentials in the price of goods and capital appear to have narrowed during the 1980s. Has the world economy continued to liberalize despite discrimination or because of discrimination? Will further reliance on discrimination lead toward openness or closure? The study of the 1980s suggests that the odd combination of nondiscriminatory norms and discriminatory actions may well be preferable to either pure nondiscrimination or pure discrimination. In practice, a weak prohibition on discrimination selects against socially disadvantageous discriminatory acts without selecting against socially advantageous discriminatory acts.

Trade during the 1980s was marked by increasing discrimination. During the 1970s, the growth of Voluntary Export Restraints (VERs) and Orderly Marketing Agreements (OMAs) left a legacy of quotas that are the focus of continuing bilateral negotiation. During the

1980s, Canadian-American, Japanese-American, and intra-European Community negotiations spawned new systems of tacit and explicit preferences. At present, over half of global imports enter on an other than MFN basis. In commercial affairs, nations may shift the costs of protection and the benefits of liberalization from trading partner to trading partner at will. The study of trade shows that commercial discrimination during the 1980s was trade expanding as well as trade diverting. Bilateral and regional bargaining enlarged domestic "anti-protectionist" coalitions and helped offset domestic biases toward protection. During the 1980s, economic discrimination was a force for commercial liberalization. These points are developed in Chapter Seven, "The Politics of Bilateral and Regional Openness: Commercial Relations in the 1980s."

In financial and monetary affairs, multilateral negotiations created the impression of successful crisis management, while unresolved fundamental problems reinforced movement toward regionalism and bilateralism. In financial affairs, a slow motion default was masked by endless rounds of rescheduling agreements and the Baker and Brady Plans. The illusion of cooperation helped insulate financial centers from crisis in the periphery. But developing country debt–export ratios doubled while new private lending remained negligible.[9] I suggest that movement toward preferential repayment and refinancing is likely and may in fact be a requisite of North-South financial reconstruction. In international monetary affairs, economic summitry, the 1985 Plaza Accord, and the 1987 Louvre Accord created the illusion of management in a period of wholesale monetary turbulence and in so doing may well have staved off more serious monetary disorder. However, nations seeking monetary stability in a period of exchange rate volatility turned toward regionalism. The emergence of nascent yen, dollar, and ECU blocs is a response to the intrinsic limits of macroeconomic coordination. These points are developed in Chapter Eight, "The Politics of Debt and Deficits: Financial and Macroeconomic Relations in the 1980s."

CONCLUSIONS

The study concludes by examining differences between the 1930s and 1980s. In so doing, it reinforces the case for optimism on the survival of an open economic order. I argue that contemporary analogies to the experience of the 1930s are based on two fundamental

[9] See Jeffrey Sachs, "Introduction," and Paul Krugman, "Private Capital Flows to Problem Debtors" in *Developing Country Debt and Economic Performance: The International Financial System*, ed. Jeffrey Sachs (Chicago: University of Chicago Press, 1989).

fallacies. Analysts often unconsciously transpose their preferences onto the decision makers of the period, and in so doing misinterpret the effects of international political process. Analysts also unconsciously impute modern economic knowledge to decision makers of the period, and in so doing downplay the role that extraordinarily inappropriate domestic economic policies played in intensifying the depression. If we project modern preferences and beliefs into the past, we develop invalid analogies between the past and the present—analogies that grossly understate the strength of forces for openness in contemporary international economic relations.

PART II

Toward a Theory of
Unrestricted Bargaining

Chapter Two

THE MANAGEMENT OF SPILLOVER EFFECTS

PUBLIC, PRIVATE, AND DIVERTABLE

EXTERNALITIES

PREVAILING WINDS, ocean currents, and economic markets do not respect national boundaries. Market forces transmit the effects of economic policies abroad as surely as natural forces carry pollution to neighboring states. Domestic macroeconomic and international commercial, financial, and exchange rate policies generate international externalities.[1] As a consequence, nations do not bear all of the costs or receive all of the benefits of their actions. In the absence of countervailing pressure from abroad, nations tend to undervalue negative and positive spillover effects. International political forces retransmit externalities back home, albeit with varying degrees of efficiency. The foreign victims and potential beneficiaries of spillover effects do not sit idly by. Through Coasian bilateral bribery, Grotian appeals to institutionalized rules, and Hobbesian hegemonic leadership, nations struggle to induce each other to take account of the broader ramifications of their actions. Their struggle is the subject of this chapter.

Most work on the management of international spillover effects is grounded on the conventional distinction between *private* and *public* externalities. Unfortunately, most spillover effects do not have the properties of either private or public goods. Political economists have addressed this problem by writing of externalities with "predominantly" private or "largely" public characteristics and then retelling the first and second versions of the parable of the factory and household(s) presented hereafter. The grey area is worthy of study in its own right. *Divertable* externalities, spillover effects that can be privatized by shifting them away from one country toward other countries, are pervasive in international commercial and financial affairs. As the third version of the parable suggests, features of commercial and financial bargaining that cannot be explained in terms of the conven-

---

[1] The problem of estimating the real sign, magnitude, and distribution of spillover effects falls within the province of international economics and is largely beyond the purview of this study. I do take account of controversies among international economists that affect the politics of externalities management.

tional private–public goods distinction are rational responses to the existence of divertable externalities.

Because the efficiency of managerial approaches varies markedly by class of spillover effect, this chapter is organized by type of externality rather than by mode of management.[2] The major sections treat private, public, and divertable externalities. For each class of externality, I assess the efficiency of unrestricted political exchange and then augment the analysis by considering hegemonic leadership and institutionalized rules insofar as they bear on the management of externalities of that type.[3]

PRIVATE EXTERNALITIES

Begin with a simple parable of life in the presence of an externality with the properties of a private good. Soot from a factory settles onto a household downwind of the factory. The household finds the soot distasteful, but the factory cannot reduce its production of soot without bearing some costs. The household may choose to bribe the factory to pollute less. If the cost to the factory of reducing soot exceeds the cost to the household of tolerating the soot, then no mutually advantageous bargain can be struck. Living with soot will be unfair and pareto optimal. If the cost to the household of tolerating the soot exceeds the cost to the factory of reducing soot production, then bribery can improve the welfare of both.

This first version of the parable of the factory and household is at the heart of what has come to be known as the Coasian position on externalities management. In a seminal 1960 essay, Ronald Coase argued that decentralized markets for externalities will yield pareto efficient outcomes even in the absence of rules limiting externalities production. Coase argued that when externalities create opportunities for mutually beneficial bribery, bargaining between the generators of externalities and those bearing the burden of externalities will result in an optimal level of externalities.[4] In an important 1980 essay, John Conybeare applied Coase to externalities problems in international relations. Conybeare argued that because nations can internalize policy externalities through bilateral political exchange,

[2] My criterion for evaluating efficiency is the usual conservative pareto standard. Under the pareto standard, an outcome is deemed to be optimal if no other outcome can improve the welfare of at least one party without leaving other parties worse off.

[3] Readers who are familiar with the conventional disciplinary controversy may wish to move directly to the section on divertable externalities.

[4] See Ronald Coase, "The Problem of Social Cost," *Journal of Law and Economics* 3 (Autumn 1960).

institutionalized systems of rules and hegemonic leadership are unnecessary.[5]

Where international spillover effects have the properties of private goods, basic Coasian arguments on externalities management through political exchange hold without modification. Relative to the public and divertable cases treated below, transaction costs are low and information on adversarial preferences is likely to be good if not perfect. Neither regimes nor hegemonic leadership will be needed to attain mutually beneficial outcomes. Bilateral bargaining between the parties affected should lead to pareto optimal outcomes.[6] The impact of this straightforward conclusion is blunted by one major problem. Private international economic externalities are rare.

My one recent example of a private international spillover effect is generated by natural rather than market forces. Prevailing winds carry acid rain from the United States to Canada. The geographical isolation of North America limits effects on other nations; the outcome of bilateral negotiations between the United States and Canada over acid rain do not have direct implications for third parties. In this instance, private spillover effects were not eliminated through bilateral compensation. As late as 1988, the American government deemed the outcome to be pareto efficient, while the Canadian government found the outcome to be unjust.

The Canadian–American acid rain dispute was ultimately ameliorated by *unilateral* American action. Acid raid devastated American as well as Canadian coniferous forests and mountain lakes, and in June 1989 the Bush administration proposed substantial amendments to the Clean Air Act of 1970. Under the new regulations, American emissions of sulphur dioxide are to decrease by half.[7] These American measures will substantially reduce the acidity of rain falling on Canada as well as the United States. Nations often take

[5] For the seminal application of Coase to international relations, see John A. C. Conybeare, "International Organization and the Theory of Property Rights," *International Organization* 34 (Summer 1980).

[6] I will dispense with the usual discussion of the effects of the existence and assignment of property rights on the efficiency of Coasian bribery. In international politics, property rights are generally not subject to reassignment. For all practical purposes, nations generating policy externalities claim the right to generate policy externalities unless compensated.

[7] The uncharitable might argue that the 1989 revisions were a response to impracticability of domestic Coasian bribery. Households in the Adirondacks and New England and owners of power companies did not and could not organize systems of bribes for power companies and factories in Pennsylvania and the upper Midwest. For a general discussion of bilateral bribery and public spillover effects, see the next section of this chapter.

actions that reduce negative spillover effects because these actions provide direct benefits to themselves. International spillover effects transmitted by market forces are rarely as confined as the Canadian–American acid rain example. The effects of domestic macroeconomic policies are diffused throughout the world economy and the effects of commercial and financial policies may be diverted from nation to nation at will.[8]

If a policy spillover effect affects only one other nation, then ad hoc political exchange between the principals will yield reasonably efficient, though not necessarily fair, outcomes. Both Coase and Conybeare claim more. They contend that their position on the pareto efficiency of bilateral bribery holds for all classes of externalities. As the next section suggests, the efficiency of bilateral bribery falls off dramatically if spillover effects have the properties of public goods.

PUBLIC EXTERNALITIES

In the classic illustration of an externality with properties of a *public good*, the factory's soot diffuses over many households in a neighborhood.[9] If the cost of compensating the factory owner for reducing soot production exceeds the collective benefits to the households of a less polluted environment, then no opportunity for mutually beneficial exchange exists. As in the private goods case, living with soot will be unfair but pareto optimal. If the households could compensate the factory owner for shutting down production and be better off than they were with the pollution, then an opportunity for mutually beneficial exchange exists. However, the households confront a classic free rider problem. If one household were to strike a bargain with

---

[8] The effects of this unilateral American action are likely to spill over into the literature on international political economy.

    If Canada takes at least one action that happens to benefit the United States within the year, then Coasians will cite the case as an example of efficient bilateral bribery.

    If Canada and the United States codify the American action in a treaty, then *International Organization* will publish an article on the acid rain regime that places emphasis on provisions for information sharing by Canadian and American scientists.

    If no treaty is negotiated and no Canadian action benefiting the United States follows the American decision, then hegemonic stability theorists will cite the case as an example of leadership by a large state with an interest in the welfare of the system as a whole.

[9] Public goods defined by jointness of consumption and nonexcludability. Jointness of consumption suggests that consumption by one does not preclude consumption by another; nonexcludability suggests that nobody can be denied access to the good.

the factory owner, other households could not be excluded from the benefits of soot reduction. Because side payments to the factory will be underprovided, soot will be overprovided.

Free Riding and the Underprovision of Bribes

Where policy externalities have the properties of public goods, Coasian ad hoc bargaining is unlikely to yield pareto efficient outcomes. As Mancur Olson argued in *The Logic of Collective Action*, because no actor can be excluded from the benefits of a public good, actors have strong incentives to free ride on the efforts of others. Unorganized markets, be they political or economic, tend to undervalue public goods relative to private goods.[10]

Consider several examples of public international externalities. Ozone depletion, the greenhouse effect, and other global commons problems are manifestations of public spillover effects. National policies on production of fluorocarbons and carbon dioxide affect global exposure to ultraviolet radiation and global temperatures, and no nation can be excluded from the costs of higher skin cancer rates or global warming.[11] The production decisions of oil exporting nations also give rise to public externalities. No oil exporter can be excluded from the benefit of higher oil prices. Because the costs of production restraint are private, free riding undercuts efforts to raise oil prices. Coasian bilateral bribery cannot provide a solution to these problems.[12]

Macroeconomic spillover effects have the properties of public

[10] See Mancur Olson, *The Logic of Collective Action: Public Goods and the Theory of Groups* (Cambridge: Harvard University Press, 1964). As Robert Keohane suggests, more recent explicit critiques of Coase demonstrate that decentralized bribery will not work well with more than two participants. See Robert O. Keohane, *After Hegemony: Cooperation and Discord in the World Political Economy* (Princeton, N.J.: Princeton University Press), 87. For a more extensive discussion of the effects of numbers of players on the prospects for cooperation, see Kenneth A. Oye, "Explaining Cooperation under Anarchy," in *Cooperation under Anarchy*, ed. Kenneth A. Oye (Princeton, N.J.: Princeton University Press, 1986).

[11] On the management of commons problems, see Russell Hardin, *Collective Action* (Baltimore: Johns Hopkins University Press, 1982); and Oran Young, *International Organization* 43, no. 3 (Summer 1989).

[12] For experimental work on the strength of the tendency toward underprovision of public goods, see G. Marwell and R. Ames, "Experiments on the Provision of Public Goods: Resources, Interests, Group Size, and the Free Rider Problem," *American Journal of Sociology* 84 (1979); and "Experiments on the Provision of Public Goods: Provision Points, Stakes, Experience, and the Free Rider Problem," *American Journal of Sociology* 85 (1980). Cited in Robert Sugden, "Reciprocity: The Supply of Public Goods through Voluntary Contributions," *Economic Journal* 94 (December 1984): 782.

goods. The international benefits or costs associated with national fiscal or monetary policies are diffused relatively evenly across a large number of countries. All share more or less equally in the benefits associated with adjustments in macroeconomic policy. None can be excluded from the benefits. But the costs associated with inducing change in other nations' domestic macroeconomic policies are largely private—offering concessions on nonmacroeconomic issues and making adjustments to one's own macroeconomic policies. As a consequence, countervailing international pressure to induce nations to take account of macroeconomic spillover effects is likely to be underprovided. The ineffectiveness of macroeconomic coordination in the 1930s and the 1980s follows logically from the largely public characteristics of macroeconomic policy externalities. If a policy externality affects many nations and if no nation can be excluded from the benefits of adjustments to policy, then free riding will weaken countervailing pressure for adjustments in policy. Externalities will not be internalized.

Efforts to salvage Coasian management by unrestricted political exchange in the public externalities case are not fully convincing. First, Duncan Snidal suggests that tendencies toward underprovision of public goods are checked by the existence of subgroups with a collective interest in assembling a bribe. Although free riding would still persist in the community at large, a determined band of households could muster their resources and offer a side payment to the factory.[13] This argument has one weakness and one strength. The weakness is theoretical. Members of the subgroup should be as inclined toward free riding as members of the community at large. The strength is practical. Public goods may be underprovided, but they are provided. Some viewers of public television contribute to fund drives, and some import-competing firms support lobbies for sectoral protection, and some households may contribute to the collective bribe fund. Snidal's analysis of subgroups points us toward an observable phenomenon. Second, John Conybeare suggests that free riding can be controlled by "converting public goods into private goods." He argues that private property rights could, at least in theory, be assigned to public externalities, and that political exchange could then ensure that levels of externalities would be optimal. Conybeare did not suggest how such international property rights might be assigned in the absence of an authoritative international legal framework.[14]

[13] Duncan Snidal, "The Limits of Hegemonic Stability Theory," *International Organization* 39 (Winter 1985).

[14] Conybeare also offers one intriguing example of linkage between public and private issues. In seventeenth century Britain, boat owners who refused to pay fees to a

Both of the counterarguments are intriguing, but neither provides a solution to the problem of free riding in the presence of public spillover effects.

Because unrestricted bargaining among large numbers of *equal* actors is unlikely to generate optimal levels of collective side payments, positive public externalities will be underprovided and negative public externalities will be overprovided. It is at this juncture that hegemonic leadership enters the debate.[15]

Structural Inequality and Externalities Management

Hegemonic stability theorists examine the implications of *inequality* on the management of public externalities. They postulate that if one nation is substantially larger and wealthier than others, it will have a substantial absolute interest in the provision of public goods and will have the capacity to contribute directly or to induce others to contribute. In their view, one large household will either deposit its money in the bribe fund or force other households to contribute.

The existence of one large actor may facilitate the production of public goods in several ways. As Olson and Zeckhauser argued in "An Economic Theory of Alliances," inequality of actors is likely to increase public goods production. In their example, a bridge serving a group of farmers is washed out. All of the farmers need the bridge to get to market, and none can be excluded from the benefits of reconstruction. If one farm is substantially larger than the others, the absolute value derived by that farm from the reconstruction of the bridge will be proportionately greater than the absolute value derived by others. The larger farm may derive sufficient *direct* benefits from the bridge to warrant either paying a disproportionate share of the costs or inducing others to pay their shares. The likelihood of provision of the public good is greater where one farm is substantially

---

lighthouse were denied access to the harbor marked by the lighthouse. Although boat owners could not be prevented from using the lighthouse as a reference point for navigation, the ban on use of the harbor denied boat owners the practical benefits of improved navigation. See "International Organization and the Theory of Property Rights," *International Organization* 34 (Summer 1980): 327–32.

[15] Regimes theorists examine the implications of *institutionalized constraints* on the provision of public goods. They postulate that preexisting institutionalized systems of rules mitigate tendencies toward free riding. In their view, a society of households can establish and maintain rules that encourage contributions to the collective bribe fund. Because these arguments are commonly applied to *divertable* externalities cases, I take up regimes in the next major section.

larger than another than in a case where numerous small farms must organize and overcome the free rider problem.[16]

The theory of hegemonic stability is an application of Olsonian analysis to problems in international relations.[17] Economic openness is assumed to be a public good.[18] A nation's absolute interest in economic openness and a nation's ability to promote openness are assumed to be a function of size and wealth. Hegemonic stability theory predicts that international systems marked by extreme inequality in the size and wealth of nations are more likely to be more stable than are systems marked by equality. The theory of hegemonic stability has been the target of substantial criticism and has received far more than its share of attention in recent years.

Consider briefly one of the major criticisms. The relationship between size and the absolute value placed on providing economic openness is more complex than hegemonic stability theorists have suggested. The *absolute* value that a large nation places on stability and openness may be *less* than that of a smaller nation, depending on the exact nature of the relationship between size and sensitivity to international disturbances. As John Conybeare suggests, large powerful nations may well have less of an interest in promoting openness than smaller nations. He contends that large nations may maximize national income by imposing optimal tariffs rather than by promoting systemic openness.[19] The variable relationship between size and the value placed on stability and openness may account for some discrepancies between the Olson–Zeckhauser hypothesis and the behavior of groups of nations confronting public goods problems.[20] This

[16] Mancur Olson and Richard Zeckhauser, "An Economic Theory of Alliances," *Review of Economics and Statistics* 48 (August 1966).

[17] See Charles P. Kindleberger, "Dominance and Leadership in the International Economy: Exploitation, Public Goods, and Free Rides," *International Studies Quarterly* 25 (June 1981); and "Government and International Trade," *Princeton Essays in International Finance* 129 (1978); Stephen D. Krasner, "State Power and the Structure of Foreign Trade," *World Politics* (April 1976); and Robert Gilpin, *U.S. Power and the Multinational Corporation* (New York: Basic Books, 1975), 258–59. For an explicit statement and test of the theory, see Robert O. Keohane, "The Theory of Hegemonic Stability and Changes in International Regimes, 1967–1977" in *Change in the International System*, eds. Ole Holsti, Randolph Siverson, and Alexander George (Boulder: Westview, 1980); and Keohane, *After Hegemony*, especially Chapters 3 and 8.

[18] Because economic openness is not a public good, the relevance of hegemonic stability theory to problems of openness is suspect. This criticism is treated in the section of this chapter on divertable externalities.

[19] See John A. C. Conybeare, *Trade Wars: The Theory and Practice of International Commercial Rivalry* (New York: Columbia University Press, 1987), 23–28.

[20] Although generally true, the assumption that larger members of a group will place a higher absolute value on a public good merits closer examination. In the example of

narrow attack weakly undermines the assumption that large states will have greater incentives to provide public goods, and will be valid *only* in circumstances where size sharply reduces the relative value placed on the public good.

The theory of hegemonic stability has received disproportionate attention as well as substantial criticism. If structural inequality is associated with stability and openness, then the postulated effect appears to be weak. Deductive and inductive inquiry into the association between the international distribution of power and systemic openness have been largely inconclusive. Most significantly, the driving variable in hegemonic stability theory is largely beyond the reach of public policy. Most causes of concentration or diffusion of international power and wealth are not susceptible to manipulation. As a consequence, the theory of hegemonic stability is largely devoid of practical significance.[21]

DIVERTABLE EXTERNALITIES

Assume that the factory can either divert soot from household to household without reducing total soot production or adjust total soot production.[22] Individual households may muster their collective re-

---

the farms and bridge, the larger farm would generally place a higher absolute value on the public good of a replacement bridge. The absolute value placed on the bridge is a function of size because the absolute value of being able to market crops is a function of the value of crops. This relationship between size and the value of public goods is indirect, since the preferences and values of individual actors may vary. For example, if a family of ten and an elderly couple are disturbed by the sound of a radio on a beach, would the larger unit necessarily bear a disproportionate share of the costs of bribing or coercing the radio owner to turn down the sound? Each member of a large family could well be far more tolerant of the sound of the radio than the elderly husband and wife. The larger unit might well place a lower absolute value on the public good of silence than the elderly couple. Indeed, one might assume that members of larger families will, in general, be more tolerant of noise than members of smaller families. With reference to the public good of silence, there may be a tendency for smaller units to bear a disproportionate share of the burden of pressuring radio players.

[21] For arguments on the sign and effect of power concentration on economic openness, see Duncan Snidal, "The Limits of Hegemonic Stability Theory," *International Organization* (Autumn 1985); Timothy McKeown, "Tariffs and Hegemonic Stability," *International Organization* (Winter 1983); and Joanne Gowa, "Rational Hegemons, Excludable Goods, and Small Groups: An Epitaph for Hegemonic Stability Theory?" *World Politics* 61, no. 3 (April 1989). For arguments on the limits of efforts to control decline, see Kenneth A. Oye, "Constrained Confidence and the Evolution of Reagan Foreign Policy," in *Eagle Resurgent? The Reagan Era in American Foreign Policy*, eds. Kenneth A. Oye, Robert Lieber, and Donald Rothchild (Boston: Little Brown, 1987).

[22] If the notion of controlling the wind seems farfetched, think of the factory owner

sources to induce the factory to reduce total soot production or may strike individual deals with the factory to divert soot away from them. As in the parable of public spillover effects, free riding will weaken the collective response. A common bribe fund earmarked for total soot reduction is likely to be undersubscribed. As in the parable of private spillover effects, an individual household may negotiate a mutually advantageous bilateral deal with the factory. Each householder could offer bribes to reduce the volume of soot falling on his home. Simple bilateral negotiations over the amount of the compensation and the extent of soot reduction could permit both to attain mutually beneficial outcomes. Such transactions between the factory owner and the householder would have benign welfare implications for both.

Unlike the private goods case, each bilateral deal has direct effects on third parties. Every diversionary agreement increases the amount of soot descending on households that have not yet struck deals. As a consequence, households have a strong incentive to strike bilateral deals with the factory sooner rather than later. As more and more households negotiate diversion, remaining households face a rising level of soot. The last household to negotiate faces three unpalatable options. It may accept the total soot production of the factory, bribe the factory owner to renege on previous deals and divert soot onto other households, or bribe the factory owner to reduce total soot production. To make matters worse, other households are most unlikely to be interested in contributing to the bribe fund. Each of these alternatives is likely to be more costly than purchasing a mere diversion of soot at an earlier stage. Because all households have an interest in not being the last to negotiate, bilateral bargaining tends to spread extremely rapidly once bilateral bargaining begins.

Economic Discrimination and Political Exchange

This third version of the parable helps account for important aspects of commercial and financial bargaining. Both commercial and financial externalities can be diverted from country to country. Importers can preference one exporter over another or grant market access on a nondiscriminatory basis. Debtors can service loans from one creditor at the expense of others or treat all creditors equally. In circumstances where collective efforts to resist protection or to manage debt appear likely to fail, nations turn toward discriminatory bilateral ne-

releasing pollutants when the wind will carry soot toward some households and away from others.

gotiations very quickly. Once bilateral or regional deals are being struck, every individual nation has an interest in being first and not last to hit the negotiating table and discriminate. This line of argument provides support for "slippery slope" characterizations of regime disintegration.

Where policy spillover effects have the properties of divertable goods, economic discrimination will be a requisite of political exchange. To strike mutually advantageous agreements, the principals to negotiations will commonly discriminate in favor of each other at the expense of third parties. Although each individual bilateral deal will improve the welfare of parties to the agreement, each individual bilateral deal will reduce the welfare of excluded parties. In many of the examples of bilateral commercial bargaining in the 1930s and 1980s, discrimination merely diverted flows of trade without affecting levels of openness. Yet in other cases, bilateral commercial bargaining appeared to have trade expanding effects. The third version of the parable does not lead directly to conclusions on whether bilateral bargaining increases, decreases, or does not affect global levels of soot production. To assess the effects of discriminatory bilateral bargaining on general levels of policy externalities, one must move beyond the simple assumptions of the third version of the parable. Economic discrimination may engender greater economic openness through two mechanisms.

One benefit follows from the effects of discriminatory international negotiations over market access on national tastes for protection. By providing export-oriented sectors with a narrow interest in campaigns against protection of import-competing sectors, international discriminatory bargaining can partially offset domestic biases toward protection. This effect of discrimination on openness is discussed in Chapter Four and is evident in many of the individual cases of commercial discrimination in the 1930s and 1980s. Liberalizing bilateral agreements negotiated under the Reciprocal Trade Agreements Act in 1934, Japanese agricultural liberalization in the 1980s, and Canadian and American acceptance of a free trade zone in 1987 were all facilitated by discrimination.

Economic discrimination may also contribute to the spread of liberal practices. Parties excluded from the benefits of discriminatory agreements have a strong incentive to join in liberalizing bilateral or regional negotiations. In the 1930s, France and Great Britain pushed the United States toward a liberalizing discriminatory policy. In the 1980s, Japanese–American bilateral liberalization, the Canadian–American free trade zone, and the European Single Integrated Market Agreement were mutually reinforcing. The tacit and explicit preferences embodied in each set of negotiations served as a spur to the other negotiations and will serve as a spur to further liberalizing bilateral negotiations.

Bilateral Discrimination and International Regimes

Institutionalized constraints on national action can preclude as well as facilitate the realization of mutual interests. I do not take exception to any of the conventional arguments offered in defense of regimes. As the extensive literature on international regimes suggests, institutionalized systems of rules can facilitate realization of mutual interests by reducing transaction costs, by providing information, and most centrally, by defining substantive rules that codify national obligations to international society.[23] However, these benefits may come at a price. The benefits of management by rules must be balanced against the opportunity costs of mutually advantageous agreements foregone to preserve substantive rules.

As Robert Keohane argues, international regimes can help nations recognize and realize mutual interests. Commitments to substantive liberal rules increase the reputational costs of departing from liberalism. Participation in international institutions provides information on the policies, values, and intentions of others—information that can expedite negotiation. Keohane writes:

> Committing oneself to an international regime implies a decision to restrict one's own pursuit of advantage on specific issues in the future. Certain alternatives that might otherwise appear desirable—imposing quotas, manipulating exchange rates, hoarding one's own oil in a crisis—become unacceptable by the standards of the regime. Members of a regime that violate these norms and rules will find that their reputations suffer more than if they had never joined at all.[24]

The factory and the households negotiated in an institutional vacuum. How might the existence of institutionalized rules affect relations among the factory and households in the divertable externalities case? First, substantive rules may obviously prohibit or limit generation of the negative externality. The General Agreement on Tariffs and Trade (GATT) plainly discourages protection, the International Monetary Fund (IMF) discourages default, and the International Energy Agency (IEA) discourages oil consumption. Second,

---

[23] For the two standard works on international regimes, see Keohane, *After Hegemony*; and Stephen D. Krasner, ed., *International Regimes* (Ithaca, N.Y.: Cornell University Press, 1983).

[24] See Keohane, *After Hegemony*, 183–216 and 257–59.

distributional rules may discourage free riding and encourage contributions to the collective good. The signatories to the IMF accept quotas for contributions and the signatories to the IEA accepted national targets for stockpiling reserves. Taken together, substantive and distributional rules decrease the likelihood that the factory will generate negative externalities and increase the likelihood that the households will pool their resources into a collective bribe fund. These considerable advantages can materialize only if nations respect both substantive and distributional obligations. Management by rules requires impartiality and generality. Nations cannot selectively comply with a rule and foster respect for a rule by other nations.

The fundamental tension between rule-based and bargaining-based modes of international economic management is most pronounced on issues where spillover effects are divertable. As noted above, political bargaining over divertable externalities generally entails economic discrimination. To confer benefits or impose costs on negotiating partners, nations offer access to markets, repayment of loans, access to credits, and conversion of currencies to some nations at the expense of others. This tension is accentuated by the tendency of discriminatory bargaining to spread rapidly when spillover effects are divertable. When rules proscribing protection or default begin to fail, nations turn toward discriminatory bilateral negotiations very quickly. Substantive rules limit the scope of bargaining, while bargaining erodes compliance with substantive rules.

To defend systems of general rules from the corrosive effects of discriminatory bargaining, regimes commonly contain a self-defense mechanism. Regimes typically consist of primary rules proscribing impediments to economic exchange and secondary rules proscribing political exchange. These secondary norms proscribing political exchange are most explicit where spillover effects are divertable. In commerce and finance, where nations are constantly tempted by the possibility of cutting a bilateral or regional bargain at the expense of third parties, secondary norms proscribing discrimination are clearly articulated.

Commercial externalities are intrinsically divertable, and prohibitions on commercial discrimination are well developed. Nations can divert the costs of protection from trading partner to trading partner through quotas, multiple list tariffs, product reclassification, and selective administration of nontariff barriers. In the postwar era, the GATT institutionalized a primary norm proscribing protection and a secondary norm proscribing discrimination. The secondary norm is reflected in provisions that explicitly favored reliance on single list tariffs rather than quotas, favored unconditional Most Favored Nation (MFN) over conditional MFN, and proscribed discriminatory applications of duties imposed under safeguard actions. Under Article 24, customs unions and free trade areas were deemed to be consistent with the GATT only if the parties notify the GATT, if the parties do not raise barriers facing third countries, and if "substantially all" merchandise trade between the parties is covered. During the late 1920s, nations at the World Economic Conference of 1927 committed themselves to convert quotas into tariffs and to insert MFN clauses in bilateral trade agreements. In 1989, participants in the Uruguay Round of the GATT are considering proposals for "tariffication" of nontariff barriers to trade. Although secondary norms against discrimination were and are commonly violated, they exist to discourage explicit bilateralism and regionalism.

Financial externalities are also intrinsically divertable. By selectively servicing loans, debtors can shift the costs of default from one creditor to another. By promising to preference some loans at the expense of others, debtors may play creditors off against each other. As a consequence, creditors support rules that discourage the privatization of debt servicing. Domestic bankruptcy law is based on the principle of equal treatment of classes of creditors. It explicitly limits the ability of debtors to cut preferential deals with individual creditors. In international finance, cross default clauses serve much the same function. Clauses in all international loan agreements stipulate that a default against one creditor is a default against all. If creditors respect cross default clauses, then debtors cannot service loans to one creditor while defaulting on others. Nondiscriminatory financial norms were constructed to serve the interests of creditors.[25]

[25] In fact, norms against discrimination may have more profound effects on the distribution of costs of managing externalities than on levels of efficiency. Consider a simple numerical example for two households and one factory case. Assume that the factory spews forth 2 units of soot to produce $2 worth of goods and that soot diversion does not affect production levels. Assume 1 unit of soot initially falls on each household and that the harm inflicted on a household by a unit of soot is $1.

Negotiating serially and independently, the factory owner could receive up to $3 to eliminate $2 worth of production. The first household would be willing to pay up to $1 to divert the unit of soot falling on it. The second household would be willing to pay up to $2 to eliminate the 2 units of soot falling on it and the factory would be unwilling to accept less than $2 to eliminate the soot.

The factory is not obligated to negotiate serially. Each household may be willing to pay close to $2 for the diversion of 1 unit of soot to avoid paying $2 to eliminate 2 units of soot. Negotiating simultaneously, the factory owner could receive close to $4 to eliminate $2 worth of production.

The households are not obligated to negotiate independently. The prospect of paying up to $2 to avoid being hit with 2 units of soot provides a powerful incentive for resisting the temptation to strike bilateral deals.

Note that the level of soot production in all of these cases is the same, but the distri-

Both modes of management are very real options and the fundamental incompatibility of bilateral discrimination and rule-based management necessitates choice. The balance between the benefits of regimes and the opportunity costs of mutually beneficial discriminatory bilateral agreements foregone is not constant.[26] The criteria that nations appear to use in choosing one approach over the other are consistent with the requirements of efficiency. Where rule-based management has drawn down general levels of protection, then nations have foregone the temptations of discrimination and respected rules. Where management by rules has failed to internalize policy externalities, nations have relied on discriminatory ad hoc bargaining. Where transaction costs of negotiation have been high, nations have tended to develop and respect general rules instead of relying on ad hoc bargaining. Where transaction costs are low, bilateral bargaining has tended to persist. Where the costs imposed on third parties by bilateral and regional arrangements have been substantial, excluded parties have negotiated away bilateral and regional preferences.

One conclusion on the choice between rule-based and bargaining-based management stands without qualification. Liberal international economic regimes contain prohibitions against such discriminatory bargaining because separate deals may undermine the regime. The extent of closure following collapse of substantive norms is likely to be determined by how effectively individual nations manage to discriminate. Once the substantive rules of the regime are shattered, what was antisocial behavior may be both individually necessary and socially useful.

CONCLUSIONS AND EXTENSIONS

Jean Monnet once quipped, "If you change the context, you change the problem." This chapter suggests that context, specifically the private, public, or divertable character of policy externalities, has per-

---

bution of costs of soot reduction is very different. If an optimal level of externalities production is reached in the privatized externalities case, the distribution of benefits is likely to be skewed in the direction of the externalities producer's end of the contract curve.

[26] Consider an example from foreign aid. Bilateral donors often require that imports financed by aid be purchased from them. The multilateral aid regime discourages tied aid. Respect for the norm against tied aid would reduce the incentive to give. Whether recipients would be better off with or without donor adherence to the norm would depend on the balance between a loss in economic efficiency resulting from restricted choice of suppliers and a gain in volume of aid received resulting from greater political efficiency.

vasive effects on the efficiency of modes of international economic management.

If externalities are private, then Coasian bilateral bribery will yield reasonably efficient outcomes. Because third parties are not affected by the terms of bilateral agreements, mutually beneficial bilateral agreements will yield optimal levels of international externalities. However, private externalities are rare. Narrow versions of the Coasian argument do not bear directly on most economic policy externalities.

If externalities are public, then Coasian bilateral bribery will not yield efficient outcomes. Free riding will undermine collective responses and positive spillover effects will be underprovided, while negative spillover effects will be overprovided. Substantial inequality in wealth and size may be a requisite of efficient management of public spillover effects. However, the weakness of the postulated association between inequality and openness and the structural nature of international systemic inequality limit the practical significance of hegemonic solutions to the management of public spillover effects.

If externalities are divertable, the intrinsic tension between bilateral discrimination and institutionalized rules will be acute. Nations must choose between Coasian and Grotian approaches. The case for management by rules is largely extrinsic: if preexisting rules place limits on externalities generation and control free riding, then nondiscriminatory collectivist approaches to externalities management should be retained. However, as is commonly the case, when Grotian approaches are unsuccessful in managing policy externalities, then continuing respect for the principle of nondiscrimination will impede rather than facilitate realization of mutual interests through economic discrimination and political exchange.

Although the three simple versions of the parable of the factory and the households capture important aspects of the politics of externalities management, the parable is a simplification. Consider four major extensions of the core argument that are treated at length in the next two chapters.

First, the case for bilateral discrimination rested on the assumption that transactions were limited to exchange. But ad hoc bargaining encompasses extortion and explanation as well as exchange. A factory may threaten to raise levels of soot production over optimal levels to extract payments from the household and may act on its extortionate threat if the household resists. A nation may increase levels of protection or fall into arrears on loans in order to extract concessions from bargaining partners. If extortion is common, then unrestricted bargaining will not be efficient. Chapter Three examines the welfare implications and incidence of all three forms of contingent action and suggests that extortion should be uncommon. The empirical chapters on the 1930s and 1980s do not include many examples of extortion.

Second, international negotiations are often not limited to single issues. The parable of the factory and the households reduced the agenda of negotiations to soot and (unspecified) compensation. During both the 1930s and 1980s, commercial, financial, and macroeconomic issues were often intertwined by both substantive and tactical linkages. Chapter Four examines the effects of cross-issue linkage on the efficiency of ad hoc bargaining, and suggests that nations often improve their welfare by joining unrelated issues.

Third, the case for reliance on unstructured political exchange in the private and divertable goods cases assumed that mutually advantageous agreements would be respected. Nations can renege. Chapter Three examines this problem under perfect information unitary actor assumptions, and suggests that reneging should be rare. Chapter Four examines this problem under imperfect information non-unitary actor assumptions, and suggests that nations may well undervalue reputational costs and renege more frequently than conventional game theory suggests.

Finally, the comparative discussion of the efficiency of bilateral discrimination and international economic regimes rested on the implicit assumption that national tastes were fixed. Regimes theorists have quite correctly observed that the existence of institutionalized international rules can affect national tastes for protection or default. Indeed, one important strand of regimes theory, neglected in this chapter, explicitly places value on institutionalized rules as part of a process of socialization.[27] Chapter Four argues that bilateral discrimination may have corresponding effects on domestic preference formation. If institutionalized rules are an important source of embedding liberalism, bilateral discrimination may be the principal force for weakening protectionism and expanding liberalism.

[27] See John Gerard Ruggie, "International Regimes, Transactions, and Change: Embedded Liberalism in the Postwar Economic Order," in Krasner, ed., *International Regimes*.

Chapter Three

THE LOGIC OF CONTINGENT ACTION

EXCHANGE, EXTORTION, AND EXPLANATION

THE OPTIONS confronting the factory and the households were limited by assumption. All parties restricted themselves to the simple exchange of soot reduction or diversion for compensation. None of the parties reached beyond these two issues to other issues in order to influence outcomes. Nations confront a far richer menu of options. Nations may link issues to project power from an issue of strength to influence outcomes in an area of weakness. Furthermore, nations may seek to influence each other through extortion and explanation as well as simple exchange. This chapter considers the implications of extending the range of issues that may be joined through negotiation and the range of tactics that may be employed in negotiation.

In situations where coercive diplomacy lacks credibility and purely verbal diplomacy lacks clout, international actors often couple issues to increase their leverage. Linkage is a common—and commonly misunderstood—form of political behavior. The literature contains a welter of contradictory statements on virtually every important question imaginable. Some characterize linkage as a tactic that results in the "intrusion" of extraneous issues into potentially fruitful single issue negotiations, corroding relations between linker and linkee.[1] Others view linkage as a technique for making side payments necessary to the attainment of mutually beneficial outcomes, improving relations between linker and linkee.[2] Still others argue that "linkages lend

---

[1] The U.S. Treasury Department expressed considerable irritation at the introduction of "extraneous political matters" into formerly "technical" issue areas when the Group of 77 linked creation of SDRs to greater access to credits and aid. When the Arab nations linked their position on the draft law of the Sea Treaty to the position of Western nations on Palestinian rights, the American delegation objected on similar grounds. In an editorial in 1979, the *New York Times* declared that the United States should reject a Saudi linkage between oil production and advanced fighters because the linkage was "blackmail."

[2] Robert D. Tollison and Thomas D. Willett, "An Economic Theory of Mutually Advantageous Issue Linkages in International Negotiations," *International Organization* 33 (Autumn 1979); John Conybeare, "International Organization and the Theory of Property Rights," *International Organization* 34 (Summer 1980); James Sebenius, "Negotiation Arithmetic," *International Organization* (Spring 1983); McGinnis, "Issue Link-

themselves to holistic prescriptions of salvation . . . (and) can be effected by cognitive means short of the holistic extreme."[3] All of these conclusions apply to *some* specific instances of linkage. The diversity of opinions as to the effects and effectiveness of linkage may be attributed, in part, to the diversity of the behavior analyzed.

Analysts have drawn lines to distinguish among classes of linkage. Paula Stern argues that "public" linkage is likely to be less effective than "private" linkage. Henry Kissinger draws a distinction between "when a diplomat deliberately links two separate objectives in a negotiation, using one as leverage on another; or by virtue of reality, because in an interdependent world the actions of a major power are inevitably interrelated and have consequences beyond the issue or region immediately concerned." David Baldwin argues that "positive sanctions" will be more effective than "negative sanctions," and many analysts distinguish between "carrots" and "sticks." There is wisdom in these distinctions, but the categories are imprecise and some of the generalizations are incorrect. Does "publicity" always trigger resistance? In a world where many issues are interrelated, how does one distinguish between Kissinger's first and second forms of linkage? A reward or punishment is usually defined in terms of a deviation from expected behavior by the linking state. What is the reference point? Finally, how do the many categories offered above overlap?

This chapter disentangles the concept of linkage, by breaking down contingent action into three exhaustive and mutually exclusive categories—extortion, exchange, and explanation—that differ as to credibility, welfare implications, and probable effectiveness.[4] It then

---

age and the Evolution of International Cooperation," *Journal of Conflict Resolution* (March 1986); and James Alt and Barry Eichengreen, "Simultaneous and Overlapping Games" (Paper delivered at NBER Conference on Political Economy of International Macroeconomic Coordination, Andover, Mass., November 6–7, 1987).

[3] Ernst Haas, "Why Collaborate? Issue-Linkage and International Regimes," *World Politics* 32 (April 1980).

[4] In earlier work I labeled these three categories "blackmailing, backscratching, and bracketing." The distinction between extortion and exchange was introduced in "On Blackmailing and Backscratching: Inter-Issue Linkage Strategies and International Political Economy" (Paper presented to the International Studies Association West Convention, Los Angeles, CA, 1977); between tactical and substantive linkage in "The Domain of Choice: International Constraints and Carter Administration Foreign Policy," in *Eagle Entangled: U.S. Foreign Policy in a Complex World*, eds. Kenneth A. Oye, Donald Rothchild, and Robert J. Lieber (New York: Longman, 1979); and among extortion, exchange, and explanation in "Towards Disentangling Linkage: Issue Interdependence and Regime Change" (Paper presented to the International Political Economy Colloquium, Institute of International Studies, University of California, Berkeley, April 1979). The tactical-substantive linkage distinction was introduced by Ernst Haas in "Why Collaborate? Issue-Linkage and International Regimes," *World Politics* 32

considers a series of cognitive, situational, and organizational factors that could be expected to influence the effects and the incidence of these forms of contingent action. It concludes by examining how the completeness or incompleteness of information on adversarial preferences conditions the effects and the incidence of each of the forms of contingent action.

TYPES OF CONTINGENT ACTION

As an introduction to the concepts, consider the following story. Rose, a flower lover, and Mutt, a dog lover, are next-door neighbors. Mutt's dog tends to wander into Rose's garden, to the detriment of Rose's flowers. Rose builds a fence that is just high enough to keep Mutt's dog out of her yard. The fence is unsightly and costly, but functional. Now consider the following actions.

If Rose were to state, "I'll take down the fence if you pay me $1,000," Rose would be offering an exchange. She is simply requesting compensation for taking an action that is adverse to her interests. Mutt might not find it worth $1,000 to remove the fence, and might worry about the possibility that Rose would keep both the $1,000 and the fence, but would regard the offer as a simple backscratch.

If Rose were to state, "I'll add ten (ugly) feet to the height of the fence if you don't pay me $1,000," Rose would be engaging in extortion. She is threatening to take an action that is adverse to her interests (visually and monetarily) unless compensated. In responding to this proposal, Mutt would be angry at what he would see as an attempt to extort $1,000, concerned over the possibility that Rose might be tempted to engage in extortion in the future, and hopeful that Rose might not execute her threat were he to resist her attempt at blackmail.

If Rose were to declare "I'll take down the fence if you shoot your dog," she would be explaining her situation to Mutt.[5] Her interest in retaining or removing the fence is contingent on the threat that Mutt's dog poses to her flowers. Both the promise and the threat are credible. Rose is merely providing Mutt with information on how his actions on the dog issue will affect her actions on the fence issue.

"Exchange" is an instrument of political exchange. "Extortion" is a weapon of political coercion. "Explanation" is the transmission of information on the direct consequences of actions. Definitions, welfare

---

(April 1980). Most recently, Arthur A. Stein discusses the categories of blackmailing and backscratching at length in "The Politics of Linkage," *World Politics* 33 (October 1980), though he maintains that his categories differ.

[5] If the imminent death of Mutt's dog is disturbing, substitute "leash" for "shoot."

implications, credibility problems, and possible applications of each category of linkage are discussed systematically.

Assume that we have an issue X controlled by the linker and an issue Y controlled by the linkee. The linker may choose to cooperate X(C) or defect X(D) on issue X and the linkee may choose to cooperate Y(C) or defect Y(D) on issue Y. The linker prefers that the linkee play Y(C) and the linkee prefers that the linker play X(C). The linkage is a promise to play X(C) if the linkee plays Y(C) and a threat to play X(D) if the linkee plays Y(D). Translated into plain language, "I'll do what you want if you do what I want." The definition of the three types of linkage hinges on the *linker* interest in the threatened and promised actions.

Exchange.   If the linker's interests are better served by action X(D) than by X(C), irrespective of what the linkee does on issue Y, then the linkage is exchange. The linker is threatening to act in its interest by playing X(D) if not compensated, and is offering to refrain from acting in its interest by playing X(C) if compensated.

Extortion.   If the linker's interests are better served by action X(C) than by X(D), irrespective of what the linkee does on issue Y, then the linkage is extortion. The linker is threatening to act against its interest by playing X(D) if not compensated and is promising to refrain from acting against its interest by playing X(C) if compensated.

Explanation.   If the linker's interests are better served by action X(C) if the linkee plays Y(C) *and* are better served by action X(D) if the linkee plays Y(D), then the linkage would be the explanation. By bracketing issues [X(C) if Y(C)] and [X(D) if Y(D)] the linker is drawing attention to an already existing connection between the issues, putting the linkee on notice that actions on Y affect linker interests on X. Because the linker's preferences on X(C) and X(D) depend on the linkee's actions on the related issue Y, both the threatened and promised actions will be in the linker's interest.[6]

These types of linkage do not correspond to carrot and stick or reward and punish or threaten and promise. The definitions rest solely on the interest of the linker in the threatened and promised actions.

[6] Explanation is synonymous with what Robert Nozick terms "non-threatening warning" and what lawyers refer to as "predictions." See Robert Nozick, "Coercion," in *Philosophy, Science, and Method: Essays in Honor of Ernest Nagel,* eds. Sidney Morgenbesser, Patrick Suppes, and Morton White (New York: St. Martins, 1969), 453–58.

Exchange

Exchange can be a pareto efficient form of linkage, at least in the simple two-actor two-issue case. Were it not for the linkage, the linker would simply go ahead with the action threatened. By joining issues, the linker provides the linkee with an option of compensating the linker for foregoing an action the linker would otherwise undertake. If the offer is not accepted, both parties are as well off as they would have been had the offer not been extended, less transaction costs. If the offer is accepted and the linker does not renege on his promise to refrain from acting against his interest, both parties are better off than they would have been had the exchange not taken place. Should the linker renege on his promise, the effect of exchange is redistributive. While exchange can be mutually beneficial, a more complete assessment of its effects on welfare requires some sense of the likelihood of alternative outcomes. Under exchange, the linkee can be certain that if he does not pay compensation, the linker will act in his (the linker's) interest.

However, the linkee may fear that the linker will renege on the promise to engage in the action X(C) that benefits the linkee and is disadvantageous to the linker. One task of the would-be backscratcher is to assuage this fear. Although reneging may have advantages in any single encounter, the backscratcher has an interest in enhancing his reputation for scrupulous honesty because he expects to be engaged in repeated encounters with the linkee. Paula Stern's observation that public linkage is likely to be less effective than private linkage is not correct in cases of exchange. Publicity raises the costs to the backscratcher of failing to make good on the promise, and thereby decreases the likelihood of reneging and assuages the backscratcher's partner's fear of reneging. This will reduce the likelihood of reaching the redistributive outcome. If the linkee believes that he is confronted by an honest backscratcher, he has no interest in discouraging exchange, because that form of linkage *raises* the level of satisfaction that the linkee can attain. From a welfare perspective, exchange tends to be a pareto efficient form of linkage.[7]

Turning from welfare to power, exchange can enhance the lever-

---

[7] This holds without qualification only for the two-actor case. In the more general multi-actor multi-issue case, variations on the Condorcet paradox may produce cycles of preferred outcomes that include "no linkage." Where such intransitivities exist, no conclusions as to the efficiency of exchange can be reached. In cases where such intransitivities are not exhibited, conclusions as to pareto efficiency may be precluded by the effects of a mutually beneficial linkage between A and B on the interest of other actors in the system. See the discussion of divertable externalities in Chapter Two.

age of the linker over the linkee. Exchange provides the linkee with an opportunity to compensate the linker for refraining from an action that would otherwise occur. Were it not for the exchange, the linkee incentive to reduce its sensitivity would correspond to the costs imposed by the threatened action; exchange reduces the preexisting incentive of the linkee to adopt sensitivity decreasing measures.[8] While extortion tends to be a power expenditure, exchange tends to conserve or even increase the linker's leverage over the linkee.[9]

Extortion

The welfare implications of extortion are malign. If extortion fails and the blackmailer executes the threat to inflict costs on the linkee, the extortionist will harm both himself and his victim. Extortion will have yielded deadweight welfare losses. If extortion succeeds, the welfare implications are redistributive. Were it not for the linkage, the linker would not even consider undertaking the threatened action; therefore, he has lost nothing by giving it up. The linkee has gained nothing, while paying compensation to the linker. If blackmailing fails and the blackmailer does not execute the threat, the effects on welfare would be neutral, minus the transactions cost of blackmailing.

Will extortion tend to result in the "no compensation-execute threat" outcome? Under extortion the linkee can be certain that if he pays compensation, the linker will refrain from acting against his interests, undoubtedly with some sense of relief. However, the linkee may hope that the linker will not make good on the threat to engage

[8] Consider one example. Throughout 1977–78, Saudi Arabia maintained petroleum production at levels well in excess of "national financial requirements." When Iranian oil production was crippled by strikes in late 1978 and early 1979, Saudi Arabia increased its petroleum production even further. The Saudis requested compensation from the United States in the form of a "special relationship" in 1977, F-15 aircraft in 1978, and a more activist American Middle Eastern security policy in 1979.

Saudi increases in production diminished the urgency of the American comprehensive energy program; a Saudi cutback in production and resulting increase in petroleum prices would have triggered more intensive American activity and thereby reduced American dependency on Saudi production. The exchange reduced the American incentive to decrease dependency to the costs, broadly defined, of the special relationship, fighter sales, and security guarantee. The exchange had the effect of perpetuating and even increasing American dependence on Saudi production.

[9] Each of these aspects of exchange has been analyzed in many different fields. The welfare implications of exchange are at the core of microeconomics, while the credibility of promises has been exhaustively examined in the literature on prisoners' dilemma and provides the functional justification for domestic contract law and international regimes.

in mutually disadvantageous activity.[10] One task of the blackmailer is to shatter this hope.

Although backing down may have advantages in any single encounter, the blackmailer will seek to enhance his reputation for apparently "irrational" ruthlessness because he expects to be engaged in repeated encounters with potential victims. Indeed, the blackmailer will often engage in the threatened action first, and then promise to refrain from acting in ways adverse to his interests in the future, in order to enhance his credibility and provide the linkee with a concrete demonstration of the costs he will bear if compensation is not forthcoming. This type of demonstration obviously reduces the welfare of both linker and linkee.

The linkee also has a reputation to protect. Given the proliferation of international issues and interest, there are many actions that potential linkers could threaten to do which impose costs on the linkee *and* are not necessarily in the interest of the possible linker. The linkee has a strong interest in discouraging blackmailing, because that form of linkage lowers the level of satisfaction the linkee can attain. By increasing the probability of future blackmailing, accession to extortion has very high costs to the linkee.

From a welfare perspective, undisguised blackmailing is likely to produce the worst of all worlds. The linkee has an interest in reducing his attractiveness to potential blackmailers, and is likely to reject the offer. The blackmailer has an interest in bolstering his credibility, and is likely to execute the threat. By its very nature, blackmail tends to become an ultimate test of credibility, with corrosive effects on the atmosphere of international relations and the interests of both blackmailer and victim.

Paula Stern's observation that public linkage is less effective than private linkage applies in many cases of extortion. Although publicity may serve the function of enhancing the credibility of blackmailing threats, by raising reputational costs of failing to execute threats for the blackmailer, publicity also raises the reputational costs of concession for the victim. Public linkage is more likely than private linkage to produce deadweight welfare losses of the no concession-execute threat outcome.

Turning from welfare to power, extortion creates an incentive for the linkee to reduce its sensitivity to the actions of the linker in order to diminish the blackmailer's leverage in future encounters. Efforts

[10] Sensible extortionists look for threats that impose significantly greater costs on their victims than themselves. The difference between "I'll blow my brains out over your nice new suit" and "I'll blow your brains out over my nice new suit" is substantial, and the second threat is likely to be more effective than the first.

to reduce sensitivity will, of course, depend on the characteristics of the issue that is the source of the blackmailer's power. For example, the Organization of Arab Petroleum Exporters (OAPEC) embargo triggered modest defensive measures by the Western states, including conservation programs, diversification of energy sources, emergency allocation schemes, intensification of the search for new sources of petroleum, and stockpiling programs. Although efforts to reduce one's sensitivity to the actions of others may be triggered by many causes, extortion creates an additional incentive. Were it not for the linkage, the blackmailer would not consider undertaking the threatened action, and there would be less incentive for the linkee to adopt defensive measures. Over the middle to long term, extortion has the effect of undermining the linker's clout on issue X; extortion is a form of power expenditure.[11]

The expectation of deadweight welfare losses may discourage rational individuals from engaging in extortion. Formal legal rules and informal legislative norms defend societal interests in discouraging blackmailing. Under British and American common law, the distinction between threats to take actions adverse to one's interests and offers to refrain from actions in one's interests is maintained in the law on water rights, theft by extortion, nuisance, and torts. In each of these four areas of law, one finds that actions *that would otherwise be legal*, which inflict harm on another without benefitting oneself, are illegal.[12]

In one nineteenth century midwestern American case, a farmer threatened to drain an underground stream that fed a very successful spa unless the owner of the spa provided the farmer with a healthy proportion of the profits. The owner of the spa refused, and the farmer dug a hole, installed a steam pump, and diverted the underground stream across a meadow and into a river. The owner of the spa sued, the farmer argued that his purpose was to irrigate the meadow, and the court found that the meadow did not require irrigation. The court enjoined the farmer from executing his threat.

In a nineteenth century Nebraska case, an artful extortionist

---

[11] Extortion gives rise to games that have been examined exhaustively by strategic theorists, notably the game of "chicken." The credibility of threats to act in ways that are adverse to your interests is a central issue in chicken. Thomas Schelling's *Strategy of Conflict* and *Arms and Influence* provide examples of many secondary tactics to enhance the credibility of blackmailing threats. Daniel Ellsberg's essay on blackmailing remains a classic statement of the problem.

[12] I would like to thank Paul Schechtman for his insights and suggestions on parallels between blackmail as defined here and extortion as defined in the Model Penal Code and the common law.

threatened to build a fence that would obstruct his neighbor's light and air, unless compensated. The threat was ignored, and a fence was built. In court, the fence builder argued that the fence served the useful purpose of protecting his home from drifting snow. The court observed that the prevailing winds were from the opposite direction. The fence builder argued that the winds frequently shifted direction in his neighborhood, and that he needed protection from the direction of his neighbor's house. The court observed that the neighbor's home afforded substantial protection from drifts from that direction and noted that the snow fence was very high only in areas directly adjacent to the neighbor's house. The court required the fence builder to remove the fence.

The distinction drawn in the case law is also drawn in the statutes and the Model Penal Code. The 1954 Code, Section 223.4, defines extortion to include any threat to inflict any harm which would not benefit the actor. The state of New Jersey also adopts the same general definition of extortion, a definition based on assessment of the linker's interest in executing the threat.

These distinctions in law are mirrored in legislative process. Well-ordered legislatures proscribe extortion while permitting exchange. In the U.S. Senate and in the California State Assembly, norms discourage threats to vote against one's interests unless compensated *without* discouraging promises to vote against one's interest if compensated. Old hands teach new senators and assembly members to differentiate between extortionate logrolling and normal vote trading, and sanction violators of the norm.[13]

Explanation

Extortion, exchange, and explanation are all undertaken to predispose the linkee toward choice Y(C). Explanation differs from the other forms of linkage in one crucial respect. While the extortionists and backscratchers are seeking to construct a connection between issues, the explainer is pointing to an already existing connection between issues. Whether or not the linkage is made explicitly, the explainer will have an interest in doing X(C) if the linkee does Y(C) and in doing X(D) if the linkee does Y(D).

For example, Peru made its support for lowering internal tariffs within the Andean Pact contingent on development of a common set of regulations on direct foreign investment. Entry into a free trade

---

[13] Ed Costantini provided the observation on the California Assembly, and Douglas Arnold provided the characterization of the U.S. Congress. Arnold notes that the norm against extortion is far less clearly developed in the House of Representatives.

zone without common regulation of investment would have negated
the purpose of Peru's relatively stringent investment regulations, for
potential investors could then gain access to the Peruvian market
without locating in Peru. The Peruvian *interest* in reducing tariffs was
contingent on the formulation of a common investment code; explanation drew attention to the connection.

Explanation is a pareto efficient form of linkage, at least in the two-
actor two-issue case. The linker has no conceivable incentive for failing to execute a threat or for reneging on a promise. If explanation
succeeds, it is because both actors prefer $X(C)Y(C)$ to the outcome
that would otherwise occur, $X(D)Y(D)$. Should explanation fail, linker
and linkee welfare will be equivalent to the no-link outcome, minus
the transactions cost of explanation.

The effect of explanation on the conservation of leverage is similar
to that of exchange. The linkee interest in reducing sensitivity to the
actions of the linker will be diminished, if the explanation is successful. In the event that explanation is unsuccessful, the incentive to reduce sensitivity will be identical to that of the "no-link" case.

Explanation has been implicitly used by neofunctionalist integration theorists, most notably Ernst Haas and Phillipe Schmitter. They
emphasize substantive connections between issues as a driving force
behind regional integration. Actions taken in one area lead to un-
foreseen changes in other areas; specifically, cooperation in one area
will often alter actor preferences in functionally related areas. Explanation simply draws attention to substantive connections between
functionally related issues. Successful explanation highlights positive
spillover effect on the linker, and unsuccessful explanation highlights
negative spillover effects as the linkee proceeds with a course of actions with a negative spillover effect on the linker. In the case studied
here, explanation and spillover served as channels for disintegration
more often than integration.

SINGLE-ISSUE CONTINGENT ACTION

Although these definitions are expressed in terms of cross-issue linkage, they may also be used to categorize interaction between two actors on a single issue. Take a linker threat to increase tariffs, if the
linkee raises tariffs, with a linker promise to lower tariffs, if the linkee
lowers tariffs. If the linker is a pure free trade liberal, the linkage
would be extortion, in that the linker would believe that lowering tariffs is in his interest, given either action by the linkee. If the linker is
a pure neomercantilist, the linkage would be exchange in that the
linker would believe that raising tariffs is in his interest, given either

action by the linkee. If the linker has a (greatly exaggerated) belief in the theory of the second best, the linkage could be explanation, in that the linker could believe that raising tariffs is in his interest if the linkee raises tariffs, and that lowering tariffs is in his interest if the linkee lowers tariffs. Take a linker threat to increase weapons spending. If the linker is a pure pacifist, the linkage would be extortion, in that the linker would believe that increasing weapons spending is not in his interest given either action by the linkee. If the linker is a pure belligerent, the linkage would be exchange in that the linker would prefer to increase weapons spending given either action by the linkee. If the linker is an international relations theorist with an exaggerated belief in interactive causes of arms races, the linkage would be explanation in that the linker would prefer to increase weapons spending if the linkee increases spending, and would prefer to decrease weapons spending if the linkee decreases weapons spending.

These examples of single-issue extortion, exchange, and explanation also illustrate the role of beliefs in the proper categorization of actions. The same threat or promise can be extortion, exchange, or explanation, depending on the linker's calculation of linker interest. To increase the credibility of threats or promises, a shrewd linker will seek to manipulate the linkee's image of the linker's beliefs. If the linkee can be convinced that the linkage is explanation, both threats and promises become entirely credible. Given the tendency for states to impute their beliefs to other actors, the possibilities for accidental miscategorization of linkage are great where belief systems differ significantly across states.

Patterns of Linkage

The effects of different classes of linkage on the nature of international relations are clear. What determines the choice of tactic? In most instances the choice among extortion, exchange, and explanation is more apparent than real. First, with respect to bracketing, the number of issues that are so closely related that one's actions on a second issue are determined by another's actions on a first issue is relatively small. Where such an intense substantive relationship between issues exists, one has nothing to lose and may have something to gain by pointing to the substantive connection and explicitly clarifying the relationship between one's choice and another's actions. Even if the relationship is not made explicit, actions on the one issue are determined by actions on the other. Since the substantive connection is structural, not tactical, effects will be transmitted from issue to issue even if the connection is not pointed out to the potential linkee.

A second issue cannot be used for exchange with any promise of success unless: (a) the costs to the linker of acting against his interests to provide a benefit are less than the benefit derived from the linkee acceding this request, and (b) the benefit offered to the linkee exceeds the cost to the linkee of acceding to the request.

A second issue cannot be used for extortion with any promise of success unless: (a) the cost imposed on the linkee exceeds the cost to the linkee of acceding to the request by a *substantial margin*, and (b) the costs imposed on the linker by executing the threat are low enough so the threat is credible.

Opportunities to link are largely products of a nation's position within the international environment. It is the exception for a potential linker to activate the power that may inhere in his situation by engaging in cross-issue extortion or exchange. Many opportunities to link issues exist. Relatively few are acted on. To explain why nations link when they do, one must consider domestic policy making processes as well as international context.

What factors are likely to bear on whether linkers will act on such opportunities? The opportunity must be recognized, interests in possible outcomes must be calculated, and the probabilities of outcomes must be estimated. The recognition of any opportunity to link and calculations of interest and effectiveness are likely to be strongly influenced by the domestic context of linkage diplomacy.

Cognitive and organizational processes are likely to shape the search for opportunities. A unit of an organization or an individual within an organization is likely to be familiar with a set of related issues, and opportunities to backscratch or blackmail across functionally related issues are more likely to be identified than are opportunities across unrelated issues. Bureaucratic interest may partially negate this expectation, as individuals or organizational units seek to shift the potential cost of a blackmailing threat or a backscratching promise onto other elements of the national bureaucracy. Nongovernmental interest groups are also likely to resist having their interests sacrificed, and such domestic resistance may well constrain a government's choice of leverage issues.

The domestic political repercussions that might result from sacrificing interests in one area to attain foreign policy objectives in another are a cost of linkage diplomacy. For example, the Carter administration's manipulation of trades and technology transfers to pressure the Soviet Union on the treatment of dissidents and the administration's assessment of linkage to affect Soviet policy on Africa revealed a fundamental disagreement between the National Security Council (NSC) and the Department of Commerce and State. The disagreement spilled over into Congress, with a member of the NSC approaching Senator Moynihan to pressure the administration to employ technology transfer as a source of leverage over the Soviets.

Reticence to link, in the face of opportunities to link, may be partially explained in terms of these domestic costs of linkage diplomacy. The significance of these intranational concerns will vary across classes of potential linker; a highly differentiated, complex, pluralist government is likely to recognize and act on fewer opportunities for exchange or extortion than a unitary, simple, oligarchic government in the same international context.

The recognition of an opportunity to explain involves high-order cognitive and organizational processes. The detection of a strong substantive connection between the actions of the linkee on Y and the interests of the linker on X may be attributable to anticipation—deduction of the interactive effects (described by the linker in his bracket) from extant belief systems—and/or the experience of continually recalculating interests on X as the linkee varies its policy on Y. However, since explanation occurs between substantively connected issues, and the course of action threatened or promised under bracketing would take place even if the linker were not to point explicitly to the bracket, the significance of governmental politics could be expected to be significantly less than under extortion and exchange.

Although institutional impediments to linking functionally dissimilar issues can be substantial, central decision makers do bridge bureaucratic divides on high salience issues. The Truman administration exacted a British pledge of cooperation on commercial issues as consideration for generous settlement of the Lend Lease account. Belgian participation in the European Payments Union was secured using a side payment of increased American economic assistance. The Eisenhower administration made American support for a floundering pound sterling contingent on British withdrawal from the Suez expeditionary force. Eisenhower also imposed a unilateral economic embargo on Cuba (ostensibly) to induce Castro to pay compensation for $1 billion of nationalized American investments and to end discriminatory taxes and licenses on American trade and investment. In August 1971, the Nixon administration made termination of the import surcharge contingent on European and Japanese actions to revalue their currencies relative to the dollar. Kissingerian detente was based on a complex linkage between American credits, trade preferences, technology, and grain sales, and Soviet foreign policy restraint in general, and Soviet pressure on North Vietnam in particular. The Carter administration tacitly linked the pace of American troop withdrawal from South Korea and the availability of some categories of American military equipment to South Korean adherence to the principles of nuclear nonproliferation. An embargo on American weapons sales to South Africa was imposed to penalize South African policies on Namibia. Cuban foreign policy in Africa was linked to normalization of diplomatic and economic relations. The Soviets were penalized for their treatment of dissidents by the temporary suspension of licenses on the Dresser Industry petroleum drilling bit manufacturing plant and by the cancellation of a Sperry Rand computer system. Security supporting assistance, economic assistance, and international credits were used to induce Somoza of Nicaragua to cease violations of human rights and to call a referendum. The Middle Eastern fighter package was designed to reward perceived Egyptian cooperation and relatively favorable Saudi Arabian petroleum production decisions. In each of these examples, the issue rose within the bureaucracy to a point where competing interests in functionally organized bureaucracies could be balanced.

Congressionally initiated linkages seem to be explained more by the politics of coalition formation than by the functional organization of committee structures. The Hickenlooper Amendment linked American aid to the prompt, adequate, and just payment of compensation to nationalized American corporations. The 1974 Trade Reform Act was replete with linkage. Under Section 502, the designation of a developing country as a beneficiary of the Generalized System of Preferences (GSP) was tied to a host of conditions. The eligibility of Communist developing countries was contingent on (a) membership in GATT and the IMF, (b) not being dominated by "international communism," and (c) being prior beneficiaries of MFN status. The benefits of GSP were not to be extended to any nation (a) that was a member of OPEC or other arrangements "the effect of which is to withhold supplies of vital commodity resources from international trade or to raise the price of such commodities to an unreasonable level," (b) that granted trade preferences to other developed states but not to the United States, (c) that nationalized American owned investments (or renegotiated contracts or imposed taxes effectively denying ownership or control to American individuals or corporations) without paying prompt, adequate, and effective compensation, or (d) that failed to take measures to halt the flow of narcotics to the United States. More recently, Congress linked American economic and security supporting assistance to the potential recipient's handling of human rights and drug enforcement efforts. In each of these instances, linkages created winning domestic legislative coalition. But the linkages were largely unsuccessful in influencing the behavior of other nation states.

EFFECTS OF INCOMPLETE INFORMATION

One fundamental point has implications for all three forms of contingent action. In the presence of incomplete information on adversarial preferences, backscratching, blackmailing, and bracketing may not be reliably distinguished from each other. The distinctions between these forms of behavior hinge on the linker's interest in making good on threats and executing promises. How does the presence or absence of complete information on adversarial preferences alter the effectiveness and incidence of the three types of contingent action?

Each of these types of contingent action is a form of signaling that conveys information on one's preferences. But it is obvious that the representations of preferences presented by each form of contingent action are not accepted naively. Why then do the distinctions make a difference?

Bracketing would be pointless in a full information world. It is precisely because Mutt does not understand how his handling of the dog affects Rose's interest in the fence that bracketing can potentially have effects on behavior. Rose is conveying information on her preferences—*not* altering her preferences—when she engages in bracketing. But because Mutt does not have knowledge of Rose's "true" preferences, he cannot know whether the bracket is a bracket or a disguised extortion or a disguised exchange. As a consequence, he will tend to discount the information provided.

Both blackmailing and backscratching work by changing valuations of outcomes. Making the statement, "If you do what I want, I'll do what you want, if you don't do what I want, I won't do what you want" changes the situation by placing reputation on the line. Although the direction of changes in preferences produced by signaling is predictable, the magnitude of changes cannot be known ex ante. Rose's interest in taking down the fence is not the same after she makes an offer that is accepted as it was before she made the offer. Rose's interest in raising the fence is not the same after a threat is issued and rebuffed as it was before she issued the threat. In each case, making the statement alters Rose's preferences by adding reputational costs. Mutt can infer the *direction* in which Rose's preferences are moved by when she issues threats and promises. But Mutt does not know how much Rose values her reputation relative to the costs associated with lowering or raising the fence. How then does the presence or absence of imperfect information affect the effectiveness and incidence of these forms of contingent action?

Cross-issue exchange permits attainment of mutually beneficial equilibria in situations where cooperation would not be rational if issues were considered in isolation. Under either perfect information assumptions or imperfect information assumptions, making good on one's promises can be a stable equilibrium point.[14]

Cross-issue extortion may lead to mutually disadvantageous outcomes. Under complete information assumptions, actors cannot credibly threaten actions that are inferior to subgame perfect strategies for issues taken in isolation. Therefore, under such assumptions, actors will not tend to rely on blackmail. If information on adversarial preferences is imperfect, however, blackmailing becomes a more attractive strategy. When information on adversarial preferences is incomplete, preferences may be misrepresented and extortion may be disguised as exchange. As a consequence, the incidence of blackmailing will tend to rise as information becomes less complete.

Cross-issue explanation of how your partner's choices affect your preferences cannot reduce welfare and can improve welfare. When information on adversarial preferences is complete, explanation cannot provide additional information and would have no effect. When information on adversarial preferences is grossly incomplete, what appears to be an explanation may be an artfully disguised extortion or exchange. As such, the information conveyed by the explanation would tend to be discounted.

CONCLUSIONS

This chapter began by defining three mutually exclusive and exhaustive forms of contingent action and examining the welfare implications of each. It then considered a series of cognitive, situational, and organizational factors that could be expected to influence the effects and the incidence of contingent action. It concluded by examining how the completeness or incompleteness of information on adversarial preferences conditions the effectiveness and incidence of each of the forms of contingent action. The last factor—the completeness of information on adversarial preferences—may appear to be the most esoteric. In fact, it is the most familiar. Students of politics have long wrestled with the problem of inferring and measuring national preferences. The very same problems that have impeded scholars impede national decision makers as they struggle to make inferences about the preferences of their bargaining partners.

[14] But as argued in the next chapter, under nonunitary actor assumptions, reputational costs are likely to be undervalued.

Chapter Four

THE CONCEPT OF PREFERENCE

BIAS AND INSTABILITY IN THE VALUATION OF OUTCOMES

TO THIS POINT, the case for discriminatory ad hoc bargaining as a mode of international economic management has taken preferences as given. As Robert Axelrod notes, there are two major problems with this common practice: "The political system is biased in the way it aggregates perceived political interests; and much of the public misperceives its own economic interests."[1] This chapter examines sources of bias and instability in national preferences.

The first half considers connections between internal biases and external bargaining strategies for nonunitary actors. It begins by examining domestic biases toward protection—what economists term "endogenous protection"—and then explains how external discriminatory bargaining may offset internal biases toward protection. Strategic interaction *between* actors can influence preference formation *within* actors. This section also raises the possibility that nonunitary actors are likely to undervalue reputation and discusses the implications of reneging on the efficiency of political exchange.

The second half examines inferential problems associated with using rational choice theory to explain outcomes. If what you think determines where you stand, then unstable beliefs can produce pronounced swings in national preferences. This section examines methodological problems that arise in defining and measuring changes in economic beliefs and in identifying the effects of apparent belief systems change on national preferences and policies.

NONUNITARY ACTORS AND THE ORGANIZATION OF INTERESTS

Nation states may be unitary actors in the literal sense that national policies are ultimately formulated and implemented. However, because national actions rarely have uniform domestic distributional

---

[1] Robert Axelrod, "Comment on How Should the United States Respond to Other Countries' Trade Policies?" in U.S. *Trade Policies in a Changing World Economy*, ed. Robert M. Stern (Cambridge: MIT Press, 1987), 282; cited hereafter *U.S. Trade Policies*.

consequences, interest groups, classes, and bureaucracies struggle to reshape national policies from below. National policies in liberal societies are broadly responsive to their struggles. But, as Mancur Olson has argued, when costs or benefits are concentrated on a few, effective representation of interests is more likely than when effects are diffused across many. As a consequence, "national" preferences are likely to be underweight costs that are evenly distributed and overweight costs that are concentrated.

Two points follow from these conventional observations. First, blackmailing, backscratching, and bracketing produce changes in the behavior of bargaining partners by inducing coalition reformation within negotiating partners and thereby changing adversarial preferences. Second, because the benefits of maintaining national credibility are diffuse relative to the costs of making good on promises and threats, nonunitary actors are likely to renege on blackmailing promises and fail to execute blackmailing threats more often than orthodox game theory suggests.

Bias and Compensation

Conventional Olsonian biases toward overrepresentation of concentrated interests and underrepresentation of diffuse interests sit at the core of the extensive literature on endogenous protection. Domestic political systems tend to underprovide openness and overprovide trade restrictions. The benefits of protection to import competing groups are relatively concentrated. Sector specific protection provides palpable benefits—larger market shares and increased profits. The costs of protection to export-oriented groups and consumers are relatively diffuse. From the perspective of an exporter, any specific import-restricting measure may invite retaliation and may slice into the export earnings of customers abroad. But these costs tend to be distributed across all exporters. From the perspective of a consumer, any specific import-restricting measure will raise prices slightly. But once again, these costs are generally spread thinly across consumers. As a consequence, import-competing groups have a clear and concentrated interest in lobbying for protection, while export-oriented groups and consumers have a more diffuse interest in lobbying against protection. Equilibrium outcomes produced by domestic polities are biased toward protection. As Stephen Magee and Leslie Young observe: "It would be unusual for political markets in redistribution between players of unequal strengths to yield outcomes in which the sum of the welfare of all players was maximized."[2] Of course, the demand for protection is not constant. Magee and Young show that the strength of biases toward protection is influenced by exogenous variables that drive the behavior of groups lobbying for or against protection. Changes in unemployment, inflation, and terms of trade all affect national preferences for protection. For example, they argue that rising inflation explains antiprotectionist activity in the 1960s and 1970s, as consumers and businesses mobilized to eliminate trade restrictions that raise prices.[3] But the existence of a bias toward protection is a constant.[4]

Recent work on "anti-protection" by political economists suggests that import-competing sectors are not the only entities whose interests are centrally affected by trade restrictions. I. M. Destler, John Odell, and Kimberly Elliott attribute antiprotectionist activity to import-utilizing groups such as distributors of imported products and manufacturers who rely on imported intermediate products and raw materials.[5] Helen Milner looks to the international or domestic orientation of firms within sectors.[6] These scholars have identified groups and firms that in fact have a concentrated interest in defeating specific protectionist measures. These actors are commonly at the core of trade liberalizing coalitions.

The standard Olsonian bias toward overweighting concentrated interests relative to diffuse interests hinges on a hidden assumption. This distortion emerges *only* if domestic mechanisms for offsetting the distributional effects of policy are undeveloped. If compensation neutralizes the domestic distributional consequences of policies, then no bias emerges and national preferences may be regarded as synonymous with national interests. If compensation is underprovided, the analytic utility of the unitary actor assumption is degraded.[7]

[2] Stephen P. Magee and Leslie Young, "Endogenous Protection in the United States, 1900–1984," in Stern, *U.S. Trade Policies*, 146–47.

[3] See Stephen P. Magee and Leslie Young, "Endogenous Protection in the United States, 1900–1984," in Stern, *U.S. Trade Policies*.

[4] For an explanation of biases toward protection drawing on both economic and institutionalist perspectives, see Robert E. Baldwin, *The Political Economy of U.S. Import Policy* (Cambridge: MIT Press, 1985).

[5] See I. M. Destler, John S. Odell, and Kimberly Ann Elliott, *Anti-Protection: Changing Forces in United States Trade Politics* (Washington, D.C.: Institute of International Economics, 1987). For an earlier survey, see Kym Anderson, *The Political Market for Protection in Industrial Nations: Empirical Evidence*, World Bank Staff Working Paper No. 492 (Washington, D.C.: World Bank, 1981).

[6] Helen V. Milner, *Resisting Protectionism: Global Industries and the Politics of International Trade* (Princeton, N.J.: Princeton University Press, 1988).

[7] For a more general discussion of how international bargaining processes may correct domestic biases, see Kenneth A. Oye, "On Underprovision of Compensation:

The conventional case for free trade parallels this line of argument. Economists argue for liberal policies on the grounds that an action, taken in combination with *hypothetical* systems of compensation, could improve the welfare of all members of a polity. But because such hypothetical systems of compensation remain largely undeveloped in liberal polities, policies with uneven domestic distributional consequences often prove unsustainable because adversely affected groups organize and mobilize to resist liberalization. In practice, the uneven domestic distributional consequences of foreign policies are rarely offset by *real* systems of domestic compensation. Because compensation is underprovided, national preferences do not conform to what the economists may correctly identify as national welfare maximizing strategies.[8]

Effects of External Bargaining on Domestic Biases

By offsetting domestic biases toward protection, discriminatory international bargaining strategies may serve as an important force for economic liberalization. Exogenous factors that influence the behavior of groups lobbying for or against protection are not limited to purely economic variables. Economically discriminatory international bargaining strategies offset domestic biases toward protection by broadening antiprotectionist coalitions beyond the core groups identified by Destler, Odell, Elliott, and Milner. In a nondiscriminatory international economic environment, the interests of exports in fighting specific import restrictions are limited. In a discriminatory international economic environment, where nations barter market access for market access on a sector by sector basis, the consequences of import restrictions for exporters tend to be etched with greater clarity. In fact, nations rely on bilateral and regional bargaining strategies precisely to influence the behavior of export-oriented groups and firms within negotiating partners. External economic discrimination affects internal preference formation by concentrating what were formerly diffuse interests.

Some Implications of Incomplete Information and Fragmented Actors," APSA Conventional Panel 26-2, September 3, 1988.

[8] Why is compensation underprovided? First, under eminent domain, the state claims the right to expropriate property to serve public needs and accepts an obligation to compensate owners for their loss. But why are property rights defined as they are? Second, conventional microeconomists have focused on the effects of forms of compensation on individual incentives. Do the intrinsic distortions associated with an issue covary with provision of compensation? Finally, interest groups generally mobilize to secure shifts in policy rather than to secure compensation for the effects of a policy. Does this tendency covary across states? Why?

In the case studies of trade in the 1930s and 1980s in this book, economic discrimination often yielded liberalizing outcomes by mobilizing export-oriented interests in the battle against protection. During the early 1930s, the spread of bilateral (and necessarily discriminatory) commercial policy throughout the British Empire, continental Europe, and Latin America inadvertently drove a wedge between export-oriented and import-competing sectors in the United States, and an unconditionally protectionist American policy gave way to a policy of reciprocity. In the late 1970s and middle 1980s, Indonesia enlisted British engineering firms and China used American farmers to influence the size of textile quotas. During the 1980s, tacit American bilateralism helped enlist export-oriented firms in Japan in the battle against Japanese agricultural protection. Time after time, external economic discrimination has helped enlist the formerly disinterested in antiprotectionist coalitions.

Plausible examples of domestic bias reduction through international bargaining are rare beyond political economy. Consider security affairs. Theorists of military organizations begin with the observation that the domestic benefits of weapons acquisitions are concentrated while the costs tend to be diffuse. The economic benefits to military bureaucracies and military contractors could not be more material, while the economic costs are spread relatively evenly over taxpayers. As a consequence, military organization theorists postulate the existence of biases toward weapons intensive offensive strategies and toward overprocurement of weapons. International arms control negotiations are less effective than international trade negotiations in offsetting these domestic biases. Because the benefits of arms reductions by one country are relatively evenly distributed across groups in another country, the mobilization of countervailing interests is more difficult than in trade. Of course, arms control negotiations can yield agreements and fiscal limitations can end weapons buildups. But examples of domestic bias reduction through external bargaining strategies that concentrate formerly diffuse interests are rare.

Although orthodox models of strategic interaction treat preferences as fixed, strategic interaction in practice produces changes in the behavior of bargaining partners by producing shifts in adversarial preferences. In these and other examples, bargaining strategies succeed or fail by stimulating the reorganization of interests. Although international actions and responses may be precisely those suggested by the logic of contingent action among unitary actors, the effects are produced through radically different channels.

Effects of Bias on the Efficiency of Bargaining

The benign conclusion on the effects of bargaining on domestic biases is offset by several more subtle effects of domestic fragmentation on the bargaining behavior of nations. The practical significance of the nonunitary character of nations for theories of bargaining hinges on the public, private, or divertable distribution of costs and benefits associated with specific issues. If concentrated interests are more likely to be effectively represented than diffuse interests, then the behavior of nonunitary actors may be expected to differ from idealtypical unitary actors in at least one crucial respect.

The benefits of maintaining national credibility are evenly distributed, while the costs of sacrificing particularistic interests to maintain credibility are relatively concentrated. As a consequence, credibility is likely to be undervalued in nonunitary actors. In effect, the endogenous protection argument presented above must be supplemented by an endogenous reneging argument. If reneging affects a nation's general ability to effect exchanges in the future, then no specific group, class, or bureaucracy can be said to have a greater stake in generic national reputation for honoring promises than any other. As a consequence, nonunitary actors will be biased against adhering to costly promises and executing costly threats.

If national credibility is truly a public good, then nonunitary nations may renege on promises more often than game theory suggests.[9] While Abreau's grim reaper extends the consequences of defection on one issue across other international issues and strengthens the national *interest* in making good on agreements, the costs of defection diffuse across an ambiguously larger number of domestic groups so that the gap between national interests and preferences widens. The patently nonunitary character of the nation state weakens the case for management through ad hoc bargaining as a means of internalizing international policy externalities.

Robert Keohane's defense of regimes addresses this issue. If nations are in fact inclined to undervalue their reputation for making good on promises, then unstructured negotiation may not prove to be a particularly efficient means of realizing mutual interests. The institutionalization of patterns of cooperation in defense of formal commitments provides a hedge against reneging.[10] Of course, all solutions have costs. By effectively ruling out discriminatory bargain-

---

[9] See James Alt and Barry Eichengreen, "Overlapping and Simultaneous Games" (Paper presented at the NBER Conference on Political Economy of International Macroeconomic Coordination, Andover, Mass., November 6–7, 1987).

[10] See Keohane, *After Hegemony*, 85–109.

ing, nondiscriminatory rules also preclude one important international mechanism for offsetting domestic biases toward undervaluation of openness.

BELIEFS AND THE ORGANIZATION OF EXPECTATIONS

This section examines problems associated with defining and estimating actor preferences as one step in developing explanations of outcomes. In an attack on the revealed preference, Amartya Sen wrote: "Preference can be defined in such a way as to preserve its correspondence with choice, or defined so as to keep it in line with welfare as seen by the person in question, but it is not in general possible to guarantee both simultaneously. Something has to give at one place or the other."[11] This study does not consciously rely on revealed preference. To the best of my ability, the empirical chapters rest on definitions of preferences from the perspective of the actors in question. But to define and estimate actor preferences without reference to actions, one must confront the thorny problem of defining and estimating beliefs.

The Great Depression shattered orthodox systems of economic thought while destroying national economies, but the rate at which the orthodoxy collapsed varied from country to country and individual to individual. In this intellectual vacuum, an extraordinary range of economic views came to inform or misinform heads of state, interest groups, legislators, and bureaucracies. Changes in economic beliefs had profound effects on the evolution of individual, group, and national preferences and account for substantial change in national policies. This section discusses procedures for making inferences about belief systems change and assesses the significance of biases and instability in systems of economic thought.

Bases for Inferring Beliefs

Policymakers, traditional historians, and advocates of systematic cognitive mapping confront a common inferential problem. Individuals and bureaucratic organizations generate streams of information that may provide insight into underlying beliefs. A causal connection may be included in one statement, omitted in a second, reversed in a third statement, and reversed again in a fourth. Contradictory statements may be made before different audiences on the same day. And ac-

[11] Amartya Sen, "Behavior and the Concept of Preference," *Economica* 40 (August 1973): 241–59.

tions may or may not be consistent with consistent statements of belief. How do we extract information from contradictory statements? How do we weigh sources that range from internal memoranda to public speeches to memoirs?

INDIVIDUAL BELIEFS

In most existing work on foreign policy within the cognitive genre, the individual decision maker has been taken as the logical unit to which beliefs may be imputed. All of the contributions to Robert Axelrod's *The Structure of Decision*, the pioneering pieces by David S. McLelland and Ole Holsti on the operational codes of Acheson and Dulles, and the article by Glenn H. Stassen on "Senatorial Responses to Secretaries Acheson and Dulles" fall clearly within the individual as actor category.[12]

Sources of information on the belief systems of individuals usually take as their starting point speeches or documents to which the individual's authorship (or at least acquiescence) can be established. For broad definitions of attitudes on relatively simple dimensions such as isolationism or cold war, simple content analysis of a very respectable number of statements has traditionally been used. In their work with more detailed representations of belief structures, Axelrod and others on his project have relied whenever possible on either verbatim transcripts of discussion at high policy levels or on interviews with policy makers (or surrogate policy makers). For the most part, those involved in attempting to represent more complex belief systems have relied on the qualitative content analysis of documentary sources, since traditional frequency-based content analysis techniques proved to be incapable of picking up connections in complex belief structures.[13]

When are individual beliefs likely to have effects on national policies? Foreign policies are products of organizational procedures, role pressures, and systemic forces that may limit the influence of any individual. In a review essay on cognitive approaches to the study of foreign policy, Ole Holsti points out that the individual and his belief system are likely to have more of an impact on policy formulation

---

[12] See Robert Axelrod, ed., *The Structure of Decision* (Princeton, N.J.: Princeton University Press, 1976); "Comparative 'Operational Codes' of Recent U.S. Secretaries of State: Dean Acheson" (APSA paper presented in September 1969; Glenn Stassen, "Senatorial Responses to Secretaries Acheson and Dulles" *World Politics* 25 (October 1972): 96; and "The 'Operational Code' Approach to the Study of Political Leaders: John Foster Dulles' Philosophical and Instrumental Beliefs," *Canadian Journal of Political Science* 3 (March 1970): 157.

[13] For coding rules, see Robert Axelrod, ed., *Structure of Decisions*, 291–332 and 343–48.

where the following conditions exist: (1) situations are nonroutine and SOPS are inconsequential, (2) planning is long range with high uncertainty, (3) situations are ambiguous, (4) information overloads standard organizational channels, (5) unanticipated events occur in which initial reactions are likely to reflect cognitive "sets," (6) stress impairs performance in highly individualistic ways. Holsti goes on to note that these conditions characterize decision making in foreign policy more than in other arenas.[14] In normal times, economic foreign policy making would not fall within the range of Holsti's conditions. But the 1930s were not normal times.

All potential sources of information on the beliefs of individuals may not be assumed to correspond to the actual beliefs of the individual. Any statement of beliefs will be intended to serve some purpose; the sources of information on individual beliefs must be evaluated in that context.[15] At the most obvious level, statements by negotiators for North Vietnam and the United States about the relationship between some point of contention and their respective utilities will probably be distorted for the rational reason of limiting the perceived contract curve to a more favorable section. The statements of representatives of competing bureaucracies must be analyzed with reference to the process of explicit or implicit negotiations taking place within the government. Even statements of beliefs by members of high-level ad hoc groups concerned with a world-threatening crisis situation may be affected by each individual's concern with both his own self-image and the image others in the group will have of his character after the crisis has ended. More significantly, during the course of deliberations an individual may be interested in maximizing his influence within the group, to gradually displace the dominant belief system with his own. Where forthright statements of true beliefs are perceived as having potentially damaging effects on the individual's influence, and indirectly, on the chances of attaining whatever the individual desires, statements by any individual will tend to be in line with that individual's perceptions of the dominant belief system of the group. Adlai Stevenson's loss of influence within the Kennedy administration is often regarded as a consequence of his dovish statements regarding the efficacy of the use of force in the Cuban Missile Crisis and with reference to Vietnam.

These sources of distortion share the property of being interactive; the purposes that statements of beliefs are assumed to serve are

---

[14] "Foreign Policy Formation Viewed Cognitively" in Axelrod, *The Structure of Decision.*

[15] For a comprehensive discussion of the manipulation of images in international relations, see Robert Jervis, *Perception and Misperception in International Politics* (Princeton, N.J.: Princeton University Press, 1976).

found in the individual's perceptions of his situation—his perceptions of the effects of his colleagues' or opponents' images of his beliefs on the probability of attaining his objectives. These effects of interaction range from deliberate misrepresentation of the importance of objectives in simple bargaining, through indirect effects of nondominant beliefs on influence within a decision-making structure, to the postdecisional link between advocacy of correct, but divergent, beliefs and long-term influence in government.

Statements to a "neutral" historian or social scientist will be colored by an individual's desire to increase or diminish the importance of his role in events and to increase the correspondence between alleged past beliefs and subsequent events. Even the most forthright statements made, in confidence, to a trusted friend or psychologist serve social functions. The mea culpa may be as subject to distortion as statements of a negotiator at the bargaining table. Should an individual look within himself to try to determine (with all sincerity) the elements and connections of an affect-laden cognitive net, even prior to making a decision, ambiguous and inconsistent answers may be found. The individual will be limited by his abilities in self-analysis. Postdecisional efforts at determining one's own belief system would certainly be affected by the phenomenon of postdecisional cognitive dissonance and unconscious ego gratification.

Any analysis that does not "black box" the individual's beliefs will be subject to these sources of distortion. Evaluation of the reliability of sources is not a problem for the cognitively oriented analyst alone. To the extent that the belief systems approach maps and analyzes statements of belief in an explicitly modeled social and political context, greater understanding of the dynamics of these sources of distortion—in itself an interesting problem for research—may be gained. However, if the analyst is attempting to predict actions and patterns of interaction on the basis of stated beliefs, a lack of correspondence between statements of belief and real beliefs (however defined) may be viewed as more of a hindrance to research than as a source of potentially interesting questions.

However, if statements are consistently made with intrabureaucratic, domestic, or international ears in mind, a "lock-in effect" may operate. If an individual places value on credibility, actions may come to be aligned with statements of belief. Statements of belief may become more consequential than real but unexpressed beliefs.

ORGANIZATIONAL BELIEFS

Bureaucracies, banks, parties, and multinational corporations are all accepted as potential actors of consequence in international relations. Leites codified the beliefs of the Politburo, and proposed organizational ideology as a significant explanatory factor in Soviet foreign policy making.[16] Much of the work on bureaucratic and organizational analyses of foreign policy makes use of implicit definitions of organizational beliefs as either alternatives or supplements to other levels of analysis, though in none of the work within that genre is there any systematic elucidation of organizational beliefs beyond the level of general objectives.[17] Nonetheless, in all instances, a communality or near consensus of beliefs is proposed as a prerequisite of analysis using the concept of organizational belief or goal.

We make inferences on the beliefs of organizations from statements of beliefs of individuals within the organization or from statements that are the product of bargaining between individuals within organizations. To move beyond the welter of memoranda and statements of purpose that are the ore from which organizational beliefs may be extracted, the concept of organizational belief used to structure the raw data must be considered. The use of organization rather than individual as actor allows us to exchange the scylla of tough epistemological problems inherent in attempting to determine the beliefs of individuals for the charybdis of reification and personification inherent in the use of terms and processes developed to describe individuals in the analysis of organizations of varying degrees of complexity. A distinction must be made between the ascription of individual characteristics to organizations and the search for organizational analogs to individual behavior that explicitly recognizes their artificiality, and locates "beliefs" and processes of the organization in the context of organizational constraints and structure.

The attribution of beliefs to organizations may be, paradoxically, more valid than the attribution of beliefs to individuals. It is easier to ascertain the *working* beliefs of an organization, be it party line of internal official statements of purpose, than it is to ascertain the innermost working thoughts of individuals within that organization. If the secret doves of the Johnson administration kept their feelings to themselves and acted in line with the official set of beliefs of the government, then their innermost thoughts on the wisdom of increasing the American military commitment to the Diem regime had no effect on the formation of American policy. It is only when beliefs are artic-

[16] Nathan Leites, *The Operational Code of the Politburo* (New York: McGraw-Hill, 1951), and *A Study of Bolshevism* (Glencoe: Free Press, 1953).

[17] Graham Allison, *The Essence of Decision* (Boston: Little, Brown, 1971) differs from most of the organizational and bureaucratic works in that a slightly fuller enunciation of organizational and bureaucratic beliefs on a higher level of specificity may be found, though treatment of evidence is unsystematic. For an example of general treatment of organizational and bureaucratic beliefs without attribution of sources, see Morton Halperin, "Why Bureaucrats Play Games," *Foreign Policy* 2 (Spring 1971): 70.

ulated and acted on that they become a part of that which we designate organizational beliefs. The measurement of unarticulated beliefs of individual humans involves greater difficulties than tapping into and interpreting messages passing though the communications networks of organizations. By defining the organization as the actor, the observation of paper may replace the indirect observation of concepts.

Information on the beliefs of organizations may fall into several general categories: (1) downward communications issued to coordinate the activities of members of organizations or suborganizations within organizations, or to convey information on the state of variables within that belief system; (2) upward communications designed to affect the organizational belief system or convey information on the state of variables within the organizational belief system; (3) outward communications to external actors designed to shape the organizational environment, where the "environment" includes domestic actors, other bureaucracies, bureaucracies within other states, and transnational actors.

In using the organization as actor, the institutional setting within which individual statements of belief are made should be examined. Some of the sources of individual bias in statements of working beliefs noted previously may be accounted for explicitly by setting up models of accommodation within organizations or by using the end products of bargaining as working organizational beliefs. Of course, additional sources of bias are introduced, even when the notion of organizational belief is kept in mind.

Most of the objections to the use of bureaucracies, transnational organizations, or parties as actors in international relations emphasize arguments that are not germane to this study. Krasner reasserts the primacy of the individual's cognitive baggage (especially the president's) over role, notes the lack of specificity for which bureaucratic analysis of international relations is notorious, and emphasizes the reformulation and clarification of objectives, rather than better control and direction of bureaucracy, as central.[18] The inclusion of the president as actor where his beliefs are both unique and salient, the specific articulation of bureaucratic beliefs, and the clarification of objectives through careful examination of those beliefs are central to this study. More telling objections assert that the beliefs of individuals and organizations are irrelevant in light of larger historical forces which shape the course of international relations (e.g., objections

[18] Stephen D. Krasner, "Are Bureaucracies Important?" *Foreign Policy* (Summer 1972): 159.

from a Marxian perspective); but these objections do not pertain to the analysis of any particular discrete event. Finally, international system level theorists may assert that anything less than a world systems level approach will miss most of the determining factors in national behavior.

Many of the context-oriented reasons for suspecting individual distortion of statements of beliefs hold for organizations as well. The classes of outward communications and upward communications are particularly suspect. Outward communications to other actors may be intended to serve bargaining purposes, as noted in the section on bias individuals. Messages from the bottom up could be intended to serve a dual purpose of attracting external support for an embattled and isolated minority (bias not necessarily implied); if exaggeration of elements of beliefs may be considered a valid strategy in the search for support, biases may be introduced. Even the top down message could be used as a signal (interpreted as an index) by other actors, both domestic and international. Memoranda announcing organizational goals and beliefs could also serve the function of overinstructing a negotiating team so as to convince the delegation that a negotiating position is actually the ultimate fallback position, thereby enabling the team to make a highly credible representation of this point to the opposing delegation.

A further bias may be introduced by the fact that information on organizational beliefs is likely to be drawn from downward and outward type messages, because communications within these classes are most likely to be publicly circulated and/or preserved for posterity in archives. Internal memoranda of a confidential character, particularly memoranda from the bottom up, which are likely to have been written before a decision was taken and to contain arguments against as well as for the ultimate decision, are more likely to be destroyed.

Although downward messages are potentially biased, they do serve as a reasonably good representation of organizational beliefs if coded over time. Furthermore, the sources of bias that tend to infect them most often result in differences in emphasis rather than in contradictions in the structure of beliefs.

The possibility of interpreting contradictions in extensive beliefs as belief systems change hinges on the same notion of turning point introduced in the section on individual as actor. However, attitude change may be more apparent than real, and may not be predicted by the standard models of that process. In a bureaucracy, different subunits may deal with an issue as salience increases or decreases. Changes in official organizational positions on an issue may be due to changes in the subunit dealing with the problem area. Robert Paarlberg has noted that a correspondence exists between changes in U.S. policy toward the Third World and the "salience" of the Third World to the United States.[19] An alternative to simple models of attitude change may be specified. If differences in lower echelon versus higher echelon beliefs are noted, then the relevant belief system determining the actions of that organization could shift with salience of the issue area.

Interpreting Instability of Economic Beliefs

The economic policies of nations in the 1930s were consistent with the declaratory beliefs of heads of state and of centrally positioned organizations, and beliefs tended to change shortly before policies changed. But this consistency does not, in and of itself, establish that declaratory beliefs explain changes in policy.

At end of the 1920s, the causal economic beliefs of central decision makers diverged on many points. The effects of monetary devaluation on British commercial prospects, of bank rate change on international capital movements, and of fiscal stimulation on domestic economic activity were all matters of controversy. During the 1930s, the causal economic beliefs of central decision makers shifted markedly on each of these issues. Did a change in beliefs cause the shift in British policy? In this case the explanatory power of beliefs lies as much in accounting for the persistence of a line of policy in the face of discrepant information as in accounting for the shift in policy. The specific causal chains of association that defined economic orthodoxy underpinned British assessments of national interest after the environment that shaped the orthodoxy collapsed.

In France, the political elite, petite bourgeoisie, and peasantry shared a common belief that departure from gold would lead to economic catastrophe. On other economic issues, no common set of beliefs held across virtually all strata of French society. But the franc-gold parity was viewed by all as central to maintaining confidence and avoiding hyperinflation. To preserve parity under deteriorating conditions, France pursued a relatively restrictive domestic monetary policy, established capital controls, and followed a mercantilist commercial policy. This national belief is central to any explanation of why the French held out until 1936 before permitting devaluation of the franc.

In Germany, economic ideology changed dramatically over the period. Bruening and Schacht disagreed sharply over the economic

---

[19] Personal communication, conversation circa 1976.

consequences of default. As in the United States, significant variations in the economic ideology of central decision makers were reflected in sharp changes in domestic and foreign economic policy. The covariation between the position of groups within German society, the content of economic beliefs, and the distribution of benefits from pursuit of policies that follow from beliefs weakens the case for ascribing independent significance to economic beliefs alone.

Presidents Hoover and Roosevelt exercised decisive influence over U.S. monetary and financial policy and shared power with Congress on trade and finance. The Federal Reserve did not behave as an autonomous actor during this period.[20] The disparate views of Presidents Hoover and Roosevelt on economic means-ends hierarchies were not always shared by some in their administrations, much less by political and economic elites at large.[21] Though I find more regularity than those who argue that Roosevelt accepted the views of the last person to speak with him, his declaratory economic beliefs shifted markedly over time. In international monetary affairs alone, he espoused at least four contradictory positions over three years.

Does this very instability weaken the case for placing much weight on Roosevelt's stated beliefs as a determinant of national preferences? Let me make the extreme case with respect to American international monetary preferences. If Roosevelt believed that the contending views of economists and advisors were suspect and adopted economic beliefs and associated programs on a trial basis until one seemed to work, then the specific content of trial beliefs would not explain fluctuations in American policies in anything but a trivial sense. The ultimate determinant of American policy would be environmental—those attributes of environment that selected for beliefs and a policy that worked.

There is merit in this view. But the path of Roosevelt's search—the sequence of beliefs and policies that he tried—was not random. His commitment to the belief that price raising (not demand stimulation) provided the route to economic salvation persisted longer than his beliefs on the relative effectiveness of alternative means to this end were less firmly anchored. And the environment did not select for success or failure with clarity or speed. Roosevelt appears to have interpreted ambiguity in a manner that preserved core beliefs as long

[20] The Federal Reserve did not exercise its independent powers in relevant ways during this period. Following the death of Benjamin Strong in 1928, the Federal Reserve functioned in an ancillary capacity to the Executive Branch.

[21] Perhaps, as Karl Deutsch has suggested, Franklin D. Roosevelt should be viewed as two different actors with two different belief systems; perhaps someday a political psychologist may model the internal struggle between the two Roosevelts.

as possible. In short, the evolution of Roosevelt's beliefs does explain shifting American preferences with respect to trade and monetary policy. If one wants to make sense of American policies and international bargaining outcomes, one must take account of changes in these beliefs.

CONCLUSIONS

The preceding chapters offered a somewhat qualified brief on behalf of ad hoc bargaining as a mode of international economic management. Given ordinary assumptions common to virtually all theories of rational choice, several limitations of unrestricted bargaining emerged.

As Chapter Two suggests, the efficiency of unrestricted bargaining hinges on the private, divertable, or public character of international policy externalities. The shape of policy externalities is an intrinsic characteristic of issues rather than actors. As a consequence, the performance of ad hoc bargaining should degrade as one moves from trade disputes through financial and monetary issues to problems of macroeconomic coordination.

As Chapter Three suggests, the efficiency of unrestricted bargaining hinges on the probable incidence of welfare enhancing exchange and elucidation relative to welfare reducing extortion. Most centrally, if nations commonly issue blackmailing threats and commonly renege on backscratching promises, then ad hoc bargaining may reduce rather than enhance individual and global welfare.

This chapter examined sources of bias and instability in national preferences. It suggested that amendments to the austere rational choice approach used in the initial chapters may be appropriate. In fact, the lucidity of theories of rational choice is purchased at the expense of the murkiness in the definition of preferences. An individual, an organization, or a nation is assumed to have well-ordered preferences defined over some set of outcomes. Rational choice theorists then identify utility maximizing strategies given preference sets. Normative theories of rational choice prescribe optimal strategies given preferences. Positivist theories of rational choice explain outcomes as the product of optimal strategies given preferences. By convention, the task of analyzing strategic interaction between actors and the task of defining actor preferences are treated as wholly distinct.

The first section of this chapter examined problems associated with normative rational choice theory. I suggested that strategic interaction *between* actors can influence preference formation *within* actors.

Specifically, discriminatory bargaining strategies between nations can offset biases toward protection within nations. However, because interests in reputation or credibility are also diffuse, I also suggested that nonunitary actors may renege on commitments more frequently than an unreconstructed advocate of unstructured bargaining might like.

The second section of this chapter examined problems with using rational choice theory to explain outcomes. I defined preferences from the perspective of the actor in question and then turned to problems associated with inferring beliefs and identifying the effects of apparent belief systems change on national preferences and policies. My motivation for raising these methodological issues was pragmatic. Although regularities in the management of public and divertable externalities emerge quite clearly in the four empirical chapters that follow, those regularities are obscured if one does not take explicit account of changes in economic beliefs.

PART III

Depression and Discrimination

Chapter Five

THE POLITICS OF TRADE DIVERSION

COMMERCIAL RELATIONS IN THE 1930s

DURING THE 1930s, economic discrimination was a requisite of economic liberalization. Conventional wisdom holds that bilateralism, regionalism, and economic imperialism reinforced a trend toward protectionism. This chapter suggests that discriminatory trading practices slowed and ultimately reversed movement toward closure. Decentralized bargaining over market access served as the principal international mechanism limiting closure to a politically, if not economically, pareto efficient level.[1]

In 1929, the international trade regime consisted of a weak primary cluster of norms that proscribed restraints on the exchange of goods and a slightly stronger secondary cluster of norms that imposed restraints on the privatization of national trade policies. The primary cluster of norms fostered international economic openness and the secondary cluster of norms discouraged economic discrimination. Tariff levels before the depression were moderately high and falling. Agricultural prices had triggered increases in agricultural tariffs during 1928 and 1929, but a bias for liberalization existed. The World Economic Conference of 1927 had called for general reductions in levels of protection, rates on manufactured goods were declining, and the Franco-German commercial agreement of August 1929 contained many rate reductions that were passed on to numerous most favored nations.

The slightly stronger secondary norm proscribing discrimination called for consolidating tariff schedules, replacing quotas with tariffs, and eliminating other commercial practices that permitted de facto or de jure trade discrimination. A trend in favor of inclusion of most-favored-nation clauses fell within both primary and secondary clusters of norms. By transmitting the benefits of rate reductions to third parties, most-favored-nation clauses enhanced movement toward

---

[1] Relative factor scarcity and simple comparative advantage provide another, more fundamental, check on movement toward closure. The expense of developing import substituting industries or finding alternatives to imported products limits protection. Even under the Smoot-Hawley Tariff, two thirds of American imports (by value) were admitted on a duty-free basis.

openness while proscribing discrimination. The World Economic Conference of 1927 explicitly called for general respect for the unconditional most-favored-nation treatment and provisions for tariff consolidation. These secondary norms, taken collectively, discouraged privatization of trade policy and limited narrowly bilateral bargaining.

Worldwide overcapacity in agriculture, mining, and manufacturing, taken together with a strong desire to avoid massive structural dislocations associated with structural adjustment, dominated the foreign trade policies of the United States, France, and other nations with large import-competing sectors.[2] As domestic consumption fell, these nations sought to maintain minimal levels of economic activity in distressed sectors by protecting their markets from international deflation.[3] Trade controls were applied to ensure that domestic markets would consume at least a minimum fixed quantity of goods produced by acutely distressed import-competing sectors. As deflation continued, and domestic markets shrank, the level of effective protection required to sustain minimum demand for domestic products from such sectors increased. Levels of protection rose to stave off unwanted structural dislocations. Deflation served as a largely autonomous determinant of rising minimum degrees of protection.

Norms against protection and norms against discrimination did not collapse simultaneously. The United States violated the primary norm with the passage of the Tariff Act of 1930, but did not engage in de facto trade discrimination until well into 1934. In 1930 and 1931, Canada, Italy, Switzerland, and Austria adopted discriminatory protectionist policies. France protected in 1930, and added discrimi-

---

[2] For example, the French government did not believe that it could refrain from raising levels of effective agricultural protection as international primary commodity prices dropped. Were the traditionally inefficient French agricultural sector to be exposed to the impact of falling international prices, the government feared that conservative peasants in the countryside would become landless radical former peasants in the cities. See Margaret S. Gordon, *Barriers to World Trade: A Study of Recent Commercial Policy* (New York: Macmillan, 1941); cited hereafter as *Barriers to World Trade*.

[3] Although the domestic politics of trade lies beyond the scope of this study, the connection between the existence of surplus capacity and rising protectionism merits discussion. Consider an import-competing firm or sectoral peak association contemplating the investment of political resources in a drive to secure protection. If the capacity of the import-competing sector and domestic demand are roughly equal, then price increases brought about by protection are likely to attract new domestic competitors. Those who would seek protection would capture less than the full benefits of protection. If the capacity of the import-competing sector is well in excess of domestic demand, then protection is less likely to attract new domestic competitors. Those who would seek protection would be likely to capture a greater share of the benefits of protection.

natory features to its trade barriers through 1933. In 1934, France formally revised its quota system to reserve 75 percent of each contingent for bargaining purposes. Germany protected in 1931, but did not formally break with the most-favored-nation principle or systematically use the Aski Mark system as a source of leverage until 1933. Great Britain adopted protection in November 1931, granted temporary Imperial Preferences in March 1932, formalized Imperial Preference at the Ottawa Conference in the summer of 1932, and entered into discriminatory bilateral bargaining with gusto in April 1933. The gaps between violation of the primary and secondary norm ranged from four years to no time at all.

This chapter suggests that the adoption of protection without discrimination by the United States may have resulted in the overprovision of protection. The Tariff Act of 1930 created high nondiscriminatory tariffs. The costs of American protection were diffused over American trading partners. The thesis argued here is that the nondiscriminatory nature of the American tariff, by intent and in effect, foreclosed international political exchange and thereby temporarily reduced the interest of export-oriented American sectors in serving as a countervailing influence to the import-competing sectors. The combination of disrespect for the primary norm of openness and respect for the secondary norm of nondiscrimination appears to have accelerated movement toward closure.[4]

The adoption of discriminatory policies by virtually every other major trading nation expanded opportunities for political exchange. However, one cannot simply assume that economic discrimination contributes to the attainment of politically pareto efficient outcomes. The effects of discrimination on welfare depend, in part, on whether discriminatory trade practices are used to exchange, explain, or extort. In Chapter Three, I suggested that the extortion, with its potential welfare reducing effects, should be uncommon. This chapter finds that commercial extortion was not common in the 1930s.

The effects of political exchange on the interests and actions of *third parties* is even more critical to the assessment of the welfare implications of trade discrimination. During the early 1930s, the discriminatory protectionist policies of primary commodity exporters and debtors gave rise to a flurry of political exchange that accomplished little but trade diversion. Each exchange was mutually bene-

---

[4] See the next section, "Nondiscriminatory Protection: The U.S. Tariff Act of 1930." During periods of rising protection, most-favored-nation provisions may act to accelerate movement toward closure. During periods of falling protection, most-favored-nation provisions and discrimination may act to advance movement toward openness, as is conventionally argued.

ficial, to be sure, but taken together the "privatization" of trade protection did not materially increase or decrease levels of effective protection. However, third party externalities associated with bilateral political exchanges had two very profound effects on levels of protection. The proliferation of discriminatory trading practices had adverse effects on relatively liberal nondiscriminatory Great Britain, and Britain moved toward discriminatory protection to protect her exports. These same discriminatory trading practices also had adverse effects on the protectionist nondiscriminatory United States. To protect her exports, America opted for *de facto* discrimination to secure most-favored-nation tariff concessions. In effect, though not by intent, the discriminatory trading practices of other nations caused the United States to move toward a more liberal commercial policy.

NONDISCRIMINATORY PROTECTION: THE U.S. TARIFF ACT OF 1930

To frame discussion of the Smoot-Hawley Tariff, consider the discussion of externalities management in Chapter Two. In the illustration of an economic externality with public goods characteristics, a factory's soot settles on all houses in a neighborhood. The costs imposed on householders exceed the benefits to the factory owner. As Coase has observed, an opportunity for mutually beneficial exchange exists. The householders could compensate the factory owner for shutting down production and be better off than they were with the pollution. However, the householders confront a free rider problem.[5] If one householder were to strike a bargain with the factory owner, third parties could not be excluded from the benefits of soot reduction. Householders are likely to encounter difficulty as they gather resources to bribe the factory owner to cease production. To return to international trade, unconditional nondiscriminatory tariffs and global quotas create a corresponding free rider problem. The public good of tariff reduction and quota expansion is likely to be underprovided through decentralized political exchange. By design and in effect, the international costs of the Tariff Act of 1930 were diffused across numerous American trading partners, and countervailing in-

[5] Duncan Snidal would take exception to this argument. Recast in terms of his argument on K-groups, some smaller subset of American trading partners had an interest in providing the public good of pressure on the United States to revise the trade bill. But the collective action problem would simply reappear within the K-group rather than within the universe of American trading partners. Unfortunately, the existence of K-groups does not provide a solution to the problem of managing international externalities with the properties of a public good. See Duncan Snidal, "The Limits of Hegemonic Stability Theory," *International Organization* 85 (1985): 579–614 and Chapter Two of this volume.

ternational pressure was underprovided. The agricultural depression of 1928–29 triggered a rash of tariff increases during 1929 and was the proximate cause of the U.S. tariff revision of 1929–30. As the range of American tariff revisions spread from agricultural to mining to manufactured goods and the extent of increases in rates grew, what began as a minor rate revision became the Smoot-Hawley Tariff. During the months of congressional deliberation over the tariff revision, many nations pointed to the international externalities associated with proposed American rates. Great Britain and France noted that the tariff revisions might have unfortunate effects on their ability to repay war debts, Germany pointed to the likely effects on their ability to adhere to the Young Plan, and the Swiss pointed to the devastating effects of the proposed rates on their watch industry. These diplomatic entreaties were not formally heard by Congress. In 1929 and 1930, American legislators deemed tariff rate setting a wholly domestic matter.

The United States' largest trading partner—Canada—was most profoundly threatened by the proposed rate increases on primary products. Prior to passage of the Tariff Act of 1930, Canada sought reductions in the proposed rates for agricultural products and other commodities for which Canada was the principal supplier. In 1929, approximately 68 percent of all Canadian imports originated in the United States and 44 percent of all Canadian exports went to the United States.[6] Prime Minister Mackenzie King continually spoke of the size of the American trade surplus with Canada and indicated that Canadian trade policies were contingent on American actions: "There should be in Canada the heartiest cooperation on the part of all parties to seek within the Empire any new markets to replace any that may be lost elsewhere, and to place within the Empire at home and abroad, as many of the purchases now given to any country that penalizes our trade as can be transferred *without* penalizing the Canadians."[7]

Studies of the 1930s continually referred to these threats as *retaliation*, connoting a simple desire to inflict costs on an adversary. Canadian public sentiment unquestionably favored retaliation in this

[6] League of Nations, *Review of World Trade 1933* (Geneva: League of Nations, 1934), 56–57. Contrary to Canadian expectations, the percentage of total Canadian exports to the United States was not changed appreciably by the U.S. tariff. In 1929 44.6%, in 1930 45.9%, and in 1931 44.0% of Canadian exports went to the United States.

[7] Emphasis added. For an excellent descriptive study of tariff retaliation, see Joseph M. Jones, *Tariff Retaliation: Repercussions of the Hawley-Smoot Bill* (Philadelphia: University of Pennsylvania, 1934); cited hereafter as *Tariff Retaliation*. This quote is drawn from p. 185.

sense. But the announced intention to respond to continuing American protection by shifting Canadian trade patterns toward the empire was not an extortionate threat. In the terminology of Chapter Three, it was explanation. American protection increased the Canadian interest in empire preference. The government had reason to believe that the proposed increases in rates would adversely affect Canadian exports of primary products at a time when access to alternative markets would be difficult to secure. Tariffs on agricultural products were increasing, and the Canadian government expected that in the event the proposed high rates on Canadian exports were passed, it would need the leverage derived from Canadian imports to secure access to alternative markets. From the perspective of Canada, the threat to turn purchases toward the empire simply drew attention to the logical consequences of American protection on Canadian interests. If the United States did not amend the proposed rates in the Tariff Act of 1930, then Canada had an interest in turning toward Britain. If the United States revised the rates substantially, then Canada had an interest in turning toward the United States. The Canadian interest in turning toward Britain or the United States was contingent on American actions.

Although virtually every major trading nation appealed for general or specific reductions in rates and for increasing the flexibility of rate setting under the Tariff Act of 1930, it was not revised. American import-competing sectors secured ample protection for themselves and even "protected" export-oriented sectors. For example, the export-oriented American automotive industry objected strenuously to tariff rates shielding them from foreign competition. Some products with *no* American producers and *no* close domestic substitutes were added to dutiable lists. The addition of export-oriented products and products without domestic sources poses a problem for materialist interpretations of tariff rate setting. Not all changes make sense.[8]

The Tariff Act of 1930 was designed to minimize countervailing international pressure. Students of domestic legislative process contend that unrestricted political exchange within the Congress transformed a modest tariff revision into the highly protectionist Smoot-Hawley Act.[9] Ironically, international logrolling that could have internalized

---

[8] I am indebted to Stephen Schuker for noting that the Tariff Act of 1930 added maraschino cherries to the dutiable list. This odd action created problems for both ice cream sundae lovers in the 1930s and for rational choice theorists in the 1980s.

[9] For more information on these points, see E. E. Schattschneider, *Politics, Pressures, and the Tariff: A Study of Free Private Enterprise in Pressure Politics as Shown in the 1929–1930 Revision of the Tariff* (New York: Prentice Hall, 1935); Raymond Bauer, Ithiel de

many of the international externalities associated with the tariff was precluded by several specific features of the Tariff Act of 1930. The Act provides a prototypical example of how the nature of protection conditions international political interaction directed at the internalization of externalities associated with protection.

By design, the Hawley-Smoot Tariff was high *and* nondiscriminatory. The Tariff Act of 1930 extended the range of goods protected and raised most tariff rates to near record levels. The Act also threatened nations that discriminated against American products with a 50 percent surcharge on (high) normal duties. However, the Act offered nations that granted preferences to American goods no corresponding reciprocal reductions in American rates. A modest "flexibility" provision granted the U.S. Tariff Commission the power to recommend tariff reductions or increases to the president if production costs changed. Ironically, the closeness of the final vote on the Tariff Act was due, in part, to "nays" cast by congressmen who opposed the limited flexibility provisions in the act. Import-competing interests did not want their protection traded away. The tariff was designed to be nonnegotiable, to limit the ability of other nations to offer reductions to American exporting interests in exchange for concessions on rates affecting American import-competing interests. Rates could only be changed to punish states that discriminated against American products or to reflect changes in production costs.

From the perspective of trading partners, the Hawley-Smoot Tariff created a public goods problem. Individual reciprocal tariff reductions were impossible under a single list tariff. Nondiscriminatory rate reductions on goods that might permit de facto discrimination in favor of a particular trading partner were ruled out by the requirement that rate changes under the "flexibility" provision be based on the technical grounds of changes in production costs. Rate reductions could occur only if the rules governing American rate setting, that is the Tariff Act of 1930 itself, were changed. The external benefits associated with such a change in rules governing rate setting could not be privatized.

If the benefits associated with a change in the rules would have been a public good, the costs associated with bringing about a revision in American tariff were most assuredly private. Individual trading partners could have sought exchange or extortion against the United States by making their trade policies contingent on revision of the

Act. But the penalty provision of the Tariff Act of 1930 discouraged the use of explicit tactical linkage as a means of influence. A 50 percent surcharge on duties toward any nation that discriminated against American products privatized the costs associated with unsuccessful offers to refrain from imposing additional duties on American goods. If a threat to impose additional restrictions on trade with the United States were to be rejected, the penalty provision would focus costs on the threatener.[10] Furthermore, if an offer to grant preferences to American products were to be accepted, the opportunity cost associated with using trade preferences as a source of leverage would have been the loss of other markets that could have been secured through privatized political exchange. Despite patent discrimination against American products, the penalty provision was invoked only once, against Germany.

The only call for a coordinated international response was not issued by a source with the resources to transcend the public goods problem described above. The Chamber of Commerce of Geneva called for a European entente to coordinate European protests to the American government.[11] Broader multilateral efforts to promote openness in 1930 were unmitigated catastrophes. The Preliminary Conference for Concerted Economic Action in February and March of 1930 could not achieve stabilization, much less reductions, in rates.[12] The Second International Conference with a View to Concerted Action in November deadlocked. Both Britain and the Netherlands declared that their adherence to free trade was contingent on international tariff reductions, but no reductions in tariffs were negotiated. The United States participated in neither conference. The Second Conference remanded the issue of tariff negotiations to governments for bilateral action.

By virtue of the nature of the American tariff, the United States was no longer active in the international politics of trade. However, the existence of the American tariff, taken in conjunction with world-

[10] The increase in effective level of protection associated with imposition of a 50% surcharge on the "normal" schedule under Smoot-Hawley is difficult to assess. The penalty provision would not have affected trade in categories of goods that were subjected to prohibitive normal tariffs, would have eliminated trade in the categories of goods that would be subjected to prohibitive rates under the penalty, and would have reduced trade in other goods. The height of the normal rates may have reduced the clout of the penalty provision surcharge.

[11] The Chamber's suggestion should be taken in the context of the Briand proposal for an economic federation of Europe. See Jones, *Tariff Retaliation*.

[12] The League of Nations *World Economic Survey 1931–32* indicates that the conference shelved the tariff truce idea in light of the "conjunction of depression" and the prospective United States tariff.

wide deflation, affected the politics of trade nonetheless. By imposing and maintaining a high nondiscriminatory tariff, the United States violated the primary norm of the international trade regime. The subsequent strong movement toward closure of the international economic system and the widespread adoption of discriminatory trading policies, discussed below, ultimately redounded to the detriment of American export interests and catalyzed American reinvolvement in international trade politics. However, between 1930 and 1934, U.S. tariffs remained high and nondiscriminatory.

DISCRIMINATORY PROTECTION: BILATERALISM AND IMPERIALISM 1930–1933

To return to the metaphor of the households and the factory, if a factory owner can control the amount of soot reaching individual households, each householder may offer bribes to reduce the volume of soot falling on his home. Simple bilateral negotiations over the amount of the compensation and the extent of soot reduction could permit both to attain mutually beneficial outcomes. Such transactions between the factory owner and the householder would have benign welfare implications for both.[13] However, as was argued in Chapter Two, privatized goods are *not* private goods. The factory owner may simply redirect soot toward other householders, thereby imposing significant costs on third parties. If a third household paid for the benefit of diversion, the costs might simply be transferred to a fourth. Ultimately, the story of the discriminatory factory owner and householders is likely to end with some subset of the householders facing a choice between enduring the factory's total production of soot or bearing the full cost of bribing the factory owner to reduce soot production.[14]

[13] See the discussion of "exchange" in Chapter Three.

[14] If an optimal level of externalities production is reached in the privatized externalities case, the distribution of benefits is likely to be skewed in the direction of the externalities producer's end of the contract curve, relative to the outcome that would prevail if a hegemon were negotiating on behalf of all households in a public goods situation. In a simple case of two households, one factory, where the factory produces 2 units of soot to produce $1.99 worth of goods and where each unit of soot costs a household $1.00, outcomes under the privatized/shifting soot case would be as follows. The factory owner would divide the soot over both households (1 unit each), and the first household would be willing to pay up to $1.00 to eliminate the soot. A deal would be struck, and the unit of soot that was falling on the first house would be added to the unit of soot already falling on the second house. The second householder would be willing to pay up to $2.00 to eliminate the two units of soot. The factory owner would receive up to $3.00 to eliminate $1.99 worth of production. The public goods

This characteristic of the privatized goods case can explain the pace of discriminatory bargaining over trade in the 1930s. Each householder had a strong incentive to strike a bargain with the factory owner as quickly as possible. Successful previous negotiations increased the amount of soot diverted. Unless the factory owner is willing to break previous deals, the position of the last householder is extremely undesirable. Soot can be reduced only by purchasing reductions in factory production, and no other households have any incentive to contribute to the bribe fund. This line of argument provides support for the "slippery slope" characterization of regime disintegration. In circumstances where no strong mutual interest in proscription of protectionist policy exists to check regime disintegration, fragmentation via privatization and negotiation is likely to take place very quickly. Once deals are being struck and trade is being diverted, every individual nation has an interest in being the first and not the last to hit the negotiating table and discriminate.

During the period 1930–1933, commercial discrimination operated largely to redirect the negative externalities associated with protection from one nation to another. In a deflationary world, with surplus capacity in all sectors, control over access to markets is a potent potential source of leverage. In *The Twenty Years' Crisis*, E. H. Carr noted: "Purchasing power had become an international asset; and the fact that price was no longer the dominant factor . . . put the purchaser and not the producer in a position to call the tune."[15] In the trough of deflation, protection was regarded as vital to the survival of virtually every advanced industrial nation, and cuts in net effective levels of protection were not attained through decentralized political exchange. However, by exchanging market access for market access, nations sought to defend their share of steadily shrinking international markets. A flurry of tariff increases that were initially presented as responses to Smoot-Hawley were followed by actions that were designed to protect and to discriminate. The variety of techniques employed is worth reviewing.

The interwar period is not known as the age of the unconditional nondiscriminatory tariff. Commercial policy makers elevated the craft of trade discrimination to a high art form. What overt and covert means did they employ, and how did each means privatize costs and benefits? Overt approaches to trade discrimination included

---

case is analogous to monopsony confronting monopoly, while the privatized goods case is analogous to market confronting discriminating monopolist.

[15] E. H. Carr, *The Twenty Years' Crisis*, (New York: Harper & Row, 1964), 129. Carr went on to observe that large wealthy nations may enjoy a relative advantage in negotiations over market access.

multiple list tariffs, quotas with limits imposed by nation of origin, and exchange controls. Multiple list tariffs simply imposed different tariff schedules on different classes of trading partners. Quotas with limits based on country of origin permit direct discrimination. Finally, exchange controls, by requiring licensing of individual payments from exporters to importers, permitted very fine-tuned control over imports. All three of these overt methods were used to grant preferences at the empire, regional, and national levels.

Commercial policy makers achieved substantial degrees of privatization through more subtle means. A nondiscriminatory tariff could be manipulated by narrowing definitions of categories of goods and by adjusting rates to discriminate with respect to trading partners. For example, the category "automobile" may be subdivided by displacement of engine, and rates may be raised on automobiles with engines displacing over 2,000 cc in order to discriminate against producers of larger cars. Ores could be defined by precise composition, and watches by number of jewels. In each instance, substantial discrimination could be engineered into a single list tariff schedule. A global quota could be manipulated in much the same manner, with categories and limits defined to permit effective discrimination. Other nontariff barriers such as quarantine and inspection regulations, product quality standards, and excise taxes could be used to discriminate against particular trading partners. Import financing and transportation cross-subsidies were used to negate the effects of nondiscriminatory tariffs on goods imported from selected partners. The imagination of commercial policy makers gave rise to devices that were both sources of leverage and bargaining tactics rolled onto one. For example, Cuba imposed sliding scale tariffs, where schedules were pegged to exchange rates (to neutralize competitive devaluation) and to bilateral trade balances (to encourage trading partners to run trade deficits).

Following passage of the Tariff Act of 1930, Canada did not resort to these more subtle techniques. Canada raised its general tariff levels and increased the margin of Empire preference on many items. The new Canadian tariff policy was designed to entice Great Britain into granting preferential access to Canadian commodities by offering British manufactured goods preferential access to the Canadian market. The British did not reciprocate, and adhered to their largely free trade policies. At the Imperial Conference in London in October 1930, Canada declared that the mild British preferences accorded members of the Empire were inadequate. Canada demanded that Britain place a 10 percent duty on foreign food products to leave the British market free for the products of the Empire. The offer was rejected and Canada did not extend the British greater preferences in its Tariff revision in 1931.[16]

Italy also sought to protect and discriminate to offset the loss of American markets. Mussolini summarized his views on Italian trade policy in an article cited by Jones from *Il Popolo D'Italia*:

> Italy will defend herself in her own way. We will make purchases only in those countries which buy our agricultural products, our marble, our cars, our ships, our silk, our wool and cotton manufactures. We will buy in the United States only the amount of goods the United States will buy in Italy. We will purchase the rest elsewhere. Our ships will load foreign goods for Italy only if they be allowed to return to the same ports with Italian goods. These are the precise limits of the new problem.[17]

The Mussolini program began with tariff increases directed at American automobiles and radios. The syndicalist Italian economy was, at least in theory, responsive to government direction and Italian firms began importing oil and wheat from the Soviet Union at about the same time as the Soviet Union began importing Fiats.[18]

In one interesting linkage between trade and finance, the Swiss negotiated a bilateral clearing and payments agreement with Austria in November 1931. The Swiss promised the Austrians a 33 percent surplus of exports over imports if the Austrians would earmark the surplus for payment to Swiss holders of Austrian securities. This linkage between commercial and financial issues was accepted. However, the agreement was of little consequence. The Austrian schilling was grossly overvalued and demand for Austrian exports in Switzerland at official par was so small that the guaranteed export surplus was very small in absolute value.[19]

French trade policy was conditioned by constraints imposed by fragments of the old trade regime. The Franco-German agreement of 1927 limited tariff increases, so the French turned to quotas on primary products to protect their domestic markets from inexpensive foreign agricultural and mineral products. During 1930 and 1931,

[16] This account is drawn largely from Jones, *Tariff Retaliation*, 189–201; J. Henry Richardson, *British Economic Foreign Policy* (New York: Macmillan, 1936); and the League of Nations, *World Economic Survey*.

[17] Jones, *Tariff Retaliation*, 79.

[18] Jones, *Tariff Retaliation*, 95. See G. Agnelli, "East-West Trade: A European View," *Foreign Affairs* (Summer 1980) for more recent thoughts on the subject. The choice of American automobiles as the object of the tariff was recommended by the Agnelli family, as was the strategy of seeking trade agreements with the Soviet Union.

[19] William Adams Brown, Jr., *The International Gold Standard Reinterpreted 1914–1934*, vol. 2 (New York: National Bureau of Economic Research, Inc., 1940), 1193; and Gordon, *Barriers to World Trade*, 121.

France allocated quotas for primary commodities on a relatively non-discriminatory basis. This initial round of quota setting was largely intended to protect French import-competing sectors. When France sought to extend the quota system to manufactured goods in 1932, Germany objected on the grounds that such quotas violated the terms of the Franco-German commercial agreement. Jones reports that France overcame Germany's natural reluctance to void the treaty by offering Germany a choice between two alternatives. In his words:

> Either the Germans should agree to an extension of the French quota system to manufactured products, the contingents to be determined and the quotas to be allocated after and upon agreements between interested manufacturers in France and Germany or they should submit to an arbitrary system of contingents decreed by the French government without any regard for German interests. Of these two evils the Germans naturally chose the former.[20]

French quotas were initially administered in a fashion that afforded Germany a modest degree of preference. The quota system, originally regarded as a means of protection, was predictably transformed into a source of leverage. France did not wait long to use her quota system to secure access to markets for French exports. The manipulation of base years and categories permitted a substantial amount of de facto discrimination even before France turned to de jure discrimination. By 1934, France settled on an overtly politicized system of quotas with 75 percent of each quota reserved for purposes of political exchange.

The British departure from the gold standard in September 1931 reinforced movement on the continent toward closure and discrimination. During the first two months after suspension of convertibility, nations that remained on the gold standard suffered a 30 percent appreciation in the value of their currencies relative to sterling. To maintain de jure parities, the continental nations expanded their quota systems and effected de facto devaluations through exchange controls and multiple exchange rate systems. Monetary and commercial restrictions were designed to offset British commercial advantages caused by the depreciation of sterling. Similar commercial consequences of international monetary developments also followed from the American decision to depart from gold in April 1933.

Narrowly bilateral commercial bargaining can provide benefits to parties to a given negotiation at the expense of third parties. As Chapter Two suggested, the politics of trade diversion creates strong

[20] Jones, *Tariff Retaliation*, 143.

TABLE 5.1
World Bilateral and Triangular Trade

	1929	1931	1932	1933
Bilateral trade	79.7	81.5	82.5	83.4
Triangular trade	20.3	18.5	17.5	16.6

Source: League of Nations, Survey of World Trade 1933, 66–68.

Note: The League defined bilateral trade as trade in which "exports and imports balance in each direction."

incentives to discriminate and negotiate as quickly as possible. The League of Nations *World Economic Survey 1931–32* reports that in 1931 alone:

1. France, Belgium, and Czechoslovakia introduced systems of licensing imports;
2. Austria, Bulgaria, Czechoslovakia, Estonia, Finland, Germany, Greece, Hungary, Latvia, Yugoslavia, Argentina, Brazil, Chile, and India imposed exchange controls;
3. Czechoslovakia, France, Italy, Latvia, Netherlands, and Turkey introduced quotas;
4. Czechoslovakia, Denmark, Estonia, Poland, Turkey, and Colombia imposed prohibitions;
5. Estonia and Sweden restricted imports through state monopolies;
6. Austria, Argentina, Australia, Belgium, Brazil, Bulgaria, Denmark, France, India, Italy, Latvia, Lithuania, Netherlands, Poland, South Africa, and Switzerland increased duties; and
7. France and Canada imposed customs surcharges for depreciated exchange.[21]

These shifts in commercial policy redirected international trade through increasingly bilateral channels. The League of Nations reported that between 1929 and 1933, reliance on discriminatory commercial practices had produced a marked decline in triangular trade. The modest global changes in Table 5.1 mask sharp swings at the national level. Between 1929 and 1933, the proportion of triangular trade for the French dropped from 23.5 percent to 6 percent, for the Swiss from 11.6 percent to 1.7 percent, and for Canada from 21.8 percent to 13.2 percent. The relatively unsystematic Italian program of trade discrimination resulted in an increase of triangular trade from 6.2 percent in 1929 to 10.2 percent in 1933.

[21] Ibid., 288.

The increasingly discriminatory and bilateral nature of trade in 1930–31 threatened the exports of (relatively) nondiscriminatory Great Britain. The British decision to protect and to discriminate followed in part from the desire to secure leverage to protect export interests. In addition, import-competing sectors within Britain feared that rising protection abroad would divert imports toward (relatively) open British markets. Taken together, these two factors pulled Great Britain toward discriminatory protection.[22] The Conservative party argued for a departure from free trade as necessary to restore free trade abroad. Stanley Baldwin argued: "you cannot get these tariffs reduced so long as you leave this market the only dumping ground of the world. . . . I believe that only those who can speak on an equality regarding tariffs can do business. We cannot do that. . . . For the sake of the home market and the foreign market you must try to pull down the tariffs of the world which will ultimately strangle you if you do not."[23] With the formation of the National Government in 1931, British commercial policy shifted quickly. The passage of the Abnormal Importations Act in November 1931 empowered the Board of Trade to assess duties of up to 100 percent on manufactured goods, and the Horticultural Products Act empowered the Minister of Agriculture to assess duties of up to 100 percent on "luxury" plant products.[24] These temporary measures were superceded by the permanent Import Duties Act in March 1932. That act levied a general tariff of 10 percent on most imports,[25] exempted the dominions, colonies, and territories from the duties until November 1932, created procedures for raising or lowering general duties, and provided for imposition of penalty duties of 100 percent against goods from nations that discriminated against British goods.[26]

[22] Forrest Capie observes that developments in 1931 should not be divorced from a longer term British trend toward protection. In his words, "the emphasis should be shifted from viewing the tariff as a sudden, unpremeditated response to the world economic depression that began in mid-1929; rather it should be seen as being the outcome of a variety of economic causes that date essentially from the First World War and flourished in the 1920s." The argument offered here does not contradict Capie. The factors emphasized here may have accelerated this long-term trend. See Forrest Capie, *Depression and Protectionism* (London: Allen and Unwin, 1983).

[23] J. B. Condliffe, *The Reconstruction of World Trade* (New York: W. W. Norton, 1940); Gordon, *Barriers to World Trade*; Richardson, *British Economic Foreign Policy*; and Jones, *Tariff Retaliation* provide the materials in this account. The quotation is drawn from Jones, p. 223.

[24] These included tulip bulbs and fresh fruits and vegetables.

[25] Exempted products included raw materials and staples.

[26] This summary is compiled from Gordon, *Barriers to World Trade*; Jones, *Tariff Retaliation*; and the League of Nations *World Economic Survey 1930–31* and *World Economic Survey 1931–32*.

The Ottawa Agreements in the summer of 1932 reinforced the discriminatory aspects of British commercial policy. The British agreed to continue existing preferences by maintaining the 1932 Import Duty Act provisions for a 10 percent tariff against foreign goods and for duty-free access for empire products, to add new duties on foreign wheat, corn, butter, cheese, and other products that had been exempted under the Import Duty Act, and to establish an import quota on meat in order to give the dominions a greater share of the British market. In return the dominions granted a variety of trade preferences affecting a broad range of British products, while safeguarding their own infant industries.[27]

The Ottawa Agreements provided Great Britain with considerable negotiating strength vis-à-vis non-empire nations. The extent of the British commitment to the empire was unclear, and British trading partners feared that the dominions might succeed in capturing even stronger preferences in the future. This fear of additional trade diversion provided the impetus for a series of bilateral commercial agreements. Like the factory owner in the story in Chapter Two, Britain struck relatively soft deals with the first group of householders at Ottawa and drove progressively harder deals in later rounds of discussions.

As Britain consolidated its ties to the empire, Norway, Sweden, and Denmark sought preferential access to the British market. Between April and May of 1933, Britain concluded reciprocal trade agreements with the Scandinavian nations. Denmark was granted 62 percent of the British quota for non-empire bacon, granted an egg and butter quota just below 1932 levels, and granted preferential access to the financial resources of the city. In return, Denmark agreed to admit a wide range of British goods duty free; to reduce duties on other goods; to freeze duties on other products; and to purchase 80 percent of its total coal imports from Britain.[28] In the reciprocal agreement with Norway, Britain agreed to import fish at not less than 90 percent of the average levels between 1923 and 1933, to keep timber products on the free list, and to reduce duties on other Norwegian products. In turn, Norway agreed to purchase 70 percent of coal imports from Britain, to reduce duties on textiles and other goods, and to extend their free list. In the agreement with Sweden, Britain agreed to reduce duties on specialty steels and not to impose quantitative limits on Swedish bacon, hams, butter, and eggs. Sweden

---

[27] Brown, *International Gold Standard Reinterpreted*, vol. 2, 1165–66; and Jones, *Tariff Retaliation*, 235–37.

[28] Brown, *International Gold Standard Reinterpreted*, vol. 2, 1167.

agreed to reduce duties and to purchase 47 percent of coal imports from Britain.[29] In a contemporaneous agreement with Germany, Britain reduced tariffs on a number of goods produced in Germany, and Germany agreed to purchase at least 180,000 tons of British coal per month and to increase the British quota in proportion to German coal consumption.[30]

In May and September of 1933, Britain protected its commercial, financial, and monetary interests through reciprocal trade and financial agreements with Argentina. Britain gave less and received substantially more than it had in earlier agreements with Scandinavia and the dominions. The British agreed to impose no quantitative restrictions and to freeze duties on an array of Argentine goods, to accept as much Argentine chilled beef as they had imported in 1931–32,[31] to place no additional restrictions on frozen meat, and to provide a sterling loan. Argentina agreed to reduce duties on a number of industrial goods provided largely by Britain, to continue to admit coal on a duty-free basis, to provide the British with preferential treatment on loan repayments, and to peg the peso to sterling and abandon the French franc.[32]

In February 1934, Britain concluded a trade agreement with the Soviet Union. Britain granted most-favored-nation status to the Soviet Union, with the proviso that the agreement could be suspended if the Soviets engaged in dumping. The Soviets agreed that the proceeds from sales in Britain would be spent in Britain "in a gradually increasing proportion until at the end of five years there would be an approximate equality of payments, both visible and invisible, between the two countries."[33]

The compartmentalization of the world economy through bilateral bargaining and reliance on the empire increased the export shares of the discriminatory protectionist states. The British Empire's share of world exports decreased from 26.3 percent in 1929 to 23.8 percent in 1931. After Britain adopted Imperial Preferences and an active bilateral discriminatory negotiating strategy, the empire share of world exports increased to 25.9 percent in 1932 and to 27.2 percent

[29] Richardson, *British Economic Foreign Policy*, 105.

[30] Richardson, *British Economic Foreign Policy*, 105–6.

[31] This guarantee was subject to a 10 percent reduction if necessary to "keep prices at a remunerative level."

[32] Richardson, *British Economic Foreign Policy*, 106–8, Brown *International Gold Standard Reinterpreted*, vol. 2, 1167–68.

[33] Richardson, *British Economic Foreign Policy*, 108–10. Richardson notes that in the period 1931–33, British imports from the Soviet Union were approximately 124 million pounds sterling and Soviet imports from Britain amounted to 40 million pounds sterling.

in 1933. The export share of France and her colonies increased steadily from 7.6 percent in 1929 to 8.2 percent in 1931 to 8.6 percent in 1932 to 9.0 percent in 1933.[34] In short, nations that engaged in bilateral discrimination and empire preference increased their world export shares.

This position on the effects of discrimination on the export performance of parties to discrimination is not uncontroversial. Barry Eichengreen contends that the rising British share of world exports was caused largely by monetary rather than by commercial policy.[35] The depreciation of sterling by approximately 40 percent relative to other key currencies in 1931, discussed in Chapter Six, unquestionably improved the British export position. However, the existence of real exchange rate effects does not necessarily imply that commercial policy had negligible effects on the British share of world exports. Because Britain turned toward commercial discrimination and monetary devaluation simultaneously, it is difficult to disentangle the independent effects of commercial and monetary policy on British shares of world exports. The French case provides a relatively clear basis for inferring that discriminatory commercial policies had effects on export performance. In the French case, the turn toward discrimination and empire preceded nominal depreciation of the franc by six years. French export shares rose *after* France had turned toward discrimination, *after* Britain had permitted sterling to depreciate, and *before* France had devalued the franc. In short, discriminatory French commercial policy between 1930 and 1936 increased French shares of world exports despite the effects of real franc appreciation.

It is not surprising that commercial discrimination provided narrow benefits to parties that engaged in discrimination. However, the case against reliance on discrimination centers on the effects of discrimination on third parties. Increases in export shares inevitably come at the expense of other exporters. This section has shown that loss of market shares and the expectation of loss of market shares turned nation after nation toward discriminatory trade policies. As critics of commercial discrimination suggest, bilateralism and regionalism tend to spread quickly through commercial systems. The next section demonstrates that loss of global markets pushed the United States toward discrimination. The United States was the last nation to move to defend its export share through discrimination, and American options were limited accordingly. In the face of preexisting bilat-

[34] Figures are drawn from the League of Nations, *Survey of World Trade 1933*, 59, 61.

[35] Personal communication. See also Alec Cairncross and Barry J. Eichengreen, *Sterling in Decline: The Devaluations of 1931, 1949, and 1967* (London: Basil Blackwell, 1983); and Barry J. Eichengreen, *Sterling and the Tariff*, Princeton Studies in International Finance, no. 48 (September 1981).

eral and regional preferences, the American defense of export-oriented interests took the form of a discriminatory liberalizing trade strategy.

DISCRIMINATORY LIBERALIZATION:
U.S. RECIPROCAL TRADE 1934–1938

The 1934 Reciprocal Trade Agreements Act (RTAA) altered both the process and the substance of American commercial policy fundamentally. To limit the effects of domestic political exchange on commercial policy, the Congress shifted the principal responsibility for trade policy making to the executive branch.[36] To harness the effects of international political exchange on behalf of American export performance, the Congress empowered the president to trade market access for market access.

The RTAA was foreshadowed by developments in the early 1930s. In his study of the reciprocal trade policy of the United States, Henry J. Tasca describes several abortive early proposals for reversal of the American policy of nondiscriminatory protectionism. In June 1931, Representative Cordell Hull called for pursuit of reciprocal trade pacts. In August 1931, Senator K. McKellar called for repeal of the Tariff Act of 1930, unilateral tariff cuts of 25 percent to nations that increased their purchases of American products by 25 percent. As the American export position declined during 1932, eccentric individual proposals became Democratic party policy. The Collier Tariff Bill, passed in May 1932, included provisions for tariff reductions, an international conference on trade, and reciprocal trade negotiations. The reciprocity section of the bill was restored after deletion in anticipation of British adoption of the Imperial preference system at Ottawa.[37] According to Robert Pastor, President Hoover vetoed the bill because he believed that continuing tariff protection was essential to the well-being of the American people, that tariff policy should continue to be treated as a solely domestic question, and that reciprocal negotiations would produce preferential agreements at variance with the traditional open door policies of the United States.[38]

Following Hoover's veto of the Collier Bill, the Democratic party

[36] See Stephen Haggard, "The Institutional Foundations of Hegemony: Explaining the Reciprocal Trade Agreements Act of 1934," *International Organization* 42 (Winter 1988) for analysis of the interaction between international environmental change and domestic institutional evolution.

[37] Henry J. Tasca, *The Reciprocal Trade Policy of the United States: A Study in Trade Philosophy* (Philadelphia: University of Pennsylvania Press, 1938), 14–16, cited hereafter as *Reciprocal Trade*.

[38] Pastor, *Congress and the Politics of U.S. Foreign Economic Policy*, 84; see also Tasca, *Reciprocal Trade*, 16.

added a plank to the party platform calling for "reciprocal tariff agreements with other nations and an international conference designed to restore international trade and facilitate exchange."[39] In his Sioux City address in September 1932, Franklin Roosevelt repeatedly attacked the Republican tariff policy by noting that it:

> "has largely extinguished the export markets for our industrial and our farm surplus; it has prevented the payment of public and private debts to us and the interest thereon, increasing taxation to meet the expense of our government, and finally it has driven our factories abroad. . . . We must consent to the reduction to some extent of our duties in order to secure a lowering of foreign tariff walls over which a larger measure of our surplus may be sent.

Roosevelt quickly backed down from this position, as import-competing agricultural and industrial groups began inquiring as to which tariffs Roosevelt wished to cut.[40]

During 1933, President Roosevelt did not move to implement the Democratic platform plank on reciprocal trade negotiations. The administration confronted a trade-off between securing powers necessary to increase access to markets for American exports and several critical domestic objectives. The First New Deal sought to promote national recovery by raising domestic prices. Both the National Recovery Act (NRA) and the Agricultural Adjustment Administration (AAA) imposed production limits to raise domestic prices and profits to increase general levels of economic activity. In order for these programs to succeed in raising levels of economic activity by raising production costs and internal prices, sectors falling under the codes had to be sheltered from foreign competition. Without tariff protection, an increase in prices would simply stimulate imports without increasing domestic production. Both acts contained provisions empowering the president to restrict imports that might "render ineffective or seriously endanger the maintenance of any code or agreement."[41] During the First New Deal, tariff reductions were inconsistent with the primary means to national recovery. Furthermore, a reciprocal trade agreements act could well have split the congressional coalition that the Roosevelt administration was counting on to pass the New Deal legislation. As noted earlier, Roosevelt had backed sharply away from discussions of tariff negotiations following the Sioux City address.

[39] Tasca, *Reciprocal Trade*, p. 17.

[40] Daniel R. Fusfeld, *The Economic Thought of Franklin D. Roosevelt and the Origins of The New Deal* (New York: Columbia University Press, 1956), 236–37.

[41] Tasca, *Reciprocal Trade*, 12.

Many of the inquiries as to which tariffs might be cut had come from groups that were core members of the New Deal coalition.

Through 1933, President Roosevelt's commercial policy was virtually indistinguishable from that of President Hoover. Their beliefs on commercial affairs differed significantly but their policies were similar. Hoover was unconditionally opposed to tariff reductions on the grounds that a high tariff was necessary to shield agriculture and industry from foreign competition and thereby to stimulate investment. He saw no connection between American imports policy and access to markets for American exports. Roosevelt saw tariff reduction as blunting the effectiveness of the NRA and AAA, and limiting the effectiveness of other price raising programs,[42] but also recognized that revision of American commercial policy was a necessary concomitant of improving American export performance. At first very different belief systems supported virtually identical policies, but as conditions changed, the differences in beliefs were reflected in trade policy.

By the end of 1933, the trade-off between defense of export interests and domestic recovery through price raising had shifted. First, the depreciation of the dollar following the April decision to depart from the gold standard raised the price of imports and enhanced the competitiveness of domestic producers. Second, mild reflation of the American economy decreased the desperation of import-competing sectors. Third, the AAA and NRA were safely enacted into law. These developments lowered the domestic costs associated with reducing levels of protection. Internationally, the reciprocal agreements struck by Britain with Argentina, the Scandinavian nations, and others in the spring and summer of 1933, restricted the access of American exporters to additional markets. Together, these domestic and international developments tilted the Roosevelt administration toward active pursuit of a revision of the Tariff Act of 1930.

Passing the Reciprocal Trade Agreements Act

By the end of 1933, every major trading nation except the United States had adopted discriminatory trading policies. The discriminatory nature of international trade bargaining adversely affected exporting interests *within* the nondiscriminatory protectionist United States. As Table 5.2 demonstrates, the U.S. share of world exports and the American trade surplus declined steadily. These developments were commonly perceived as effects of the discriminatory trad-

---

[42] Such as the gold purchasing program discussed in Chapter Six.

TABLE 5.2
World and U.S. Trade 1929–1933 (in millions of dollars)

	1929	1930	1931	1932	1933
World imports	35,606	29,083	20,847	13,885	11,937
World exports	33,035	26,492	18,992	12,726	11,119
U.S. imports	4,339	3,114	2,088	1,330	1,122
U.S. exports	5,157	3,781	2,378	1,577	1,149
U.S. trade surplus	818	667	290	247	27
U.S. import share	12.2	10.7	10.0	9.6	9.4%
U.S. export share	15.6	14.3	12.6	12.4	10.3%

Source: U.S. Congress, House Committee on Ways and Means, Majority Report on Reciprocal Trade Agreements, 73rd Cong. 2nd Sess.

Note: The perceptive reader will note that world imports exceeded world exports by varying amounts in these years. Systematic differences may be caused by governmental underreporting of exports and/or overreporting of imports in a world inclined toward bilateral balancing and by the definition of fob and cif valuations. The variations from year to year suggest that interwar trade figures should be regarded with substantial caution.

ing policies of other nations.[43] The deterioration of American exports ultimately provided the critical external impetus for a reversal of American commercial policy. During hearings on the Reciprocal Trade Agreements Act, Roosevelt administration officials repeatedly pointed to the "discriminations" of other states as their motivation for seeking a revision of American trade law. Ostensible unconditional economic liberals including Secretary of State Cordell Hull cast their arguments in terms of the need for the United States to defend American exporting interests and to stave off further "deterioration" in the American trade balance.[44]

Congress passed the revision suggested by the administration with only minor modifications.[45] The amendment to the Tariff Act of

[43] In reality, monetary as well as commercial policies undoubtedly contributed to the deterioration in American external trade position. In the period 1929–1933, the dollar appreciated in both real and nominal terms relative to currencies of major trading partners. As the following chapter notes, the nominal sterling-dollar rate fell by a third in the twelve months after the British left gold; differences in domestic price levels did not offset the nominal exchange rate change.

[44] In later writings, Cordell Hull discusses RTAA in terms of his ultimate end of reconstructing world trade along liberal internationalist lines rather than in terms of mercantilist goals.

[45] The minority report from the House Ways and Means Committee opposed the Reciprocal Trade Act on several grounds. First, they argued that tariff reductions would impose "greater harm" on import-competing sectors than export expansion would benefit export-oriented sectors. Second, they believed that other nations had

1930 was titled, "Promotion of Foreign Trade," and the first section began with the following clear, if somewhat less than succinct, sentence.

> For the purpose of expanding foreign markets for the products of the United States . . . by regulating the admission of foreign goods into the United States in accordance with the characteristics and needs of various branches of American production so that foreign markets will be made available to those branches of American production which require and are capable of developing such outlets by affording corresponding market opportunities for foreign products in the United States, the President, whenever he finds as a fact that any existing duties or other import restrictions of the United States or any other foreign country are unduly burdening and restricting the foreign trade of the United States and that the purpose above declared will be promoted by the means hereinafter specified is authorized from time to time to . . . enter into foreign trade agreements and . . . to proclaim modifications of existing duties and other import restrictions . . . such as are necessary to carry out any foreign trade agreements.

The bill authorized the president to raise or lower duties by as much as 50 percent, prohibited transferring articles between dutiable and free lists, and explicitly prohibited linkages between financial and commercial issues. Import-competing interests could not block negotiations exchanging their domestic market shares for improved access to foreign markets. However, American creditors succeeded in forestalling negotiations that might exchange their claims on foreigners for improved market access.[46] By engaging the interests of export-oriented sectors in the fight against protection, the discriminations of other nations were instrumental in shifting U.S. commercial policy from autonomous protection to reciprocity.

Two features of the new American trade policy require explanation. First, given the need for a more active American defense of exporting interests, why did the United States choose to offer tariff concessions rather than to threaten tariff increases? Second, why did the United States opt for trade increasing discrimination instead of trade diverting discrimination?

---

already padded their rates, and that tariff negotiations would bring only illusory reciprocal reductions. Third, they argued that the United States should strive for a balanced economy, and decrease its dependency on trade. Fourth, the Republicans argued, perhaps somewhat disingenuously, that they feared that tariff reductions would undermine the NRA and AAA's programs to stimulate the domestic economy.

[46] U.S. Congress, "An Act to Amend the Tariff Act of 1930," 73rd Cong., 2d sess., chapter 474, June 12, 1934.

Congress divided on the first issue. The Republican minority called for a policy of threatening to impose duties on items currently on the duty-free list[47] and to raise duties on the dutiable list. The Republicans argued that discouraging imports of nondutiable items would benefit the United States by creating a more balanced economy. Additional protection would benefit import-competing sectors that confronted competition from lower wage nations. From the Republicans' perspective, offering to refrain from raising duties was exchange. They dismissed Democratic arguments that other nations would retaliate against the United States if the United States were to execute threats to increase protection.

The proposal to threaten to impose duties on duty-free items attracted little support; no significant lobby on behalf of *potential* import-competing sectors existed.[48] Approximately 37 percent of American imports by value were dutiable.[49] The proposal to threaten to impose additional duties on dutiable products was undercut by the height of tariffs imposed by the Tariff Act of 1930. Many American tariffs were prohibitive, and raising prohibitive duties would not have affected flows of imports. Raising nonprohibitive rates would unquestionably have reduced the volume of these imports while benefiting import-competing sectors. Democratic advocates of mutual trade concessions argued that rate increases would perpetuate even greater rigidity and inefficiency in the American economy. From their perspective, threatening to raise rates was extortion. They spoke frequently of how threats to raise rates would cause rapid deterioration in commercial relations and spark tariff wars. Whatever the merits of the Republican and Democratic assessments of the American interest in executing threats to raise tariffs, it is clear that no other nations would have perceived threats to raise tariffs during a time of reflation as extortion. Fear of retaliation dominated other factors during deliberations on this point. The Reciprocal Trade Agreements Act authorized the Roosevelt administration to raise or lower rates. The administration chose to seek mutual rate reductions.

Fear of international retaliation against rate increases pushed the administration toward a policy of mutual tariff concessions. However, the requirements of the NRA and AAA price raising programs lim-

[47] The free list consisted largely of items not produced in the United States.

[48] Furthermore, the harm inflicted by duties imposed on goods not produced in the United States might not be great. The absence of an import-competing sector suggests that reductions in imports, hence harm inflicted on exporting nations, would be limited initially to reductions in volume induced by the price elasticity of demand.

[49] U.S. Congress, House Committee on Ways and Means, "Extending Reciprocal Foreign Trade Agreements Act," 75th Cong., 2d sess., January 1937, 61.

ited the range of concessions that could be made. Henry Tasca notes that: "the NRA was a definite factor retarding the progress of the trade agreements program. And this flowed from the antithetical relation to the tariff law. . . . it appears most probable that the State Department had to be cautious in granting concessions on industrial products."[50] Fifty-six producers covered by NRA codes filed for protection from imports under section 3(e) of the National Industrial Recovery Act. Twenty-three petitions were pending at the time that the U.S. Supreme Court invalidated the NRA in the Schecter Poultry decision in 1935.[51] The trade-off between the NRA approach to price raising and the RTAA program of export expansion through reciprocal tariff reduction was ended by judicial action.

Second, the United States could have chosen to increase American exports by seeking bilateral trade preferences rather than by seeking general reductions in levels of protection that were to be passed on to third parties through MFN provisions of trade agreements. The commercial diplomacy of other major trading nations was directed largely at diverting the incidence of protection. The United States focused on reducing levels of protection. Both views were represented within the Roosevelt administration. George Peek, Special Assistant to the President on Trade Policy, argued for narrowly bilateral policies to regain American export shares. Reversion to the conditional form of MFN status, adoption of quotas and other nontariff import controls, and government-to-government barter deals were the central elements of Peek's program of trade bargaining. The benefits derived from American purchasing power were to be reserved for the United States.[52] On the other hand, Secretary of State Cordell Hull argued for a policy directed at general tariff reductions to be transmitted through unconditional MFN provisions. The narrow objective of improving American export performance was, to Hull, secondary. During hearings on the extension of the Reciprocal Trade Agreements Act in 1937, Hull consistently answered questions on narrow benefits with lectures on the intrinsic merits of reducing international barriers to the free flow of goods.[53]

The tension between Peek's economic nationalism and Hull's economic internationalism may have been more apparent than real. During the mid-1930s, the narrow interest of the United States coin-

[50] Tasca, *Reciprocal Trade*, 95.

[51] Tasca, *Reciprocal Trade*, 95.

[52] See George Peek, *Why Quit Our Own?* (New York: Van Nostrand, 1936).

[53] U.S. Congress, House Committee on Ways and Means, *Hearings on Extending the Reciprocal Foreign Trade Agreements Act*, 76th Cong., 3d sess. (Washington, D.C.: GPO, 1937).

cided with pursuit of tariff reductions and unconditional MFN status. As the last major trading nation to defend its exports, the United States had little choice but to seek reductions in levels of protection. Other major trading states had already diverted and channeled trade through narrowly bilateral political exchanges. To expand American exports without reducing levels of protection would have entailed convincing or coercing other nations into breaking previous agreements. Like the last household in the "privatizable externalities" case discussed in Chapter Two, the United States could not simply bribe factory owners to divert soot to other households, but had to pay the full price of soot reduction.

Given the bilateral and regional trade preferences that were the products of political exchanges prior to 1934, granting and receiving of MFN status served narrow American interests. In 1937 hearings on renewal of RTAA, Assistant Secretary of State Francis Sayre described the American strategy: "What the United States does, in effect, is to trade the extension of all its concessions in bulk against the extensions to it of all concessions which the various recipient countries have granted, are granting, or may in future grant to all other countries. The reciprocal element is present in the extension of concessions just as much as it is in the original exchange. Both are bargaining-exchanges."[54] Under unconditional MFN, trade preferences that other nations had extended to their trading partners in the past would be passed on to the United States. Furthermore, in the context of generally declining tariff rates, the unconditional MFN clause would transmit to the United States the benefits of future negotiations between nations covered by MFN treaties and third parties. Or so the theory suggested.

RTAA in Practice

The Reciprocal Trade Agreements Act was designed to increase American exports by permitting American trade negotiators to barter market access for market access. Although American concessions were formally nondiscriminatory, many rate reductions were structured to benefit negotiating partners without conferring substantial benefits on third parties. American concessions centered on products for which a negotiating partner was the principal supplier. American product classifications were sometimes redefined to exclude third parties from the benefits of a rate reduction. Through these two

[54] U.S. Congress, House Committee on Ways and Means, "Hearings on Extending the Reciprocal Foreign Trade Agreements Act," 1937, 110–116.

practices, the benefits of concessions extended to all states covered by MFN agreements could be focused narrowly on negotiating partners. American tariff reductions were privatized even as the United States adhered to a nominally nondiscriminatory trading policy. In practice, the benefits of unconditional MFN to the United States and to its negotiating partners were far more limited that Assistant Secretary Sayre suggested.

In 1936, the United States and France negotiated a reciprocal trade agreement with a MFN provision that appeared to provide substantial benefits to the United States. When France granted MFN status to the United States, the United States secured more favorable treatment with respect to 4,330 tariff positions.[55] The benefits to the United States were far less substantial than this figure suggests. The principal supplier rule had been the foundation of previous rounds of French tariff bargaining. Prior French import preferences had been crafted meticulously to benefit their negotiating partners without conferring benefits on third parties. American exporters did not benefit from reductions in barriers to French imports of tropical products. In fact, French concessions covered only 21.5 percent of American exports to France.[56] The agreement neither increased nor decreased trade between the United States and France to any substantial degree. Like the Tripartite Stabilization Agreement discussed in the next chapter, the Franco-American trade agreement mattered more as a reflection of an emerging anti-Nazi coalition than because of its economic consequences.

The United States used reciprocal trade negotiations to fight for Western Hemisphere markets that had been lost to Great Britain and the continental Europeans. On the southern flank, the United States entered into bilateral discussions with a dozen Latin American and Caribbean nations. Prior to the Second World War, the United States negotiated trade treaties with Cuba in 1934, with Colombia, Brazil, Haiti, and Honduras in 1935, with Costa Rica, Guatemala, and Nicaragua in 1936, with El Salvador in 1937, and with Argentina in 1939.[57] The United States reduced barriers to imports of food and raw materials in exchange for Latin American and Caribbean concessions on manufactured products. As John Conybeare has observed, the United States obtained large concessions on manufactures while its concessions on raw materials reduced the cost base of American

---

[55] "Hearings on Extending the Reciprocal Foreign Trade Agreements Act," 112.

[56] John A. C. Conybeare, *Trade Wars*, 257.

[57] For detailed descriptions of these bilateral agreements, see U.S. Congress, House Committee on Ways and Means, *Hearings on Extension of Reciprocal Trade Agreements Act*, vol. 2, 76th Cong., 3d. sess. (Washington, D.C.: GPO, 1937).

industry. In each of these negotiations with small weak suppliers of raw materials, the United States was able to strike narrowly advantageous deals.[58] Because Argentine commerce was covered by a complex bilateral preferential arrangement with Great Britain, the terms and timing of the Argentine-United States bilateral differed from the other Latin American bilaterals. The existence of previously negotiated preferences also shaped American negotiations with Canada.

Consider the northern flank of the battle for Western Hemisphere markets. Like the first laundry to negotiate over diversion of soot, Great Britain had struck relatively advantageous deals at the expense of late negotiating third parties. To preserve the magnitude of preferences under the Ottawa system, signatories were effectively barred from extending equivalent preferences to other nations. The "binding preferential margins" of the 1932 Ottawa Agreements limited the freedom of Canada and Britain to negotiate with third parties such as the United States. Binding preferential margins were much like laws forbidding rich and poor alike from sleeping under bridges. As Ian Drummond notes, Canada had a substantial interest in expanding trade with the United States to reduce Canadian export and import dependency on Great Britain. Great Britain had relatively little to gain from negotiations with the United States.[59] Provided the United States pursued an unconditionally protectionist policy, Canadian and British conflicts over negotiations with the United States were moot. With the American adoption of RTAA, British and Canadian differences over liberalization of commercial relations with the United States surfaced.

In 1935, the Roosevelt administration initiated discussions with both Britain and Canada. British negotiators suggested that the Ottawa preferences and existing bilateral agreements precluded substantial bargaining over British-American trade. Canadian negotiators were more receptive to American overtures. Canada offered limited concessions on products not covered by the Ottawa preference system. In exchange, American negotiators offered concessions on products for which Canada was the principal supplier. These concessions were extended to Britain under the MFN principle. American negotiators did not limit the benefits of concessions to Canada through the device of narrowing subclassifications of products. For example, the United States cut duties on whiskey imports by 50 percent *without* restricting the cuts to Canadian rye and excluding British

---

[58] Conybeare, *Trade Wars*, 255–56.

[59] Ian Drummond, *Negotiating Freer Trade* (Wilfrid Laurier Press, forthcoming). The Drummond book will become the definitive study of Anglo-Canadian-American commercial negotiations in 1935–1938 and provides the basis for the account in this book.

Scotch. Ian Drummond suggests the American policy was designed to improve American access to the Canadian market *and* to entice Britain into serious trade negotiations with the United States.[60] One prong of the strategy was at least partially successful. Canada and the United States concluded a bilateral trade agreement in 1935. However, because Canada was constrained by the terms of the Ottawa preference system, the 1935 Canadian-American bilateral was limited in scope and significance. The modesty of the Canadian-American agreement underscored the importance of liberalization of trade relations with Great Britain. The United States could not substantially improve its access to any nation bound by the Ottawa system or covered by British bilateral agreements without first liberalizing British-American trade relations. Great Britain remained unreceptive to American overtures throughout 1935 and most of 1936.[61] During this period, British interests were well served by the status quo.

In 1938, the United States concluded bilateral agreements with Canada and Great Britain. Two factors had changed in the intervening period: the Ottawa Agreements were scheduled to expire in August 1937; and Nazi Germany posed an ever increasing military threat to Great Britain. Taken together, these developments pushed Britain to renegotiate the commercial status quo while creating a dilemma for British negotiators. Britain had good reason to secure supplies of commodities from the dominions by reinforcing the preference system. Supplies from the dominions could prove critical in time of war. But Britain could not afford to alienate the United States by reinforcing the preference system. The appearance of Anglo-American cooperation might deter Nazi aggression and material American support would be vital to British survival in the event that war broke out. By 1937, Great Britain was involved in two sets of interlocking trade negotiations. In one arena, Britain, Canada, and the other dominions negotiated over renewal of the Ottawa preference system. In a second arena, the United States negotiated bilaterally with Great Britain and Canada over market access.

Consider points of tension across these arenas of negotiation. Each of the principal parties confronted difficult trade-offs. The British hoped to maintain preferences that had bound the dominions to Britain while simultaneously lowering commercial tensions with the United States. The Americans hoped to improve access to the British

[60] Drummond, *Negotiating Freer Trade*, 2-2 to 2-8.

[61] British negotiators insisted that Britain would reduce its duties on American commodities only if the United States would compensate suppliers in the dominions that would be displaced by American entry into the British market. This account is drawn from Drummond, *Negotiating Freer Trade*, 2-10.

and Canadian markets and to break down the imperial preference system without weakening a crucial ally. The Canadians hoped to improve their access to the American market without losing preferential access to the British market. Each of these nations viewed bilateral negotiations between the other two with substantial suspicion. As third parties that were most assuredly affected by the outcome of bilateral discussions, each nation sought to influence the terms of agreements between the other two. The terms of Anglo-Canadian, Canadian-American, and Anglo-American bilateral agreements reflected these concerns.

In 1937, Britain and Canada concluded a bilateral agreement as part of the renewal of the Ottawa preference system. The United States was as involved in the Anglo-Canadian negotiations as the principals. As Canada and Britain negotiated, the United States indicated that the terms of British and Canadian access to American markets would be influenced by terms of Anglo-Canadian preference margins. As the principal party with the keener interest in improved access to the American market, Canada negotiated reductions in the coverage and magnitude of numerous preferences that benefited American exporters. The terms of the 1937 Anglo-Canadian bilateral partially satisfied the concerns of the United States as well as Canada and Great Britain.

In 1938, the United States concluded bilateral agreements with Canada and Great Britain. These agreements reduced or froze rates on hundreds of items and limited the benefits of liberalization to third parties. The British lowered barriers on products of interest to the United States, including wheat, ham, beef, tractors, and automobiles, while the United States reduced restrictions on products of interest to Britain, principally manufactured goods. The Canadians eased restrictions on American manufactured products, while the United States lowered barriers facing Canadian lumber, cattle, and other commodities.

The limitations of the 1938 Canadian-American and Anglo-American bilateral agreements were as significant as the gains. As Ian Drummond observes, the product coverage of the 1938 agreements was limited. The United States did not reduce rates on British woolens and lace and Great Britain did not reduce barriers to American anthracite or peanut butter. Furthermore, benefits to third parties covered by MFN clauses were severely restricted by the classic devices of rate differentiation and quota shifting. As Britain reduced rates on American automobiles, it reclassified automobiles on the basis of horsepower to exclude German products. As Britain increased the quota on American hams, it reduced quotas for Baltic and Danish hams. As the United States reduced rates on Canadian cattle, it excluded cows that weighed between 200 and 700 pounds to exclude Mexican cattle.[62] Commercial practices in the late 1930s bore a striking resemblance to practices during the early 1930s. Ian Drummond cautions that it would be a mistake to view these agreements as a major milestone in the march toward open and nondiscriminatory trade. All observers should accept his admonition.

Evaluating RTAA

The RTAA program was liberalizing and discriminatory. The average nominal rate of American tariffs fell from 53 percent in 1933 to 37 percent in 1941. American concessions varied markedly across categories of products. American tariffs fell by 43 percent on food and 31 percent on crude materials, while tariffs on manufactures and semimanufactures dropped by only 20 percent.[63] However, nominal tariff rates are notoriously unreliable indices of protection. A very high prohibitive rate is no more or less protectionist than a marginal prohibitive rate. Rate reductions on goods regulated by quotas may be meaningless. To assess the effects of RTAA, one must look beyond nominal rates of protection to volumes of trade.

Table 5.3 contrasts American trade with countries covered by bilaterals negotiated under RTAA with countries that were not covered by RTAA. Although it is tempting to infer that the overall increase in trade was caused by MFN provisions and the more rapid increase in trade with RTAA nations was caused by the bilateral and discrim-

TABLE 5.3
Increases in U.S. Trade 1934–1939

	RTAA Nations	Non-RTAA Nations
Increase U.S. exports	62.8	31.7%
Increase U.S. imports	21.6	12.5%
Increase U.S. exports Increase U.S. imports	2.9	2.5

Source: Figures drawn from Stephen Schuker, *American Reparations to Germany 1919–33: Implications for the Third World Debt Crisis*, Princeton Series in International Finance, no. 61, 103.

[62] Drummond notes that Mexican cows typically weighed between 200 and 700 pounds. See Drummond, *Negotiating Freer Trade*, 8-8.

[63] Conybeare, *Trade Wars*, 255.

inatory aspects of the new American commercial policy, one cannot reject at least two competing explanations. First, the lagged effects of American devaluation of the dollar in 1933 unquestionably account for a portion of the overall disparity between increases in exports and in imports. Second, although American trade with RTAA nations increased far more rapidly than trade with non-RTAA nations, one cannot simply infer that the new American trade policy was responsible for the difference. A selection bias could well exist. Countries that negotiated trade agreements were countries interested in increasing trade with the United States. Some of the differences between these groups of countries is explained by predisposition as well as bargaining process.

However, these alternative explanations do not account for the difference in the ratio of increases in exports to increases in imports. While exports and imports rose substantially for both RTAA and non-RTAA countries, the ratio of export increases to import increases was higher for nations covered by bilateral trade agreements. Although George Peek lost his battle with Cordell Hull, the program that he opposed appears to have served his narrowly nationalist goals well. In practice, American trade negotiators struck deals that served exporters well while minimizing damage to import-competing interests. From a mercantilist perspective, the RTAA program was a clear success.

Conclusions

At any given moment during the 1930s, discriminatory economic practices appeared to be antithetical to liberalism. As nations exchanged market access for market access, nations relied on a variety of discriminatory devices to deny third parties the benefits of concessions. The extensive literature on commercial diplomacy during the 1930s contains hundreds of examples of bilateral, regional, and imperial agreements that were crafted to benefit some trading partners at the expense of others. Throughout the depression years, quotas, differential tariff schedules, rate differentiations through product subclassification, and imperial preferences distorted patterns of trade.

To evaluate the effects of discrimination on openness, one should not view acts of economic discrimination as discrete events. By focusing the benefits of concessions on the parties to negotiations, discriminatory economic practices helped preserve openness on a limited basis as general levels of protection rose. By denying third parties the benefits of market access, discriminatory economic practices encouraged excluded nations to join in future rounds of negotiations. Most centrally, discriminatory international economic practices helped offset domestic biases toward protection. The discriminations of other nations disadvantaged export-oriented interests in the nondiscriminatory protectionist United States. Bilateralism and regionalism abroad mobilized export-oriented interests at home in the struggle against protection. Over time, economic discrimination was a significant force for liberalization.

As consumption and prices fell, all nations increased levels of protection to defend domestic prices and employment. In 1929–30, the United States adopted a nondiscriminatory protectionist policy and then stood to the side of trade bargaining for four years. Virtually every other nation in the world pursued discriminatory protectionist policies. Quotas, rate differentiation, and other discriminatory practices spread at an extraordinary rate. The pace and scope of this change followed directly from the divertiable character of commercial policy externalities. Because bilateral and imperial preferences operate to the detriment of third parties, nations had a strong incentive to lock in preferences sooner rather than later. As nations exchanged market access for market access, flows of goods were redirected along bilateral and imperial lines. As the world economy closed, it compartmentalized.

The bilateralization and regionalization of the world economy ultimately produced a check on movement toward closure. The systems of bilateral and imperial preferences negotiated by other nations operated to the detriment of American exporters. A discriminatory international environment selects against exporters from nations with nondiscriminatory trade policies. French quotas, British imperial preferences and bilateral agreements, and the German aski mark system mobilized American export-oriented sectors in support of the RTAA program. The discriminations of other nations inadvertently pushed the United States away from unconditional protection.

The American RTAA program was discriminatory and liberalizing. As the last major nation to adopt a discriminatory bargaining strategy, the United States confronted an array of preexisting bilateral and imperial arrangements. To defend American export interests, the United States attacked bilateral and imperial preferences. Ironically, the American war on bilateral and imperial preferences was waged using the weapon of de facto economic discrimination. Between 1934 and the onset of the Second World War, the United States relied on the principal supplier rule in extending concessions to negotiating partners and used the device of rate differentiation to exclude third parties from the benefits of liberalization. Although Ian

Drummond and others have condemned the discriminatory aspects of the RTAA program, discrimination was a precondition for continuing liberalization. In 1938, the United States used weight classifications to accept Canadian cattle and exclude Mexican cattle. In 1942, the United States and Mexico concluded a bilateral trade agreement. Parties that are excluded from the benefits of one round of bargaining have a material interest in joining in the next.

These findings may have implications for contemporary debates over the merits of relying on inherently discriminatory bilateral strategies of reciprocity or adhering to the intrinsically nondiscriminatory norms of the GATT.[64] As noted previously, the wholesale turn toward commercial discrimination had the unintended consequence of mobilizing export-oriented interests within the United States against the established American policy of unconditional protection. In more general terms, a bilateralized and discriminatory international environment provided a partial correction to conventional Olsonian biases from below by concentrating the interests of export-oriented sectors in lobbying against protection.[65] This general argument on the effects of international bargaining processes on internal preference formation lies at the core of the analysis of bilateralism and regionalism in contemporary trade in Chapter Seven. By offsetting domestic biases toward protection, economic discrimination may have liberalizing consequences.

[64] See Robert Keohane, "Reciprocity in International Relations," *International Organization* (Winter 1986) for a general discussion of reciprocity. See William Cline, *Reciprocity: A New Approach to Trade Policy?* (Washington, D.C.: Institute of International Economics, 1983) for a specific attack on bilateral discrimination in trade policy.

[65] For a more general discussion of how international bargaining processes may correct domestic biases, see Kenneth A. Oye, "On Underprovision of Compensation: Some Implications of Incomplete Information and Fragmented Actors," APSA Conventional Panel 26-2, September 3, 1988.

Chapter Six

THE POLITICS OF DEFAULT
AND DEPRECIATION

FINANCIAL AND MONETARY RELATIONS
IN THE 1930s

THE LATE 1920s and 1930s provide examples of virtually every conceivable mode of international financial and monetary management and mismanagement. Between 1929 and 1933, the global monetary and financial orders disintegrated. Multilateral financial clearing arrangements collapsed in the face of wholesale defaults, while the gold exchange standard gave way to serial devaluation and the formation of monetary blocs. Between 1933 and 1936, the monetary and financial orders began to reintegrate. International lending resumed, albeit on a limited bilateral basis, while the leaders of three monetary blocs agreed to manage swings in exchange rates. This chapter offers an explanation of why these changes took place and assesses the extent to which these arrangements served mutual financial and monetary interests.

The onset of the depression eliminated whatever perceived mutuality of interest may have existed in the preservation of the old monetary and financial orders. As price levels fell and real debt burdens increased, the cost of servicing debt rose. As domestic economic activity spiraled downward, the interests of key currency countries with overvalued currencies were not well served by defending parities through domestic deflation. But even had the depression not taken place, change was inevitable. In retrospect, the dramatic collapse of monetary and financial relations during the 1930s was rooted in both the effects of depression and the intrinsic fragility of these systems as they evolved over the 1920s.[1]

The gold exchange standard was predicated on the assumption that growth of private and official holdings of sterling, francs, and dollars could create international liquidity without undermining confidence in convertibility of these currencies at fixed parities.[2] The task

[1] The collapse of international monetary and financial relations during the depression is perhaps less noteworthy than the survival of these systems during the 1920s.

[2] The Genoa Conference of 1922 explicitly limited the number of countries expected to hold reserves in gold. Other nations were encouraged to hold the currencies of the

of walking a monetary tightrope without falling into a liquidity crisis on one side or a confidence crisis on the other was rendered more difficult by the overvaluation of sterling relative to the dollar and franc.[3] Prevailing winds tended to drive sterling toward a confidence crisis and devaluation. In short, the gold exchange standard relied on the willingness of private and official holders of sterling to refrain from converting their balances under circumstances when devaluation of sterling was inevitable.[4]

The core of the international financial system of the 1920s consisted of two unbalanced cycles of lending. Under the intergovernmental debts cycle, private loans flowed from the United States to Germany, reparations payments moved from Germany to Great Britain, France, and Belgium, and war loans payments moved from the allies to the United States. Long-term American public claims on the former allies and long-term public British, French, and Belgian claims on Germany declined slowly, while medium- and short-term private American claims on Germany accumulated. In short, public international financial stability hinged on the willingness of private lenders to issue new loans and roll over old loans even as German financial obligations grew greater than German earnings potential. Under a second lending cycle, funds flowed from the City of London, New York, and Paris to debtor nations in Central Europe and to the non-European periphery. Some funds returned to the financial centers in the form of export earnings and some funds were retained abroad in dollar and sterling balances that were in turn deposited in money center banks. Under this cycle, the financial centers accumulated claims of increasingly questionable worth and short-term obligations subject to short-term liquidation. In short, private international financial stability hinged on the willingness of private and public claimants to refrain from liquidating their balances in the face of losses from either a sterling devaluation or a crisis of confidence in the financial system.

Collapse of either intrinsically unstable order could bring down the other. The interruption of forward movement in any of several critical areas could collapse the interconnected financial and monetary

---

three key nations as a fraction of their reserves. These holdings permitted expansion of international liquidity above the fixed supply of monetary gold.

[3] This interpretation of a liquidity-confidence trade-off implicit in the gold exchange standard of the 1930s obviously borrows from Robert Triffin's prescient identification of the "paradox" at the heart of the dollar-gold exchange standard.

[4] In 1931, the Macmillan Committee estimated that sterling was overvalued by approximately 15 percent. Following suspension of convertibility, the pound dropped by 30% in two months.

systems. Nations accumulating debt required fresh credits and deposits to service existing loans. British banks required fresh short-term deposits to continue longer term lending. The Bank of England relied on official and private accumulation of sterling balances to preserve parity. The satisfaction of all of these conditions was necessary to the maintenance of the unrestricted system of multilateral payments and the gold exchange standard. The collapse of either the financial or monetary system would cause the contraction of international liquidity.[5]

International norms governing foreign economic policies addressed most of these potential sources of financial and monetary instability. The international monetary regime centered around a primary cluster of norms that proscribed actions that might jeopardize exchange rate stability and gold parities and a secondary cluster of norms that imposed restraints on the privatization of national monetary policy. The central monetary powers were obligated to maintain existing parities and convertibility of their currencies by contracting their domestic money supply and shipping gold if under pressure and by offering credits, intervening on foreign exchange markets, and refraining from liquidating devisen to support other currencies under pressure. Other nations were obligated to hold balances of key currencies as reserves in lieu of gold and to maintain the parity and convertibility of their currency in terms of gold. The secondary cluster of norms proscribed privatized de facto devaluation through exchange controls, multiple exchange rates, and licensing schemes.

The international financial regime consisted of a primary cluster of norms to forestall financial collapse and a secondary cluster of norms that proscribed privatization of default but did not inhibit politicization of lending. Central and commercial banks in Great Britain, the United States, and France were obligated to issue fresh credits and renew short-term loans to debtor institutions and nations in short-term financial distress. Governments in debtor nations were obligated to restore confidence in the strength of their economies and financial

---

[5] Financial collapse would contract liquidity by stimulating withdrawals from banks, causing banks to adopt more conservative reserve requirements, and forcing write-downs on bank assets. Taken together, these effects would dramatically reduce the monetary base. Collapse of the gold exchange standard would contract liquidity by stimulating conversion of devisen into gold. Proponents of the orthodox gold standard correctly observed that the gold exchange standard was unstable, but rarely noted that a shift to the gold standard would of necessity entail substantial monetary contraction. This argument on the effects of monetary collapse on liquidity is a short-term argument. Over the medium term, nations would be more free to adopt expansionary policies without the tie to gold, and this effect would tend to offset the immediate contraction resulting from liquidation of devisen.

institutions. Measures to restore confidence included official guarantees of foreign financial obligations, Central Bank support to bail out ailing private financial entities, and the adoption of deflationary fiscal and monetary policies to raise foreign exchange needed to service debt. The secondary norm against privatization of default supported the primary norm by facilitating cooperation among lenders.

During the 1930s, primary and secondary norms governing financial and monetary affairs collapsed. As in the case of trade, the dissolution of primary norms fostering exchange rate stability and unrestricted multilateral capital mobility encouraged resort to mechanisms of political exchange. Nations violated secondary norms against privatization of international economic policies to secure a measure of exchange rate stability, to increase the likelihood of debt repayment, and to acquire access to international capital.

In practice, the collapse of the multilateral clearing system and the disintegration of the gold exchange standard were intimately related. With the exception of the U.S. decision to depart from gold in 1933, each major shift in international monetary relations was caused by monetary crises that were exacerbated by short-term capital flows. Conversely, each major financial crisis focused on the institutions of nations with overvalued exchange rates. Although this chapter treats financial affairs and monetary affairs in separate sections, real ties between these issue areas cut across this organizational divide.

FINANCIAL BREAKDOWN AND RECONSTRUCTION

International lending prior to the depression was substantial and multilateral. The Dawes and Young Plans channeled fresh American loans to Germany, reparations payments to France, Britain, and Belgium, and war debt payments to the United States. London, Paris, and New York provided credits to Central European debtors and to nations in the periphery. Temporary crises of confidence during the 1920s were contained by the infusion of fresh credits from London and other money centers. During the 1920s, a transnational network of central and merchant bankers managed the international financial order under the leadership of Montague Norman, the Governor of the Bank of England. Although the French occasionally linked private lending to political goals, they neither influenced the behavior of the Germans nor seriously destabilized the international financial order.[6]

---

[6] When Germany balked at the schedule of reparations payments in the spring of 1929, French and Belgian banks called loans and withdrew funds from Germany in an

In many respects, the effects of the depression on international financial preferences mirror the effects on trade. Economic contraction eliminated dilemmas of collective action by removing the mutuality of interest in cooperative outcomes. Groups of lenders frequently confront situations where the possibility of default creates a strong incentive for each individual lender to reduce exposure by halting fresh lending. Yet if all lenders act on this individual interest, default is assured. The severity of the depression may have transformed this difficult n-person prisoners' dilemma into a "game" of simple unanimous defection. First, deflation greatly increased the real servicing burden of debtor institutions and nations. Even if fresh funding had been forthcoming at customary levels, default would have been difficult to avoid. Second, deflation greatly reduced the ability and interest of creditor institutions and nations in fresh international lending. Domestic defaults and cash withdrawals depleted the reserves of private banks, and countercyclical international lending would have undermined confidence in their solvency. The obvious risks of lending to a nation or institution in extreme financial distress provided a strong incentive for private lenders to limit their exposure.[7] It is precisely under such circumstances that central banks and other public international financial actors are expected to serve as both lenders-of-last-resort to stave off immediate default and defenders-of-financial-orthodoxy to impose discipline on the policies of borrowers and thereby encourage eventual repayment. To what ex-

effort to bring about an exchange crisis and thereby force Germany to accept their terms. Reichsbank President Hjalmar Schacht maintained that the withdrawal of funds and resulting exchange crisis provided Germany with an opportunity to use German weakness as a bargaining asset. He instructed the Agent for Reparations from the Bank for International Settlements to communicate the following message to France: "If the calling in of these—not very considerable—French debts at German banks creates an obvious menace to German currency, such as we have seen recorded in the exchange market during the past few days; if German currency is shaken by the repayment in foreign exchange of borrowed capital, it is surely obvious that payments of reparations, such as the French still dream of, are simply out of the question. If the French banks do not rescind their orders forthwith, I shall express my thanks at the next session to the French delegation for having given me such striking proof of the impossibility of transferring the payments of reparations which they still demand." Schacht maintains that French withdrawals ceased and the French reduced their reparations demands. *Confessions of the Old Wizard: The Autobiography of Hjalmar Horace Greeley Schacht* (Westport, Conn.: Greenwood Press, 1974), 221–22.

[7] Even when governments were willing to arrange financing, the private markets often failed to provide funds. Under the Hague Agreements of 1930, new international long-term loans were promised to Hungary to extend a program of financial reconstruction begun under the League of Nations in 1924. The central monetary markets could not or would not provide funds. Brown, *International Gold Standard Reinterpreted*, 2: 862.

tent did the intense economic contraction convert what had been a dilemma of collective action facing lenders-of-last-resort into a preference not to lend regardless of the actions of others? To what extent did the contraction render internationally sanctioned discipline counterproductive?

The Collapse of the Multilateral Clearing System

In the first phase of the financial crisis, the Bank for International Settlements and American and British central banks underestimated the severity of the Central European crisis, cooperated under what they saw as a conventional dilemma of collective action, and imposed discipline that proved counterproductive. In later phases of the global financial crisis, central bankers appreciated the severity of the contraction, accepted the inevitability of collapse of the old multilateral clearing system, defected without regard for the actions of others, and turned to increasingly privatized channels of international lending.

The Austrian financial and monetary crisis began with the run on Credit-Anstalt Bank in May 1931. The Bank of International Settlements responded by raising a \$14 million credit from the central banks of eleven countries and arranging a standstill agreement with major foreign creditors, subject to provision of an Austrian government guarantee of eventual repayment of Credit-Anstalt's foreign obligations. The total credit raised came to less than foreign withdrawals during the preceding two weeks of the crisis, and the run on Credit-Anstalt became a run on the Austrian schilling. As the monetary and financial crisis deepened, the Austrian central bank asked the Bank for International Settlements to arrange a second credit. The Bank for International Settlements arranged a \$14 million credit, subject to the provision that the Austrian government secure a medium-term private loan to strengthen the Credit-Anstalt. At the prompting of the French government, Lazard Freres and Rothchilds linked their participation in the private loan to Austrian withdrawal from Anschluss.[8] This private bank linkage between financial and political issues blocked the private loan that the Bank for International Settlements had, in turn, linked to its credit. The Bank of England provided an equivalent \$14 million credit and neutralized the French connection. Although the burdens of providing fresh international credits were not equitably shared, both the Austrian banking system

---

[8] The French interest in supporting Austria financially was partially contingent on the extent to which Austria was likely to increase German strength.

and Austrian schilling were temporarily stabilized by British financial leadership. However, the Austrian government could only meet the international obligations that it incurred in exchange for credits and the standstill agreement through domestic austerity and monetary exchange controls. Paradoxically, the partial success of the international financial rescue mission may have contributed to the intensity of the depression by encouraging deflationary domestic economic policy.[9]

During June and July of 1931, German banking and the Reichsmark came under pressure. The Austrian standstill agreement immobilized German financial assets in Austria, and thereby undermined confidence in an already deflation weakened German banking system. The international response to the German financial and monetary crisis was marked by the same pattern of political linkage, limited cooperation, and inappropriate international discipline that marked the Austrian case. The timing of credits was affected by French efforts to secure political benefits from financial leverage. On July 7, France tied credits for the failing Danat Bank to the abandonment of Anschluss, prohibition of military demonstrations, and cancellation of a naval cruiser.[10] On July 15, the French offered to provide credits if Germany promised to abandon the Sollverein, resume reparations payments after expiration of the Hoover moratorium, and cease agitation for reform of the Versailles Treaty.[11] In neither case did the French achieve their political ends, but both linkages delayed arrangement of international credits. Despite French financial linkage, substantial cooperative efforts were mounted. The Bank for International Settlements provided a two-week $100 million credit on June 15, the Hoover administration announced a one-year moratorium on war debts and reparations payments on June 20, an American syndicate of commercial banks permitted the Gold Discount Bank of Germany to draw on an old unused $50 million credit line on July 7, and a seven power conference approved a three-month renewal of the $100 million Bank for International Settlement's

---

[9] This account is drawn largely from Stephen V. O. Clarke, *Central Bank Cooperation: 1924–1931* (New York: Federal Reserve Bank of New York, 1967), 185–89. Details on French linkage strategy are drawn from Brown, *International Gold Standard Reinterpreted*, 2: 1040.

[10] Kindleberger, *World in Depression*, 156. The Danat Bank closed on July 13 and was taken over by the Dresdner Bank. Schacht uncharacteristically fails to mention French political conditions on provision of credits in his account, *Confessions of the Old Wizard*, 266.

[11] Brown, *International Gold Standard Reinterpreted*, 2: 1043.

credit and a standstill agreement, covering $1,250 million in private bank obligations, on July 23, 1931.[12]

These international credits and payments moratoria alone were insufficient to alleviate pressure on Germany. The Reichsbank moved the discount rate from 5 percent at the start of the crisis to 15 percent at the peak of the crisis.[13] To prevent capital outflows, the Reichsbank imposed exchange controls. Even with these domestic measures and controls, Germany could not meet the obligations it accumulated under the two financial cycles. International creditors had little recourse but to ratify the reality of default. In March 1932, the seven powers approved a 10 percent reduction in the principal of the Bank for International Settlements credit. In April, the Bank for International Settlements extended the standstill agreement to cover municipal and public loans. In June, the Lausanne Conference postponed resumption of reparations payments indefinitely and formally terminated the Young Plan. Default, whether or not ratified by creditors, shattered the multilateral payments system and choked off new international lending. The ability and the inclination of lenders to provide capital contrasted sharply.

The concept of capital scarcity is as fundamental to the disintegration of international finance as the concept of surplus capacity was to the disintegration of international trade. With respect to trade, global surplus capacity in agriculture, mining, and manufacturing taken in conjunction with strong national preferences for avoiding structural adjustment caused movement toward closure, and the potential leverage associated with manipulation of access to markets caused movement toward discrimination. Both closure and discrimination were rooted in surplus capacity. With respect to finance, global capital scarcity taken in conjunction with strong national preferences for reserving capital to facilitate domestic recovery caused movement toward closure of international financial channels. In a capital-scarce world, major lending nations rationed their capital by using explicitly discriminatory criteria to actualize potential financial leverage. In a deflationary world where debtors staggered under enormously increased real debt burdens, borrowers resorted to discriminatory defaults to actualize their potential financial leverage. Thus, the

[12] This account is compiled from Brown, *International Gold Standard Reinterpreted*, vol. 2: 1040–46; Clarke, *Central Bank Cooperation*, 375–88. For an excellent account of the effects of the standstill agreement on creditors and a review of the composition of German short-term debt, see C.E.S. Harris, *Germany's Foreign Indebtedness* (London: Oxford University Press, 1935), 15–31.

[13] Clarke, *Central Bank Cooperation*, 190.

breakdown of the old multilateral clearing system and capital short-age gave rise to a compartmentalized system of international finance.

The Restoration of Lending through Discrimination?

As lenders ceased both refinancing and fresh lending and as borrow-ers defaulted, privatization of lending and payments should have in-creased the volume of international finance relative to levels that would have been produced by nondiscriminatory lending. Under conditions of severe deflation and credit contraction, borrowers that could not conceivably meet all international obligations and lenders that would not conceivably provide general distress funding reached bilateral and bloc financial accords. Debtors agreed to earmark a por-tion of export earnings to service their payments to particular credi-tors in exchange for preferential access to markets and fresh loans.[14]

Great Britain turned to a bloc approach to privatize its financial policy. British policy may be broken out into the following phases. Following the financial crisis of 1931, the government discouraged all new international lending and prohibited new lending outside of the empire.[15] As might be expected, in 1931–32 the empire share of all new lending fell from 41.6 percent to 25.6 percent, while foreign lending fell from 10.4 percent to 0.35 percent. Starting in April 1933, the British Treasury granted exceptions to nations in the emerging sterling bloc that sought financing to purchase British goods and ser-vices.

Like most countries in the periphery, Argentina faced a payments crisis. Britain had purchased over 80 percent of Argentine beef ex-ports, and the British turn toward empire was squeezing Argentine export earnings. In 1932, Argentine export earnings failed to cover one third of its total exchange needs. In anticipation of negotiations with the British, the Argentine government used its system of ex-change controls to bloc peso balances of British companies and cred-itors. The Roca-Runcimin agreement reached in 1933 spanned vir-tually all economic issues. The British offered a fresh sterling loan and a market for beef.[16] Argentina agreed to earmark its bilateral

---

[14] Chapter Five discusses the Austria-Switzerland bilateral clearing and payments agreement of November 1931.

[15] During this period, several techniques of prohibiting new lending outside of the empire were used. September 1931–June 1932: informal governmental influence. June 1932–September 1932: official nonbinding request from Chancellor Chamber-lain. September 1932–April 1933: formal embargo on new foreign issues.

[16] This guarantee was subject to a 10% reduction if necessary to "keep prices at a remunerative level."

trade surplus with Britain for British companies and creditors. Argentina was to make available sterling remittances equal to exchange derived from Argentine sales in Britain after retaining a "reasonable sum" to service other foreign obligations. In addition, it reduced or eliminated duties on goods provided largely by Britain and pegged the peso to sterling.[17]

In July 1934, the British government formalized a policy of permitting sterling loans to nations in the sterling bloc and to finance British trade with any nation, subject to explicit government approval. Government approval was contingent on preferential repayment terms, deposit of a portion of borrower export earnings in London accounts, trade concessions, and other political goods.[18] But even with these policies in effect, the empire share of new British capital issues held at 22.5 percent and 26.9 percent in 1933–34, then fell sharply to 9.4 percent in 1935. The foreign share of new British issues rose to 6 percent in 1933 as backlogged issues were floated, then plunged to 2.0 percent in 1934 and 1.6 percent in 1935.[19] These figures suggest that the criteria for granting ad hoc exemptions to the prohibition on foreign loans were less restrictive than the formal criteria put in place in 1934 or that British private investors were wary of loans to foreign nations that met the formal criteria.

Ironically, Germany was a major recipient of the limited fresh lending going to foreign nations. Investors had particular reason to be wary of Germany. German financial strategies were hardly straightforward in the period leading up to the Central European financial crisis. As Stephen Schuker observes, German strategies became even less straightforward in the aftermath of crisis.[20] The Standstill debt was held largely by the British banks, while the Dawes and Young loans and German bonds were held largely by American banks and individual bondholders. Schacht favored the British banks over American banks and especially bond holders. He reserved his leverage for the one major class of creditor with influence over national commercial and financial policies. Germany serviced the Standstill debt. Germany sought trade credits, support for a moratorium

[17] Richardson, *British Economic Foreign Policy*, 106–8; and Brown, *International Gold Standard Reinterpreted*, 2: 1167–68.

[18] Richardson, *British Foreign Economic Policy*, 69–75; and Brown, *International Gold Standard Reinterpreted*, 2: 1135.

[19] Total new British capital issues rose steadily during this period. See Richardson, *British Economic Foreign Policy*.

[20] The following account is based on his *American Reparations to Germany 1919–33: Implications for the Third-World Debt Crisis*, Princeton Studies in International Finance 61 (July 1988).

on the Dawes and Young loans, and improved access to the British market. In negotiations with British banks, Schacht stressed the substantive connection between these issues. He pointed out how British trade concessions and trade credits and a moratorium on the long-term American loans would permit him to continue to service the Standstill debt. Most of these goals were realized in the Anglo-German Trade and Payments Agreement of 1934, and British banks continued to extend trade credits to Germany until the late 1930s. Schacht serviced foreign bondholders in a special script convertible at a 50 percent discount relative to the official mark rate, then further reduced the conversion rate on the script. As the price of German bonds plummeted, Schacht reduced German external debt by quietly entering the market to purchase German bonds. The moral of this story is ambiguous. German discrimination in favor of British banks and against underrepresented small American bondholders was a natural response to the collapse of the multilateral clearing system. The British banks did issue substantial trade credits to Germany and exert internal pressure for a trade agreement. Trade between Germany and Britain did increase. And Germany secured credits and material to prepare for war against Britain.

As in the trade case, the effects of discriminatory financial policies on the extent of closure hinge on two factors. First, to what extent were threats and promises of credit and repayment extortion, exchange, or explanation? To the extent that international financial discrimination was used to extort, especially unsuccessfully, discrimination could have accelerated movement toward closure. To the extent that financial discrimination was used for exchange or explanation, the effects of financial discrimination on the extent of financial interaction between two parties may have been benign. The extraordinarily low levels of fresh lending taking place following the collapse of the old multilateral clearing system supports the inference that traditional lenders saw no interest in issuing fresh credits. The attachment of preferential repayment provisions to new loans increased the likelihood of repayment and should be regarded as explanation. The attachment of demands for unrelated compensation to new loans should be regarded as exchange.

Second, how did third-party externalities associated with bilateral and bloc financial diplomacy influence the extent of financial openness or closure? In the case of trade, third-party externalities pushed Britain toward closure and the United States toward openness. What happened in the case of finance? The externalities problem must be addressed in the context of specific international financial circumstances. Discriminatory default and preferential repayment in a multilateral clearing system clearly impose cost on unfavored creditors. The collapse of the old multilateral system produced a rash of standstill agreements, defaults, and payments moratoria; debts were frozen and payments were scarce. The new bilateral and bloc-based system encouraged fresh lending on politically private terms, and effectively replaced global financial closure with compartmentalized financial openness. Borrowing and lending can be *private* activities, and the financial system founded on that assumption produced a modest revival of international lending.

INTERNATIONAL MONETARY COLLAPSE AND RESTORATION

The collapse of the gold exchange standard in the early 1930s is commonly viewed as a paradigmatic example of a failure of collective action. The characterization of the international monetary issue area as a dilemma of collective action rests on the existence of both individual incentives to defect and a mutual interest in cooperation. Were these conditions satisfied?

The first condition—the existence of incentives to defect—was satisfied. Individual monetary powers could derive commercial benefit by permitting or encouraging depreciation. Such exchange rate changes would increase the price of imports on domestic markets and reduce the price of exports on international markets, and thereby increase short-term domestic economic activity at the expense of nations that did not devalue.

These short-term incentives to resort to competitive devaluation for commercial reasons would exist under any international monetary system, but one intrinsic feature of the gold exchange standard reinforced this commercial incentive and rendered that system especially vulnerable to the shock of depression. In practice, payments of key currency countries were the primary source of growth in international liquidity and, over the short term, liquidity creation reduces the costs associated with maintaining stable exchange rates. Intervention to alter foreign exchange market conditions is distinctly less domestically disruptive than deflation. But over the long term, payments deficits may well promote exchange rate instability by giving rise to virtually insoluble n-person games where all players are vulnerable to one shot defection.[21] Under the gold exchange standard, governmental and nongovernmental actors in many countries must continue to accept and hold the reserve currency even as doubts

[21] See Robert Triffin, *Gold and the Dollar Crisis* (New Haven, Conn.: Yale University Press, 1961), 3–14.

about its future value may materialize. Under the gold exchange standard, holders of a reserve currency could not convert into gold without heightening pressure on pars between the reserve currency and gold. If a currency is under pressure, dumping reserves denominated in that currency is individually rational. Failure to convert, if others do so, may produce substantial one time losses in the value of one's holdings. But mass conversion—into gold or other assets—is certain to bring about depreciation of the reserve currency. Unless currency holders are insured against exchange risk, defection is likely.

The currency holder's dilemma gives rise to a second problem. Holders' interest in retaining balances of a reserve currency are contingent on the actions of the reserve currency country as well as the decisions of other holders. Unless the reserve currency nation is willing to stem depreciation of its currency *and* holders are willing to act on the assumption that the reserve currency nation will subordinate domestic economic goals to stem depreciation, the value of the reserve currency will oscillate sharply. Holders have a strong incentive to defect first, for reserve losses may be minimized by preemptive conversion into gold. Issuers of the reserve currency have a strong incentive to defect early, to forestall conversion of outstanding currency balances into gold at a higher rather than a lower exchange rate.

These two sets of individual incentives, one rooted in the nature of trade and the other in the specific nature of the gold exchange standard, account for the widespread preferences for the defect-cooperate option over the cooperate-defect outcome.

The second condition—a mutual interest in cooperation—was not satisfied. Conventional wisdom holds that the benefits of defection were outweighed by the detrimental effects of exchange rate instability on the volume of international financial and commercial transactions. In this view, early defectors should have preferred maintenance of the gold exchange standard to international monetary disintegration. If this view is incorrect, the disintegration of the gold exchange standard may not be a valid example of a failure of collective action. For a dilemma of collective action to exist, all must prefer mutual cooperation to mutual defection. Would adherence to the rules of the gold exchange standard have satisfied national preferences better than mutual defection? The evidence suggests that no monetary collective action dilemma existed when Great Britain departed from gold in 1931 or the United States departed from gold in 1933. In each instance, the suspension of convertibility and modification of gold parities took place when at least one nation did not prefer mutual cooperation to mutual defection. Deteriorating domestic macroeconomic circumstance and shifting economic beliefs strengthened preferences for suspending convertibility and modifying gold parities to such an extent that mutual adherence to the gold standard would have been inferior to mutual departure from the gold standard.

Monetary Disintegration: The British and American Devaluations

In September 1931, Great Britain decisively violated the primary norm of the gold exchange standard that it created in 1925. By suspending convertibility and permitting sterling to depreciate relative to gold-backed currencies, Great Britain reversed the direction of an international monetary policy that had been committed to maintaining an overvalued pound. To place the decision to depart from the gold standard into perspective, consider the evolution of economic beliefs, macroeconomic conditions, and British international monetary policy between 1925 and 1931.

By returning to the prewar parity with gold and the dollar in 1925, Great Britain sought to preserve sterling's role as a preeminent international currency and the City of London's role as a preeminent international financial center.[22] To defend the overvalued pound at prewar parities without resorting to the traditional expedient of domestic deflation required great ingenuity. Great Britain succeeded in encouraging Austria, Hungary, Belgium, Norway, Italy, and other smaller monetary powers to keep their reserves in sterling while Britain maintained very modest reserves in dollars and gold.[23] The Bank of England found that manipulation of the bank rate served to defend the pound against short-term pressure without shipping gold or suffering domestic deflation. In his testimony before the Macmillan Committee in March 1930, Montague Norman declared that market operations were generally not necessary to effect a change in bank rates. Short-term capital inflows were responsive to changes in the bank rate, and generally proved sufficient to strengthen the pound and obviated the need for market operations.[24] Lord Norman's views

[22] In the aftermath of the First World War, Great Britain turned toward invisible exports to maintain British supremacy. A return to the prewar parity was viewed as the most effective way of maintaining confidence in the City of London. See Diane B. Kunz, *The Battle for Britain's Gold Standard in 1931* (London: Croom-Helm, 1987), 8–28 and 189–91.

[23] As per the *Report of the Financial Commission of the Genoa Conference* of 1922.

[24] Macmillan Committee Transcript, as reproduced in R. S. Sayers, *The Bank of England* 1891–1944 (Cambridge: Cambridge University Press, 1976), 2.

on the effectiveness of these relatively costless means of preserving the gold standard should be taken as part of his larger views on the importance of the gold standard. Lord Norman saw central bank cooperation in defense of the gold standard as a requisite of international financial stability.[25] If the principal instrument for resisting exchange rate change without substantial deflation—manipulation of the bank rate—were ineffective, then his central goal of international financial cooperation could not be realized at reasonable cost. The persistence of Lord Norman's beliefs on manipulation of the bank rate even as the crisis of 1931 intensified may be properly viewed as a clear illustration of the power of cognitive consistency. Lord Norman saw domestic economic performance, export performance, and financial position as complementary interests best served over the long term by maintenance of parity.

In his questioning of Lord Norman, John Maynard Keynes presented a radically different view of the relationship among these economic objectives. Keynes believed that market operations and consequent credit tightening were necessary to effect an increase in the bank rate. Therefore, parity could only be preserved at the cost of export performance. Although Norman believed that the relatively costless manipulation of the bank rate would influence capital movements and relieve pressure on sterling, Keynes believed that internal deflation was a requisite of exchange rate stability. Where Norman saw complementary interests, Keynes saw a trade-off across financial position, export performance, and domestic economic performance.[26]

During the summer of 1931, the Austrian financial crisis and ensuing sterling crisis resolved the debate over the existence of the international monetary—domestic economic performance trade-off. At the same time, domestic deflation tilted the terms of the trade-off. The traditional expedient of adjusting the bank rate without engaging in market operations proved insufficient to stem conversions of sterling into gold. The freezing of British long-term credits in Central Europe and withdrawal of foreign balances from Britain were the proximate causes of a monetary crisis that was rooted in the overvaluation of sterling. Although foreign central banks offered to support sterling with credits and intervention, international stabilization efforts could not preserve sterling-gold parity without substantial adjustments in British domestic economic policy. Fiscal austerity was a

---

[25] See Kunz, *Battle for Britain's Gold Standard in 1931*, chapters 4 and 5.
[26] Macmillan Committee Transcript, as reproduced in Sayers, *The Bank of England*.

precedent for continued access to foreign funds, while monetary contraction was necessary to effect changes in the bank rate.

After the British had exhausted intervention credits borrowed from the United States and France, the British asked the New York Federal Reserve to raise funds to increase British resources. Because the New York Federal Reserve Bank was prohibited by statute from lending directly to a foreign government, Governor Harrison asked Morgan Guaranty to raise funds from commercial banks. Governor Harrison informed the British that "an American contribution would be forthcoming only if an adequate program of economy obtained the approval of Parliament." An "adequate program" referred to belt tightening measures to reduce budgetary deficits along the draconian lines suggested by the May report.[27] This linkage between finance and fiscal policy was a case of explanation: it rested on the belief that unless the British budget were brought into balance and the British economy were put through a tighter deflationary wringer, Britain would be forced to request additional resources to defend sterling and would not ultimately be able to make good on its international financial and monetary commitments.[28]

The domestic economic consequences of monetary contraction more than offset the dubious benefits of maintaining parity. Even prior to the depression, British economic performance lagged. During the international boom of the late 1920s, British unemployment did not fall below one million and British industrial activity did not keep pace with other advanced industrial nations.[29] During 1930 and 1931, British domestic economic activity declined from this already low baseline. The penalties associated with adopting a restrictive domestic monetary policy under conditions of rising unemployment and declining industrial activity were unacceptable. Because the only path to sustaining the gold exchange standard involved trekking through deflationary swamps, mutual cooperation became less attractive than mutual defection. In effect, the depression converted what was a monetary n-person prisoners' dilemma into noncontingent defection. Great Britain had no interest in monetary cooperation.

Preventive political exchange was impeded by an intrinsic feature

[27] The May report projected very substantial budgetary deficits and recommended austerity measures including reductions in the hole.

[28] The best account of this episode is found in Sayers, *The Bank of England*, 2: 397–99.

[29] The British economic malaise was caused, in part, by the overvaluation of sterling. See Charles Loch Mowat, *Britain Between the Wars: 1918–1940* (Chicago: University of Chicago Press, 1955), chapters Five through Seven on structural causes of sluggish British economic performance.

of the gold exchange standard. Central monetary powers could not offer to refrain from devaluing their currencies as a form of leverage because any indication that a change in parities was possible would have triggered a run on their currencies. Private and public holders of sterling confronted a dilemma of collective action. Their willingness to refrain from converting devisen to gold was contingent on confidence that parities would not be changed. This attribute of the gold exchange standard effectively prohibited linkage between monetary issues and other international economic issues. Only *after* the gold exchange standard had disintegrated, and holdings of foreign currencies had dropped to insignificant levels, were monetary linkages possible.

Reconstructive political exchange was impeded by the public nature of monetary externalities. The British decision to suspend convertibility of the pound imposed substantial costs on nations that remained on the gold standard. The United States, France, Germany, and other gold bloc nations found that the costs of maintaining gold parities were increased by the depreciation of sterling. Each of the gold bloc nations was forced to adjust to the British decision. But the gold bloc nations did not move effectively, either individually or collectively, to forestall the British move or to induce the British to check the slide of sterling. The dearth of political coercion and political exchange directed at influencing British monetary policy requires explanation.[30] The public nature of externalities associated with the suspension of convertibility and depreciation of sterling accounts for the absence of action aimed at bringing about a revision of British policy. All of the nations on the gold standard would have benefited had Britain established a new parity and intervened to check the slide of sterling. None could have been excluded from the benefits. And none chose to expend political capital by bringing pressure to bear on Great Britain.

To what extent could the British privatize externalities associated with the suspension of convertibility and depreciation of the pound? The British were unwilling to privatize the effects of depreciation through multiple exchange rate systems and exchange controls. Indeed, the British explicitly rejected de facto devaluation through exchange controls in favor of de jure devaluation. The British rejected a characteristic French suggestion that the British privatize French losses by converting Bank of France reserves of sterling into gold at

[30] Each of these nations expressed their preference for a British return to convertibility, with varying degrees of emotional intensity. But none expended political resources to effect a change in general British monetary policy.

the old parity to the detriment of other central banks. The primary means by which the British privatized the externalities associated with devaluation was by encouraging other nations to peg their currencies to sterling instead of gold. The members of the empire followed as a matter of course. As noted earlier in the study on trade, the British used financial and commercial benefits to encourage Argentina and the Scandinavian states to move toward a sterling standard. By floating—or sinking—together relative to the gold bloc, members of the sterling bloc could pursue more expansionary monetary policies, enjoy a degree of exchange rate stability with respect to each other, and secure a commercial advantage over nations on gold. Great Britain also benefited directly from the use of sterling as a reserve asset and medium of exchange, unfettered by a connection to gold.

Nations that remained on the gold standard found that the new British monetary policy increased the difficulty of maintaining parities. Following the depreciation of sterling, short-term capital outflows pushed the dollar to the gold selling point. The Hoover administration was adamantly committed to maintaining the dollar-gold parity. Hoover believed that international monetary stability was the key to restoring world trade, building confidence, promoting dishoarding, stimulating investment, and ultimately ending deflation. His orthodox views on the importance of maintaining existing parities were shared by the French. The principal difference between American and French views centered on the desirability of the gold exchange standard, as distinct from a pure gold standard. Since 1928, the Bank of France was committed in principle to liquidate its foreign exchange holdings. Following the British suspension of convertibility, the French developed systematic plans to dispose of sterling and convert dollars into gold. This Franco-American divergence of views on the relative merits of the gold standard relative to the gold exchange standard was of more than theoretical interest. A wholesale liquidation of $600 million in Bank of France balances could have turned the late 1931 run on the dollar into a full-scale crisis. Under such circumstances, the costs of maintaining the dollar parity through gold sales, intervention, and discount rate changes would have been high.

The French offered to refrain from liquidating their dollar balances if the United States would refrain from pursuing any policy that would endanger the gold standard and would increase the United States interest rate to make employment of French funds in New York more profitable.[31] The New York Federal Reserve formally

---

[31] This account is drawn from Brown, *International Gold Standard Reinterpreted*, 1179–

rejected this explicit linkage,[32] but met French terms by raising the discount rate from 1.5 percent to 3.5 percent.[33] This rise in the discount rate was accomplished on October 9 and 15, 1931. To place these rates in real perspective, domestic prices were falling rapidly during this period. The GNP implicit price deflator in 1929 was 30 percent higher than the deflator for 1933. The French refrained from converting further dollar balances during the run on the dollar. It should be noted that the compensation sought by the French—the rise in the New York discount rate—also contributed directly to stemming the run on the dollar. France and the United States succeeded in realizing a mutual preference for sustaining gold parities in the face of a conflict of preferences over the timing of liquidation of devisen. Tacit political exchange was facilitated by the private nature of externalities associated with wholesale conversion of Bank of France dollar balances.[34] The French resumed their gold withdrawals when the crisis ended in December 1931 and completed their conversion program in June 1932.

Germany derived one benefit and many costs from sterling depreciation. The appreciation of the Reichsmark relative to sterling reduced the servicing costs of sterling denominated foreign debts, but increased pressure on the Reichsmark by placing Germany at a commercial disadvantage. The German commitment to maintaining formal parity between the Reichsmark and gold was unusually intense. Under the terms of the Young Plan, the Reichsbank was bound to keep Germany on a de jure gold standard. Future international funding was explicitly tied to this commitment. This international legal obligation was strongly reinforced by the recent German experiences with hyperinflation. The customary gold bloc belief that gold backing was a precondition of the restoration of confidence was backed by images of wheelbarrows of worthless paper. However, a commitment to maintaining de jure parity did not preclude de facto devaluation. German exchange controls, compensation agreements, multitiered exchange rate systems, and myriad other devices permitted Germany

---

82. Brown notes that Great Britain, the Netherlands, Germany, and Switzerland also liquidated their dollar balances during this period. He also indicates that the French sought to link their policy on liquidation of dollar balances to modification of the Hoover moratorium. Given the French interest in reducing their holdings, their threat appears to make sense even in the absence of a tie to the question of reparations.

[32] Kindleberger, *World in Depression*, 168.

[33] *Economic Report of the President 1982*, Table B-3.

[34] This example of tacit policy coordination between France and the United States clearly served the preferences of both governments. However, I do not argue that preferences and interests coincided. The two-point increase in the discount rate in 1931 unquestionably intensified the depression.

to sustain formal parity without resorting to full-scale deflation by reducing the effective value of the mark in international trade and finance. These devices also permitted Germany to privatize, albeit imperfectly, its international exchange rates policy. Licensing arrangements and blocked accounts were used to reduce the international purchasing power of Reichsmarks in Germany and to encourage trading partners to import German goods. The German exchange control system evolved into a primary instrument of political leverage in trade, even as German trade policy evolved into an instrument for neutralizing other effects of the British devaluation. Sterling bloc nations encountered sliding scale tariffs that were pegged to the cross rate between sterling and the Reichsmark.[35]

The de jure depreciation of the sterling and de facto depreciation of currencies of weaker gold bloc nations placed pressure on the dollar. The American departure from the gold standard in 1933 is best understood in terms of the conjunction of the effective appreciation of the dollar with shifts in domestic economic circumstances and beliefs. With its large gold reserves, the United States could have adhered to the rules of the gold standard by shipping gold to sustain parity. The United States was not pushed off the gold standard by a deteriorating international position. It stepped off gold to permit domestic economic recovery.

Differences between the economic beliefs of Herbert Hoover and Franklin D. Roosevelt had consequential effects on international monetary relations. As noted earlier, Herbert Hoover was willing to tighten the domestic money supply to maintain dollar parity because he believed that international monetary stability was a requisite of domestic economic recovery. Given these views, no tension between international and domestic objectives existed. During the First New Deal, Franklin D. Roosevelt believed that domestic price raising was instrumental to domestic recovery. Roosevelt saw two paths to the proximate goal of reflation.[36] The core programs of the First New Deal, the AAA and NRA, sought to raise the process by restraining production.[37] Roosevelt also subscribed to the view that a general rise

[35] This account is drawn from Howard S. Ellis, *Exchange Control in Central Europe* (Cambridge: Harvard University Press, 1941), 158–289; Frank C. Child, *The Theory and Practice of Exchange Control in Germany* (The Hague: Nijhoff, 1958); and Brown, *The International Gold Standard Reinterpreted*.

[36] The core approach of the Second New Deal, public works as fiscal stimulus, seemed unattractive in 1933. Roosevelt frequently complained of the lack of useful purpose of many early public works projects.

[37] See Ellis W. Hawley, *The New Deal and the Problem of Monopoly: A Study in Economic Ambivalence* (Princeton, N.J.: Princeton University Press, 1966) on domestic problems associated with production restraints.

in prices could be effected through either the conventional means of manipulating the discount rate or unconventional means of purchasing newly mined gold at a premium price.[38] Defense of the old gold-dollar parity could simply not be reconciled with price raising by either of the two means. Given these economic beliefs, Roosevelt confronted a substantial tension between international monetary orthodoxy and domestic economic recovery.

The United States suspended convertibility between the dollar and gold in April 1933 and permitted the dollar to fall relative to gold and sterling. Although the action was widely denounced, countervailing political pressure was limited. During preparatory discussions for the World Economic Conference, the British indicated that depreciation of the dollar had increased British difficulties in meeting war debt payments and suggested that monetary stabilization and intergovernmental debts should be jointly discussed at the London Conference. The United States indicated that it would not participate in the conference if intergovernmental debts were placed on the agenda. The French reiterated their commitment to the international gold standard, and indicated that the depreciation of the dollar might force them to tighten their system of contingents to maintain parity between the Poincaré franc and gold. The United States indicated that it might be prepared to discuss stabilization, and encouraged the French to dismantle their system of contingents. These British and French linkages highlighted real substantive connections among financial, commercial, and monetary issues. Roosevelt also considered a joint French and British proposal for temporary currency stabilization during the World Economic Conference. He instructed the American delegation to seek agreement on ever higher dollar/sterling rates.[39] When one of his offers was accepted by the British and French, Roosevelt withdrew his offer so as to preserve his freedom to pursue a reflationary domestic strategy. Although Roosevelt was clearly suspicious of the British, believing that any agreement that met British requirements was undoubtedly less advantageous than it appeared, his decision appears to be best explained in terms of his desire to pursue a reflationary domestic policy. Rumors of a possible stabilization agreement during this period triggered a precipitous decline in stock and commodity prices. This may have reinforced his views on the desirability of further dollar depreciation. From Roosevelt's perspective, acceptance of any of these offers would have

[38] See George F. Warren and Frank A. Pearson, *Gold and Prices* (New York: John Wiley & Sons, 1935) for a fuller exposition of these views.

[39] See Feis, *1933: Characters in Crisis*, 178–258 for a colorful and sensitive account of this episode.

compromised the central proximate objective of the Roosevelt administration's first recovery program. None of the British and French proposals were accepted because the concessions offered were simply incommensurate with the perceived costs of exchange rate stabilization. Over the remainder of 1933, the dollar continued to depreciate relative to sterling and gold.[40]

Monetary Reconstruction: Tripartite Stabilization

By the end of 1933, adjustments to dollar depreciation appeared to be complete. International exchange rates and domestic prices were steady. In early 1934, Roosevelt established a lasting temporary parity at the $35 per ounce rate that had been produced by the float. In the middle of 1934, Great Britain pegged sterling to the dollar at the $4.95 rate that had been produced by the float.[41] The devalued but fully convertible dollar and the floating but pegged pound exerted continual pressure against gold bloc nations. Pressure on the franc had increased sharply following the American devaluation. The three-month future price for francs on franc-sterling markets fell from a 0.1 percent premium over spot prices in the summer of 1933 to a 33 percent discount by the summer of 1936.[42] The French supported the overvalued franc through rigorously deflationary domestic fiscal and monetary policies, by expanding their system of quotas on imports, and by drawing down their gold reserves.

The willingness of the French to continue to support the franc-gold par through deflation, despite domestic stagnation, can only be understood in terms of the widespread French belief in monetary orthodoxy. In Great Britain the commitment to the 1925 sterling-gold par was an article of faith within financial circles and an article of controversy within commercial circles. In the United States, the Republican party's belief in the complementarity between domestic recovery and supporting the dollar-gold par was not embedded in the general culture. Indeed, disputes over the merits of gold, silver, and greenback monetary standards had been common since the economic contractions of the late 1800s. In France, the putative virtues of the

[40] The depreciation was helped along when Roosevelt followed the Warren and Pearson gold purchasing prescription in the summer and fall of 1933.

[41] The United States sought to privatize benefits associated with restoration of full convertibility between the dollar and gold. Nations on the gold standard were free to convert dollars into gold, while members of the sterling bloc were denied conversion rights. However, because the British were free to trade in the gold backed Poincaré franc, the United States did not effectively privatize its international monetary policy.

[42] Paul Einzig, *The Theory of Foreign Exchange* (London: Macmillan, 1937), insert following p. 286.

orthodox gold standard were accepted by peasants, artisans, the middle class, manufacturers, and financiers. Even the Popular Front had campaigned in 1936 on a slogan of "neither deflation nor devaluation," and Leon Blum declared that he would not lead a "coup d'etat monetaire."[43] France moved off gold only after the tension between domestic reflation and preservation of the franc-gold par became extraordinarily acute. The Blum Popular Front government rejected fiscal austerity in the late spring of 1936, and accelerating gold shipments drew down French reserves. Domestic tolerance of deflation and official reserves of gold both neared exhaustion during the summer of 1936.

The devaluation of the franc in the autumn of 1936 was the last in a series of uncoordinated devaluations that began in 1931. As in the British and American cases, France could not simultaneously support an overvalued currency and reflate a stagnant domestic economy. France opted for domestic reflation and exchange rate depreciation. As in these earlier cases, exchange rate realignment did not bring about exchange rate stability. The two-stage depreciation of the franc and the depreciation of the pound and franc relative to the dollar were as steep as the sterling devaluation of 1931 and the dollar devaluation of 1933. However, in contrast with these earlier cases, the devaluation of the franc did not trigger offsetting devaluations, intensified commercial conflict, or imposition of exchange controls. Despite profound exchange rate instability, the hounds of monetary and commercial conflict did not bark. What factors permitted the emergence of extensive monetary consultation and limited monetary coordination in the late 1930s?

Consider factors affecting national preferences. During the two years before the franc devaluation, both American and British officials gradually recognized that the French defense of an overvalued franc had adverse effects on commercial interests. In a 1935 memorandum to Cordell Hull, State Department economic advisor Herbert Feis wrote:

> From a long range standpoint, a prolonged effort by the gold bloc countries to maintain present gold parities might be at least as damaging to us as a sudden collapse of their currencies, because such an effort would involve increasingly severe restrictions on trade and a chronic gold drain to the United States. In this connection, it is significant that while the dollar value of our exports to all countries increased 32 percent from 1932 to 1934, our exports to the five principal European countries which

[43] Martin Wolfe, *The French Franc Between the Wars* 1919–1939 (New York: Columbia University Press, 1951), 144.

have maintained their pre-depression gold parities—France, Germany, Italy, Holland, and Belgium—rose less than 3 percent.[44]

Feis went on to argue that a 25 to 35 percent devaluation of the franc would permit French payments to balance without additional commercial restrictions, and would provide a reasonable basis for stabilization negotiations. In the summer of 1936, Chancellor Neville Chamberlain stipulated that British support for a fair rate of exchange hinged on freedom from the quotas and other trade restrictions that were used by the French to defend the franc. With the devaluation of the franc in 1936, none of the three key international currencies were clearly over- or undervalued. All three governments hoped that limited coordination of international monetary policies would permit reconciliation of export expansion, exchange rate stabilization, and domestic reflation.[45]

This emerging economic mutuality of interest in stabilization was reinforced by developments in security affairs. In 1936, governing elites in Great Britain, France, and the United States were suspicious of nascent German rearmament programs and disturbed by Hitler's occupation of the Rhineland. An economically and militarily strong France could serve as a barrier to a rapidly militarizing Germany. All three monetary powers saw further deterioration in the French economic position as undesirable, and saw devaluation of the franc as a necessary condition for French economic recovery. However, given the widespread French belief in the sanctity of gold, devaluation itself could well have undercut the fragile Blum coalition and further polarized French politics. By sanctioning and legitimating devaluation, Britain and the United States could lessen the domestic French political repercussions of devaluation. The possible common security threat from Germany tempered British and, especially, American pursuit of narrow national advantage. In explaining the Tripartite Agreement to his staff, Treasury Secretary Morganthau exclaimed: "This is a threat to Italy and Germany. . . . This is a notice to the boys—Achtung!"[46] Both British and American officials saw an inter-

[44] See Herbert Feis, "Economic Stabilization," National Archives, Record Group 59, 800.5151/88 1/2, 4th Draft, 7–8.

[45] On Chamberlain, see Sayers, The Bank of England, 2: 478–79. For general discussions of the consequences of exchange rate misalignment, see Walter A. Morton, British Finance 1930–1940 (Madison: The University of Wisconsin Press, 1943); and League of Nations, International Currency Experience: Lessons of the Interwar Period (Geneva: League of Nations, 1931).

[46] Morganthau Diaries, September 18, 1936, Book 32, 10. Cited in Scott Eric Ratner, "The Politics of Quiet Diplomacy: Henry Morganthau Jr. and the Efforts of the Amer-

est in French economic performance and political stability, an interest best served by acceptance of franc devaluation.[47]

The mere existence of a mutual interest does not guarantee realization of the common good. Reductions in the vulnerability of nations to defection by others were an important factor that facilitated cooperation. During the turbulence of the preceding five years, nations prudently drew down the foreign exchange component of official reserves. The foreign exchange component of official French reserves dropped from 51 percent in 1928 to 3 percent in 1936. The elimination of holdings of foreign exchange altered the structure of the situation by reducing one-time gains from unilateral defection and one-time losses from unrequited cooperation. Although these nations could have derived commercial advantage from unilateral devaluation, commercial benefits could be largely negated through future retaliation. Because export levels are slow to respond to exchange rate changes, the benefits of unilateral defection and the costs of unrequited cooperation at any one time were limited. Although devaluation could affect medium-term commercial prospects and threats to devalue could affect short-term capital flows, exchange rate changes no longer jeopardized the value of official monetary reserves.

How did Great Britain, France, and the United States realize these emerging mutual interests? In the autumn of 1936, the central monetary powers issued three parallel declarations that are known as the Tripartite Stabilization Agreement. The declarations were ambiguously defined and carefully hedged. Under the Tripartite Agreement, Britain, France, and the United States promised to refrain from seeking "unreasonable competitive advantage" through manipulation of exchange rates, without specifying what exchange rates might be deemed unreasonable. The three treasuries promised to consult on the buying and selling prices of gold targeted by their exchange equalization funds, without pooling resources, committing lines of credit to the defense of other nations' currencies, or establishing mechanisms for enforcement. Finally, this innocuous agreement was subject to termination on twenty-four hours notice.[48]

---

ican Jewish Establishment to Aid the Jewish Victims of Nazism." B.A. Thesis, Princeton University, 1984, p. 121.

[47] On French efforts to reinforce perceptions of the connection between security and economic issues, see R. S. Sayers, *The Bank of England*, 476–77; and Wolfe, *French Franc Between the Wars*, 145–46.

[48] To the Deputy Governor of the Bank of France, the agreement was "ni accord, ni entente, uniquement co-operation journaliere." To an official British operator, "flimsy and ineffective." Quoted in Sayers, *The Bank of England*, 2: 480–81. For a superb ac-

The form of the Tripartite Agreement limited potential losses in the event of collapse. The treasuries of Britain, France, and the United States were well aware of how exchange risks had heightened monetary conflict in the past, and consciously sought to maintain a favorable setting for cooperation. Under the Tripartite Agreement, the parties committed to settle outstanding balances in gold on a daily basis to ensure that gains from unilateral devaluation would be limited. That provision was both a response to unsatisfactory recent experience and part of a strategy to reduce vulnerability to defection by others.

To what extent did Britain, France, and the United States cooperate under the loophole ridden Tripartite system? The initial slide from 80 to 130 francs per pound was accepted by all; harmony prevailed because all preferred a moderate depreciation of the franc to no depreciation. Indeed, the Blum government sought and received explicit support for the devaluation of the franc from Britain and the United States. The ambiguities of the Tripartite Agreement and the instability of exchange rates add weight to the significance of international monetary stabilization during the late 1930s. The real test of cooperation began after the initial devaluation. French business, fearful of the Blum Popular Front, continued to move capital toward London and New York even after devaluation. Pressure on the franc from capital flight was compounded by French domestic inflation. By mid-1937, rising internal prices more than offset the effects of the initial franc devaluation. The British, the Americans, and the French had underestimated continuing pressures on the franc. Throughout most of 1936 and 1937, the three-month franc-sterling forward rate ran at a substantial discount under the spot rate.[49]

How did the central monetary powers respond to this situation? Despite French efforts to support the franc by selling gold, capital flight pushed the franc below levels that would balance French exports and imports. The British Treasury offered to assist in floating a loan on private London markets if France would swallow conservative medicine by tightening fiscal policy and attenuating Popular Front reforms. The French adopted some of the British suggestions

---

count of how agreement was reached, see Stephen V. O. Clarke, *Exchange-Rate Stabilization in the Mid-1930s: Negotiating the Tripartite Agreement*, Princeton Studies in International Finance 41 (Princeton: International Finance Section, 1977). For trenchant commentary on the weaknesses of the Tripartite Stabilization Agreement, see Ian M. Drummond, *London, Washington, and the Management of the Franc, 1936–39*, Princeton Studies in International Finance 45 (Princeton: International Finance Section, 1979).

[49] Paul Einzig, *The Theory of Forward Exchange* (London: Macmillan, 1937), 480; and Wolfe, *French Franc Between the Wars*, 138–71.

and used funds raised in London to support the franc. The British pegged sterling to the franc, and utilized their exchange equalization fund to resist changes in the sterling-franc rate.

The U.S. Treasury continued to utilize its exchange equalization fund to maintain parity between the dollar and gold, and thereby provided indirect support for the franc. American support for France stopped short of credits. France was in default on war debts and the Johnson Act prohibited loans to governments in default on official obligations to the United States. Treasury Secretary Morganthau horrified the British by advising the French to impose capital controls and offering to track down fugitive private French assets in the United States. Morganthau's indignation at French capital flight may well have been intensified by fraternity among New Dealers, for Blum explicitly based elements of the Popular front program on the New Deal. The French rejected Morganthau's advice as impracticable, and continued to draw down their gold reserves to slow the decline of the franc.[50]

In January 1937, the French Stabilization Fund announced that it had exhausted its entire gold allotment in defense of the franc-gold parity. Although Fund resources were partially replenished through a Bank of France loan, pressure on the franc intensified. In February 1937, the Blum government announced a pause in social and economic reforms, cancellation of some public works expenditures, and other measures to check capital flight by restoring the confidence of the business community. Although these actions succeeded in stemming pressure on the franc for a few months, renewed capital flight in June 1937 exhausted the resources of the French Stabilization Fund. During the ensuing financial crisis, Blum's government fell.[51] The deep depreciation of the franc in 1936 and 1937 elicited consternation, but not reprisals, from Britain and the United States. France supported the franc by selling gold and altering domestic policies. Britain and the United States did not regard French efforts to support the franc, ineffectual though they may have been, as an effort to obtain unreasonable commercial advantage, and both offered limited support to the French.

Why did cooperation continue under the tripartite system? Each of the nations was free to defect. Consider the substantive issue of exchange rate stabilization. The American commitment to the $35 per ounce parity was explicitly revocable, Great Britain refused to estab-

[50] Because New Deal capital controls were never tested by strong capital outflows, the American experience was of limited relevance to France.

[51] This account is drawn from Ian Drummond, *London, Washington, and the Management of the Franc*, and Wolfe, *French Franc Between the Wars*.

lish any official parity between sterling and gold or other currencies, and France was free to engineer a large or a small drop in the value of the franc. Yet the United States maintained par, Britain pegged sterling to the franc, and France engineered a modest devaluation of the franc and then sought to defend a new par. The persistence of mutual interests and relative invulnerability to defection explains both the emergence and robustness of cooperation. A very large devaluation of the franc might have stemmed capital flight from France and advantaged French exporters, but France feared retaliation by Britain and the United States. The expectation of retaliation in the future reduced the French incentive to defect in the present. Raising the dollar price of gold might have raised domestic American price levels and advantaged American exporters, but the United States feared retaliation by Britain and did not want to weaken the economy of France. Engineering a drop in the value of sterling might have stimulated the British economy and advantaged British exporters, but Britain was wary of weakening France and was fearful of retaliation by the United States. The realignment of exchange rates over the previous five years and the emerging German security threat created a mutual interest that could be realized through cooperation. The disorder of the previous five years caused these nations to limit their vulnerability to one shot devaluations. The experience of the previous five years clearly demonstrated the willingness and ability of these nations to pursue strategies of monetary reciprocity. And the consultative mechanisms established under the tripartite system provided a means of continually revising and updating definitions of cooperation in light of changing circumstances and provided early warning of defection. Although the tripartite system was not marked by monetary stability, cooperation among the central monetary powers prevented the decline of the franc from triggering another round of monetary and commercial conflict.

Conclusions

The course of disintegration of the international financial and monetary regimes appears to be better understood in terms of the changing structure of games rather than how the games were played. The conjunction of intrinsically flawed monetary and financial systems, deteriorating macroeconomic conditions, and economic ideologies converted the n-person prisoners' dilemmas of the 1920s into the noncontingent defections of the 1930s. With the collapse of primary norms governing international monetary and financial relations, nations brushed aside secondary norms proscribing discrimination and sought to realize limited mutual interests through bilateral and bloc-oriented political exchange. In finance, privatization may have raised levels of lending and payment above what would have prevailed in the absence of financial discrimination. In monetary affairs, the emergence of monetary blocs accommodated divergent tastes for monetary expansion and deflation between blocs while affording some measure of exchange rate stability within each bloc. Finally, a combination of international monetary systemic changes, the German military threat, and improvements in macroeconomic circumstances in the United States and Great Britain converted unconditional preferences for defection in monetary affairs into a dilemma of collective action. In this one case, a clear multilateral mutual gain existed and was realized.

PART IV

Prosperity and Hypocrisy

Chapter Seven

THE POLITICS OF BILATERAL AND
REGIONAL OPENNESS

COMMERCIAL RELATIONS IN THE 1980s

FIFTY YEARS AGO, nations relied on overtly discriminatory practices to manage or mismanage international economic affairs. Today, nations profess respect for nondiscriminatory norms even as they engage in discriminatory practices.[1] During the 1930s, discrimination was pervasive. Commercial, financial, and monetary relations were organized along bilateral, regional, and imperial lines. Today, the incidence of discrimination varies markedly across issues. Discriminatory practices are common in contemporary trade negotiations, uncommon in financial bargaining, and rare in macroeconomic discussions. If the 1930s were an economic state of nature, the 1980s may be characterized as a faintly corrupt civil society. De facto discrimination and de jure nondiscrimination coexist uneasily in a political economy of hypocrisy.

By historical standards, the contemporary international political economy is also relatively open. Restrictions on movements of goods and capital are low and falling and cross-national differentials in the price of goods and capital appear to have narrowed during the 1980s. Has the world economy continued to liberalize despite discrimination or because of discrimination? Will further reliance on discrimination lead toward openness or closure? This chapter on trade relations and the following chapter on financial and macroeconomic relations suggest that the combination of (oft violated) nondiscriminatory norms and discriminatory actions may well be preferable to either pure nondiscrimination or pure discrimination.

This chapter begins with a general argument on the benefits of hypocrisy in international political economy. As was argued in the theoretical chapters at the start of this book, the efficiency of ad hoc bargaining is affected by both the incidence of extortion and the magnitude of the costs that bilateral deals impose on third parties.

---

[1] Practitioners and scholars use the word *minilateral* to describe bilateral or regional bargaining. This linguistic convention may reflect discomfort with the tension between nondiscriminatory ideals and discriminatory practice.

The existence of norms against discrimination may affect the content of discriminatory bargaining. Norms proscribing discrimination are unlikely to be invoked by the principals to mutually beneficial transactions. However, they are likely to be invoked by aggrieved third parties and victims of extortion. In practice, a weak prohibition on discrimination should select against socially disadvantageous discriminatory acts without selecting against socially advantageous discriminatory acts.

The balance of these two chapters examines the causes and implications of discrimination in commercial, financial, and macroeconomic affairs. The characteristics of policy externalities provide only a partial explanation of the uneven incidence of discrimination. Macroeconomic spillover effects cannot readily be diverted from country to country. As a consequence, economic discrimination cannot play a major direct role in macroeconomic coordination. Both commercial and financial externalities can be diverted from country to country. In commercial affairs, nations barter market access for market access on a bilateral or regional basis though they affirm their devotion to the GATT. Even as the Uruguay Round of trade talks stalemated, discriminatory bilateral and regional negotiations succeeded in extending openness, albeit on a limited basis. Yet in financial affairs, creditors respect cross default clauses and debtors do not accord preferential treatment to some creditors at the expense of others.

The OECD reports a significant shift toward discrimination and away from GATT Article 19 during the past twenty years.[2] During the 1970s, the growth of Voluntary Export Restraints (VERs) and Orderly Market Agreements (OMAs) left a legacy of quotas that are the focus of continuing bilateral negotiation. During the 1980s, Canadian-American, Japanese-American, and intra-European Community negotiations spawned new systems of tacit and explicit preferences. At present, over half of global imports enter on an other than MFN basis.[3] In commercial affairs, nations may shift the costs of protection and the benefits of liberalization from trading partner to trading partner at will. This section shows that commercial discrimination during the 1980s was trade expanding as well as trade diverting. Bilateral and regional bargaining enlarged domestic "anti-protectionist" coalitions and helped offset domestic biases toward protection.[4]

[2] OECD, "Costs and Benefits of Protection," *OECD Observer* no. 134 (1985): 18–23.

[3] Richard Pomfret, *Unequal Trade: The Economics of Discriminatory International Trade Policies* (London: Basil Blackwell, 1988), 1, 6–7; cited hereafter as *Unequal Trade.*

[4] The literature on "endogenous protection" establishes the existence of substantial domestic biases toward protection. See Stephen P. Magee and Leslie Young, "Endogenous Protection in the United States, 1900–1984," in *U.S. Trade Policies in a Changing*

During the 1980s, discrimination was a force for liberalization in trade.

THE POLITICAL ECONOMY OF HYPOCRISY

The juxtaposition of discriminatory ad hoc bargaining, nondiscriminatory norms, and openness in the contemporary political economy creates an inferential problem. To identify the causes of openness, one must disentangle the effects of surviving elements of the postwar liberal economic regimes from the effects of discriminatory bargaining. Consider three basic positions on this problem.

Most political economists attribute continuing openness during the 1980s to the lingering effects of the postwar liberal economic regimes. Robert Keohane notes that important elements of the trade and monetary regimes persist. Commitments to substantive liberal rules increase the reputational costs of departing from liberalism. Participation in international institutions provides information on the policies, values, and intentions of others—information that facilitates fruitful negotiation. Robert Gilpin concurs, noting that inertia "has carried the norms and institutions of a decreasingly relevant liberal world into the 1980s." Both Keohane and Gilpin note that liberal norms and institutions are threatened by the spread of discriminatory practices.[5]

Most economists also contend that world economy has remained open despite the rise of discrimination. At best, open discriminatory systems such as Customs Unions and Free Trade Zones are less efficient than open nondiscriminatory systems. Preferences introduce distortions that reduce global and national welfare. At worst, discrimination invites retaliation that leads to closure. Threats to reduce market access on a bilateral or regional basis may trigger trade wars. Finally, empirical studies find that sectoral discrimination and sec-

---

World Economy, ed. Robert M. Stern (Cambridge: MIT Press, 1987), 146–47. I suggest that discriminatory international bargaining may offset, at least in part, domestic biases.

[5] Keohane demonstrates that international regimes provide rules that constitute standards for evaluating state behavior and facilitate contacts that provide information on policies, intentions, and values. See Robert O. Keohane, *After Hegemony: Cooperation and Discord in the World Political Economy* (Princeton, N.J.: Princeton University Press, 1984), 183–216 and 257–59. Gilpin concurs with Keohane only in the narrow sense of attributing continuing international liberalism to the persistence of liberal regimes. Keohane and Gilpin clearly differ in their normative orientations toward liberalism and toward Grotian regimes. See Robert Gilpin, *The Political Economy of International Relations* (Princeton, N.J.: Princeton University Press, 1987), 3, 25–64, and 208.

toral protection are strongly correlated. In the 1970s and 1980s, discrimination was most common in sectors where barriers were high.[6]

By contrast, the theory of unrestricted bargaining presented in the first four chapters of this book suggests that bilateral and regional bargaining may well have reduced barriers to movements of goods and capital in the 1980s. The internationalization of production and finance invariably entails domestic dislocation as falling prices of goods and credit squeeze the inefficient. By mobilizing the efficient against the inefficient, discriminatory bargaining strategies may have sustained and extended liberalism. Furthermore, the correlation between closure and discrimination exists because closure begets discrimination. It is precisely in situations where market access is restricted that bilateral and regional negotiations over market access are most likely.[7]

My argument on the political economy of hypocrisy straddles these positions. Although the case for discrimination remains central to my interpretation of political economy in the 1980s, I draw on elements of the first two positions to modify the case. The persistence of elements of the liberal postwar regimes helps explain why discriminatory bargaining has lead toward the economist's second best world of discriminatory openness rather than toward the economist's worst case world of discriminatory closure.

The conventional case for *corruption*, for entering into private transactions in violation of public rules, is straightforward. The case for *hypocrisy*, for feigning respect for rules while violating them, is more complex. The conventional defense of corruption reduces to one simple point. Bribery can be efficient. The perverse literature on the economics of bribery rests on the assumption that private transactions in violation of rules can yield more efficient outcomes than adherence to rules. As a form of exchange, bribery improves the welfare of principals to corruption at the expense of third parties. Because the gains to the principals often (though not invariably) exceed the losses of third parties, bribery can enhance efficiency. If corruption can be efficient, what societal interests are served by feigning respect for rules while violating rules?

First, the existence of a general rule proscribing discrimination will

---

[6] For clear statements of this position, see William R. Cline, *Reciprocity: A New Approach to World Trade Policy* (Washington, D.C.: Institute of International Economics, 1982); and Pomfret, *Unequal Trade*.

[7] For work that defends discrimination, see Carolyn Rhodes, "Reciprocity in Trade: The Utility of a Bargaining Strategy," *International Organization* 43, no. 2 (Spring 1989); and John A. C. Conybeare, "International Organization and the Theory of Property Rights," *International Organization* 34, no. 3 (Summer 1980).

discourage extortion more effectively than exchange. So long as the principals to an act of corruption are left better off by the act, neither has an incentive to denounce the transaction. If a general rule proscribing corruption exists, the principals to a mutually advantageous exchange will keep the transaction secret. In practice, rules proscribing corruption are extraordinarily difficult to enforce. Preferential deviations from a general rule are commonly undetected. The principals to such agreements—health inspectors and restaurant owners, purchasing agents and suppliers, and international economic negotiators—have no interest in drawing attention to the discriminatory character of their transaction.[8]

If corruption takes the form of extortion rather than exchange, then the existence of a general rule prohibiting discrimination provides a dissatisfied principal with a possible escape. When a party to a prospective act of corruption would be harmed by the transaction, an appeal to general rules is likely. Of course, an appeal to general rules is a predictable result of extortion and parties to transactions try to anticipate each other's actions. As a consequence, in situations when a general rule proscribes private transactions, extortion is rare. In domestic life, successful prosecutions for corruption are infrequent; almost invariably such prosecutions are limited to acts of extortion. In international political economy, appeals to norms of nondiscrimination by principals are virtually nonexistent. Because negotiators can anticipate such appeals, they rarely rely on extortionate threats. This line of argument suggests that the existence of a general rule barring discrimination has the effect of discouraging extortion without severely limiting exchange.

Second, the existence of a general norm proscribing discrimination will limit, but not eliminate, rent-seeking behavior. The redistributive consequences of corruption can be more pronounced than the standard microeconomic defense of corruption assumes. As students of rent-seeking suggest, the principals to corruption may enrich themselves by redistributing rather than creating wealth. Associations with Manila under Marcos, Jakarta under Sukarno, Managua under Somoza, Port au Prince under Duvalier, and New York under Koch are both unavoidable and apt. These cases suggest that the outrage of third parties ultimately imposes limits on kleptocratic polities, at least outside of the United States. However, the interests of third parties

---

[8] By forcing discriminatory exchanges underground, the existence of a general rule proscribing discrimination may create modest problems of enforcement. Reneging on an open agreement will do more harm to reputation than reneging on a private agreement. In underground domestic economies, these problems are handled by structuring transactions to limit the feasibility and desirability of reneging.

are characteristically underrepresented in corrupt political economies. Because the costs of corruption tend to be diffused across large numbers of third parties, third parties must transcend dilemmas of collective action to defend their interests effectively.

How do norms prohibiting corruption and discrimination offset this bias toward underrepresentation of the interests of third parties? Where third parties are substantially and materially harmed by the actions of principals, the existence of a general norm proscribing corruption or discrimination provides third parties with an avenue for defending their interests. In domestic political economy, corruption enriches the principals at the expense of sick restaurant patrons, unsuccessful bidders, and overburdened taxpayers. In international political economy, bilateral and regional discrimination benefits the principals at the expense of nations that are not preferenced. Where the harm is significant, third parties may at least delegitimate harmful behavior by appealing to norms proscribing corruption or discrimination. Prudent principals to transactions should anticipate such appeals to norms by third parties and limit the redistributive consequences of their actions to make such appeals to norms less likely. By contrast, in cases where third-party externalities are minimal, the existence of a norm proscribing corruption and discrimination will have less significant effects on outcomes. If third parties are not materially damaged by a transaction, then third parties are unlikely to invest even minimal political resources in challenging the transaction.

In brief, the general argument on the benefits of hypocrisy presented above reduces to the following. The efficiency of unstructured bargaining is affected by the incidence of extortion and the existence of substantial third-party externalities. Norms proscribing discrimination are likely to be invoked by aggrieved third parties and by victims of extortion. These norms are unlikely to be invoked by the principals to mutually beneficial transactions. In practice, a prohibition on discrimination selects against socially disadvantageous discriminatory acts without selecting against socially advantageous discriminatory acts.

COMMERCIAL DISCRIMINATION AND LIBERALIZATION

International externalities associated with trade are privatizable. Nations can manipulate the terms of market access to favor or punish specific trading partners or regions at will. Multilateral, regional, and bilateral modes of management are all possible. All of these modes of management are used to govern at least some aspects of contemporary trade. This section argues that discrimination may foster openness in the contemporary trading environment. By offsetting domestic biases toward protection, discriminatory international bargaining strategies are an important force for economic liberalization.

The association between economic discrimination and economic openness postulated in this section hinges on the existence of domestic biases toward protection.[9] The extensive literature on what economists term "endogenous protection" suggests that levels of protection in the 1980s reflect a bias toward protection. As Stephen Magee and Leslie Young observe: "The replacement of tariffs with less efficient nontariff barriers in the last two decades supports a view that special interests can counter Pareto moves by general interests in sophisticated ways."[10] During the 1980s, bilateral and regional international bargaining strategies offset domestic biases toward protection by broadening antiprotectionist coalitions within trading states. This effect of external economic discrimination on internal preference formation is anticipated by an example from the depression. During the 1930s, the wholesale turn toward commercial discrimination had the unintended consequence of mobilizing export-oriented interests within the United States against the established American policy of unconditional protection.[11] A bilateralized and discriminatory international environment provided a partial correction to conventional Olsonian biases by concentrating the interests of export-oriented sectors in lobbying against American unconditional protection.[12]

In the 1980s, de facto bilateral discrimination has, at least on occasion, had parallel effects. With increasing frequency, trading nations exchange market access for market access without passing on the benefits of liberalization to third parties. As trading nations discriminate, they broaden and strengthen the forces of antiprotection within negotiating partners beyond traditional core free trade

[9] For an explanation of biases toward protection drawing on both economic and institutionalist perspectives, see Robert E. Baldwin, *The Political Economy of U.S. Import Policy* (Cambridge: MIT Press, 1985).

[10] Stephen P. Magee and Leslie Young, "Endogenous Protection in the United States, 1900–1984," in *U.S. Trade Policies in a Changing World Economy*, ed. Robert M. Stern (Cambridge: MIT Press, 1987), 146–47.

[11] In more general terms, American trade preferences reflected conventional Olsonian biases toward protection. The benefits of protection to import-competing groups were palpable. The costs of protection to export-oriented groups were diffuse: the general possibility of retaliation against all American exports and the general contraction of markets as export earnings of trading partners declined.

[12] For a more general discussion of how international bargaining processes may correct domestic biases, see Kenneth A. Oye, "On Underprovision of Compensation: Some Implications of Incomplete Information and Fragmented Actors," APSA Conventional Panel 26-2, September 3, 1988.

groups. I. M. Destler, John Odell, and Kimberly Elliott attribute antiprotectionist activity in the 1980s to import utilizing groups such as distributors of imported products and manufacturers who rely on imported intermediate products and raw materials.[13] Helen Milner looks to the international or domestic orientation of firms within sectors.[14] Stephen Magee and Leslie Young argue that rising inflation explains antiprotectionist activity in the 1960s and 1970s, as consumers and businesses mobilized to eliminate trade restrictions that raise prices.[15] Discriminatory bargaining can broaden antiprotectionist coalitions beyond the core groups identified by these authors. By providing an incentive for otherwise disinterested export-oriented interests to battle import-competing interests, discriminatory bargaining can strengthen the forces of liberalism.

CONTEXT

The political economy of trade in the 1980s is framed by the successes and failures of GATT multilateral trade negotiations. The 1967 Kennedy Round and 1979 Tokyo Round of multilateral negotiations under the GATT succeeded in reducing tariffs on manufactured goods to unprecedented lows. Consider the effect of GATT negotiating rounds on American tariff rates. In Table 7.1, the figures to the right are the percentage ad valorem equivalent tariff rate on dutiable and total imports. Reductions in tariffs for other advanced industrial nations were comparable to these figures on the United States. The virtual abolition of the tariff as a barrier to trade in manufactured goods through multilateral negotiations should not be lightly dismissed.

However, half of world trade is totally or completely unregulated by the GATT. Trade in agriculture and services remain largely beyond the purview of the GATT. Barriers to flows of agricultural products and services are overt.[16] Furthermore, nontariff barriers to

[13] See I. M. Destler, John S. Odell, and Kimberly Ann Elliott, *Anti-Protection: Changing Forces in United States Trade Politics* (Washington, D.C.: Institute of International Economics, 1987). For an earlier survey see Kym Anderson, *The Political Market for Protection in Industrial Nations: Empirical Evidence*, World Bank Staff Working Paper No. 492 (Washington, D.C.: World Bank, 1981).

[14] Helen V. Milner, *Resisting Protectionism: Global Industries and the Politics of International Trade* (Princeton, N.J.: Princeton University Press, 1988).

[15] See Stephen P. Magee and Leslie Young, "Endogenous Protection in the United States, 1900–1984," in Stern, ed. *U.S. Trade Policies*.

[16] On areas of coverage by the GATT, see Jock A. Finlayson and Mark W. Zacher, "The GATT and the Regulation of Trade Barriers: Regime Dynamics and Functions,"

TABLE 7.1
GATT Negotiating Rounds and U.S. Tariff Rates

Year	Event	Dutiable (%)	Total (%)
1930	Hawley Smoot Trade Act	53.0	18.0
1956	Four initial GATT rounds	25.0	9.0
1961	Dillon round concluded	22.5	8.1
1967	Kennedy round concluded	12.0	7.0
1979	Tokyo round concluded	8.3	6.2
1987	Tokyo round implemented	5.8	4.3

Source: Figures on all except Dillon round from Richard Whalley, *Trade Liberalization Among Major World Trading Areas* (Cambridge: MIT Press, 1985), 16. Figures for Dillon round computed from Gilbert R. Winham, *International Trade and the Tokyo Round* (Princeton, N.J. Princeton University Press, 1985), 60.

trade on manufactured goods rose as tariffs fell. Modern protection has taken on a variety of forms: "temporary" safeguard actions against imports that do substantial and material damage to import competing sectors; countervailing duties in cases of export subsidization and dumping; government procurement codes that disadvantage foreign suppliers; health and safety certification procedures that delay or prohibit imports; VERs, OMAs, and bureaucratic red tape have all been used to restrict imports. Nations have addressed these significant issues in multilateral forums. The participants in the Uruguay Round are considering proposals to move agriculture and services under the GATT. A bold proposal to convert all nontariff barriers into equivalent tariffs that may then be reduced through conventional multilateral bargaining has stirred attention.[17] However, to date the Uruguay Round has not made progress on these problems.

Nations have relied on discriminatory bilateral and regional bar-

in *International Regimes*, ed. Stephen D. Krasner (Ithaca, N.Y.: Cornell University Press, 1983).

[17] The effective height of a nation's nontariff trade barriers may be imputed from differences between domestic and global price levels. Proposals for "tariffication" call for the creation of formal tariffs based on price differences and the destruction of all other policies that create the price differences. If tariffication proposals are accepted, it is not clear how the more subtle forms of nontariff protection could be identified and eliminated.

gaining strategies that violate the spirit and often the letter of the GATT principle of nondiscrimination. Nations paid lip service to the principle of equal access while paying bribes to secure preferential market access. The advanced industrial nations have varied substantially in the extent to which they have departed from unconditional MFN. Table 7.2 presents Brian Pomfret's estimates of the percentages of 1985 imports entered on an unconditional MFN basis. Pomfret's figures on non-MFN imports take account of visible and explicit systems of preferences. Imports under the Lome Convention and the Generalized System of Preferences are handled on a better-than-most-favored-nation basis. Imports from Eastern Bloc nations are often handled on a less-than-most-favored-nation basis. Most trade between European Community members ($353 billion in 1985) is on a better-than-most-favored nation basis. Trade regulated by VERs and OMAs is on a worse-than-most-favored-nation basis.[18]

In the illustrations presented below, the effects of discrimination on openness vary. At times, discrimination has simply diverted the incidence of protection from one trading partner to another without raising or lowering levels of protection. At other times, discrimination promoted greater openness. However, in all of the following illustrations, economic discrimination mobilized export-oriented interests against import-competing interests.

Trade Diversion under OMAs

Within the shadow world of OMAs, bilateral bargaining over quota size is pervasive. Like the laundries in the privatizable goods case,

Table 7.2
Percentages of Imports Entering on MFN Basis in 1985

	MFN Imports (% of total)	Total Imports ($ billions)	Imports (% of world)
Japan	94	131	7
United States	90	362	19
Canada	90	81	4
EFTA	12	110	6
European Community	19	664	34

[18] This table is compiled from Pomfret, *Unequal Trade*, 5–6.

individual exporters negotiate to divert protection to other exporters rather than to reduce overall levels of protection.

To place specific illustrations of trade diversion through bilateral discrimination into context, it is useful to have some sense of the level and distribution of explicit nontariff barriers. Nogues, Olechowski, and Winters estimated NTB coverage ratios for industrial countries in 1983.[19] Figure 7.1 summarizes their findings on industrial nation NTBs on manufactured goods and agricultural products. Agricultural NTBs are proportionate to the distance between zero and the top of each line. NTBs on manufactured products are proportionate to the distance between zero and the bottom of the line. As Figure 7.1 shows, NTB coverage of agriculture was far more extensive than NTB coverage of manufactured goods and cross-national variations in coverage were substantial.[20] The United Kingdom and the United States were very average countries in their reliance on NTBs in man-

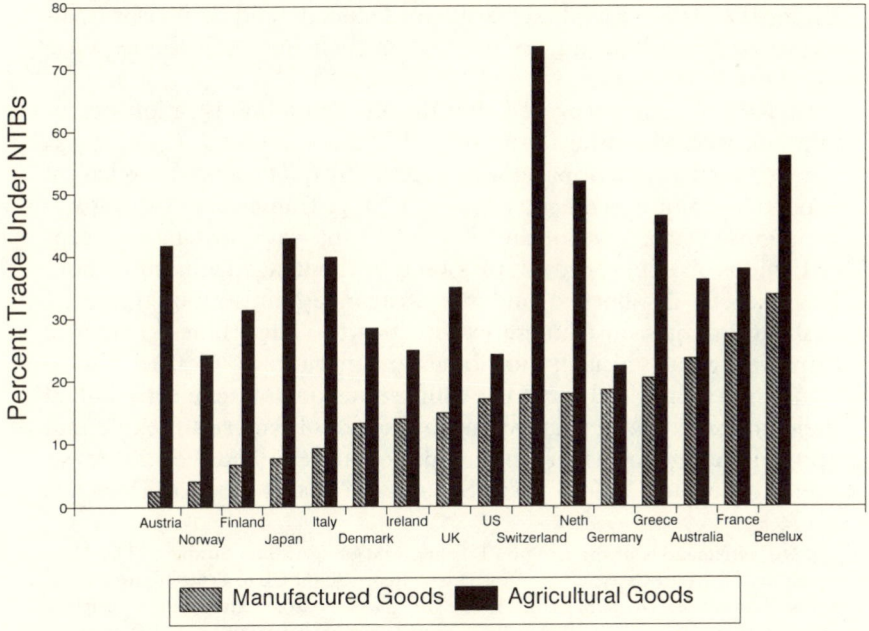

Fig. 7.1. Nontariff Barrier Coverage Ratios 1983

[19] Julio J. Nogues, Andrzej Olechowski, and L. Alan Winters, "The Extent of Non-Tariff Barriers to Industrial Countries' Imports," Discussion Paper, Report DRD 115, World Bank 1985 as cited in Alan V. Deardorff and Robert M. Stern, "Current Issues in Trade Policy," in Stern, *U.S. Trade Policies*, 29.

[20] Figure 7.1 is based on numbers in Alan V. Deardorff and Robert M. Stern, "Current Issues in Trade Policy: An Overview," in Stern, *U.S. Trade Policies*, 29.

ufactured goods. Consider two very simple examples of trade diversion through bilateral discrimination involving these countries.[21]

In the late 1970s, textile interests in Great Britain secured a reduction in the Indonesian quota under the Multi Fibre Agreement (MFA). The government of Indonesia responded by threatening to switch from British to American engineering firms on several major Pertamina petrochemical projects. Quite predictably, British engineering firms developed an interest in lobbying on behalf of increasing the Indonesian textile quota. The British government restored the Indonesian quota at the expense of other textile producers and the Indonesian government reaffirmed the petrochemical construction contracts of British engineering firms. The structure of the MFA taken as a whole and the aggregate quotas of any given importing nation should be taken as givens. While bringing down the MFA as a whole or enlarging overall quotas would benefit all textile producers, countervailing pressure in support of collective interests is minimal. Under the MFA, individual textile producers defend their private interests by bribing producers to increase their quotas at the expense of others.[22]

In 1983, China discovered that the Reagan administration's commitment to free markets was somewhat less than total. Chinese exports of textiles and apparel were limited by quotas under a bilateral export restraint agreement within the MFA framework. During negotiations over renewal of the bilateral, China was unwilling to accept reductions on export growth proposed by the Reagan administration. Negotiations deadlocked and the Reagan administration imposed unilateral quotas on Chinese export growth. The Chinese response displayed great sensitivity to domestic American politics. In discussions with grain bowl senators, Chinese negotiators explicitly linked their imports of American wheat to the size of American textile and apparel quotas. A former Chinese diplomat described the strategy as "getting Senator Dole to beat Senator Helms."[23] Senator Dole was

---

[21] For explanations of the rise of VERs and OMAs, see Susan Strange, "The Management of Surplus Capacity: Or How Does Theory Stand Up to Protectionism 1970s Style?" *International Organization* 33 (1979); Douglas R. Nelson, "The Political Structure of the New Protectionism," World Bank Staff Working Paper No. 471 (Washington, D.C.: World Bank, 1981); and Sima Lieberman, *The Economic and Political Roots of the New Protectionism* (Totowa, N.J.: Rowman and Littlefield, 1988).

[22] Pertamina is an Indonesian public enterprise that controls oil exploration, development, and processing. This brief account is drawn from *The Financial Times of London*. For a comprehensive study of evolution of the MFA, see Vinod K. Aggarwal, *Liberal Protectionism: The International Politics of Organized Textile Policy* (Berkeley: University of California Press, 1985).

[23] Interview with Pu Shou Chan, Chinese Academy of the Social Sciences, Beijing, June 1985.

only partially successful in defending the interests of Kansas farmers and Chinese weavers. The final American quotas on Chinese textiles and apparel were larger than the unilateral quotas imposed by the United States but smaller than the quotas would have been allowed under the old bilateral agreement. In turn, China resumed purchases of wheat but cut back on the size of their orders.[24]

The Indonesian and Chinese cases are typical of bilateral bargaining within areas regulated by OMAs. In both cases, bilateral bargaining strategies diverted trade without increasing or decreasing levels of trade. In both instances, overall levels of protection—the sum of quotas—were determined by factors beyond the scope of bilateral negotiations. Bilateral bargaining affected the size of slices without affecting the size of the pie.

TARGETING AND EXPORT CREDIT SUBSIDIZATION

During the 1970s and 1980s, de facto bilateral economic discrimination played a significant role in reducing export credit subsidization. Under conditions of global surplus capacity, trading nations commonly offer long-term trade credits at interest rates below their cost of borrowing. When the domestic costs of liquidating excess capacity appear to exceed the costs of subsidizing export financing, nations subsidize to stave off adjustment.[25] Since 1960, the GATT has classified subsidization of credits of nonprimary products as prohibited direct export subsidies. The multilateral agreement was widely ignored. During the deep recessions of the 1970s, many industrial nations, most centrally France, increased export credit subsidies to move primary and manufactured products. Multilateral efforts to enforce and renegotiate the GATT ban on export credit subsidization failed. The Carter administration responded with an explicitly bilateral strategy. It created a war chest of export credits and targeted credit subsidies against France. Specifically, the American Export-Import Bank matched or exceeded French export credits in critical third country markets. By raising the cost of dumping, the Carter administration strategy helped mobilize the French Ministry of Finance against export credit subsidization. France reduced its export

[24] Destler, Odell, and Elliott, *Antiprotection*, 16. For a comprehensive discussion of agricultural trade politics, see Robert Paarlberg, *Managing World Farm Trade*. The decline in Chinese grain purchases from the United States was proportionately smaller than the overall decline in Chinese grain imports during this period. By increasing domestic grain production, agricultural reforms had sharply reduced Chinese dependency on all grain imports.

[25] See Richard E. Feinberg, *Subsidizing Success: The Export-Import Bank in the U.S. Economy* (Cambridge: Cambridge University Press, 1982).

credit subsidies. In the final year of the Carter administration, an OECD agreement barring long-term export credit subsidization was negotiated. When the Reagan administration assumed office, it sharply reduced funding to the Export Import Bank war chest and shifted toward a nondiscriminatory policy of terminating American export credit subsidies. At that juncture, France rejected the OECD draft agreement on "technical" grounds and increased its export credit subsidies. Negotiations stalemated. After the Reagan administration returned to the Carter administration strategy of targeting export credit subsidies against French products in third country markets, France managed to set aside its reservations on technical issues and agreed to a formal OECD agreement barring export credit subsidies. In this case, a discriminatory bargaining strategy was central to the reformulation and enforcement of a nondiscriminatory rule.[26]

BILATERAL LIBERALIZATION AND JAPANESE-AMERICAN TRADE

Critics of reliance on explicitly bilateral bargaining strategies observe, quite correctly, that exchanging market access for market access can lead toward closure if agreements are not reached and trade wars break out. The record of Japanese-American bilateral bargaining suggests that American threats have generally been followed by Japanese concessions. As Figure 7.1 showed, Japan relied heavily on formal NTBs on agricultural products but not in manufacturing. Of fourteen advanced industrial nations, Japan ranked eleventh in formal NTB coverage of manufactures and fifth in NTB coverage of agriculture. By contrast, the United States ranked seventh in manufactures and thirteenth in agriculture.[27] Throughout the 1980s, the

---

[26] For a full account of this case, see Andrew M. Moravcsik, "Disciplining Trade Finance: The OECD Export Credit Agreement," *International Organization* 43 (Winter 1989): 1.

[27] Explicit NTBs in Figure 7.1 do not encompass all NTBs. To measure the strength of informal NTBs, economists have relied on indirect estimation methods. First, they predict "expected" import penetration using traditional variables such as income, distance and transportation costs, economic size, and tariffs. Second, they treat observed departures from expected values—imports not explained by conventional factors—as a measure of the strength of NTBs. This approach is obviously sensitive to differences in specification and estimation of the models used to predict expected import penetration. As a consequence, the magnitude and sign of imputed NTBs varies significantly from study to study.

Barbone summarized studies of Japanese informal NTBs as follows: Balassa and Lawrence found that informal NTBs were substantial in both manufacturing and agriculture; Bergsten and Cline, Noland, Saxonhouse and Stern, and Leamer found no significant departures from overall expected imports. Barbone's own study found significant underimporting in agricultural and manufactures, but also found that overall

United States relied on a de facto strategy of implicitly linking continued Japanese access to the American market for manufactured goods to Japanese liberalization of agriculture and services. This implicitly discriminatory American strategy has gradually drawn down effective levels of Japanese protection.

Unlike most nations, Japan's propensity to protect does not span all import-competing sectors. Inefficient sectors within manufacturing are generally liquidated rather than protected. The horizontally integrated Japanese trading companies span both import-competing and export-oriented sectors.[28] The benefits of expanding export-oriented sectors and the costs of liquidating import-competing sectors are internal to single firms.[29] However, there are important import competing segments of Japanese society that do not benefit directly from export expansion. As Daniel Okimoto has argued, the Liberal Democratic Party (LDP) subsidizes and protects agriculture, services, and construction to preserve the political status quo. Over the long term, the political centrality of inefficient interest groups is slowly being reduced by demographic and economic changes, while the substantial costs of subsidizing and protecting inefficiency provide impetus for rationalization. In the near term, these pockets of inefficiency are deeply embedded.[30] In the absence of international pressure, tacit and explicit protection of politically significant pockets of inefficiency is an equilibrium outcome.

American tacit bilateral bargaining strategy upset this equilibrium. Congressional threats to restrict imports of Japanese manufactured products had the effect of mobilizing export-oriented manufacturers in Japan on behalf of liberalization of agriculture, government procurement codes, and services. In turn, negotiators in the Department

---

imports were in line with expected imports. The intrinsic difficulty of assessing the magnitude of informal NTBs has been a substantial problem for academics and negotiators alike. See Luca Barbone, "Import Barriers: An Analysis of Time-Series Cross-Section Data," *OECD Economic Studies* 11 (Autumn 1988): 155–68.

[28] Because American industrial organization tends to be along vertical sectoral lines, winners and losers from liberalization are not within the same company.

[29] This argument on horizontal integration was triggered by a Peter Gourevitch observation on family organization. To explain differences between British and German agricultural trade policy during the 1873–96 crisis, he observes that British landholding aristocracy had intermarried with the rising industrial bourgeoisie while German junkers had not. As a consequence, the British aristocracy's losses in agriculture were offset by gains in manufacturing. See Peter Gourevitch, *Politics in Hard Times: Comparative Responses to International Economic Crises* (Ithaca, N.Y.: Cornell University Press, 1986).

[30] See Daniel I. Okimoto, "Political Inclusivity: The Domestic Structure of Trade," in *The Political Economy of Japan: The Changing International Context*, eds. Takashi Inoguchi and Daniel I. Okimoto (Stanford: Stanford University Press, 1988), 331–34.

of Commerce and the Office of the United States Trade Representative (USTR) have pointed to general protectionist sentiments in Congress to strengthen their hand in sector specific bargaining over Japanese import restrictions.

Market Oriented Sector Specific Negotiations

The 1982–1986 Market Oriented Sector Specific (MOSS) negotiations provide an example of tacit bilateralism in action. To stave off American protectionism, Japanese negotiators had to serve as *sensei*. Before bargaining over market access, Japanese negotiators had to teach naive American negotiators how to extract concessions from Japan. American trade negotiators initially defined the problem in terms of general market access while Japanese negotiators wished to bargain over specifics. As Syed Maswood has observed, the strong Japanese preference for dealing with specific restrictions was based on Japanese negotiators' appreciation of the strength of Japanese forces for protection. If Japanese negotiators were to succeed in pressuring a Japanese domestic industry or ministry to accede to liberalization, then American negotiators had to single out specific sectoral problems. As Maswood notes, American negotiators and legislators may not have fully assimilated the teachings of their Japanese counterparts. Under Secretary of Commerce Lionel Olmer expressed frustration in testimony before the Senate: "In several discussions when we would lay out the case, one or more members of the (LDP Chairman) Esaki mission would reach into a briefcase and pull out large volumes of data to deal with us on a selective issue or other rather than to discuss in a more general basis what I believe and what the administration believes is a pervasive problem of market access generally."[31] The MOSS negotiations eventually centered on specific problems of market access in leather, medical instruments, forestry products, and telecommunications equipment. Bargaining focused on government procurement, residual quotas, government standards and certification procedures, the government tobacco and salt monopoly, and the application of sales tax on a CIF basis for imports and on an ex-factory basis for domestic goods. While Maswood reports that the MOSS talks resulted in Japanese concessions on many of these issues, by 1986 only twenty-three of twenty-seven quotas covering products treated by the talks were removed.[32] The MOSS discussions were but one of many settings for bilateral bargaining.

[31] See Syed Javed Maswood, *Japan and Protection: The Growth of Protectionist Sentiment and the Japanese Response* (New York: Routledge, 1989), 92.
[32] Ibid., 96.

Throughout the late 1980s, American threats were followed by Japanese liberalization. In 1987, the Reagan administration imposed a 100 percent tariff surcharge on $300 million worth of electronics imports from Japan in retaliation against violations of a semiconductor pricing agreement, and the U.S. Congress considered an explicitly anti-Japanese omnibus trade bill. Japan moved to increase imports through a combination of domestic stimulation and yen revaluation. In 1988, the U.S. Congress considered yet another explicitly anti-Japanese version of an omnibus trade bill, and American negotiators objected to a large number of specific import restrictive measures. Japan promised to abolish quotas on eight processed agricultural products, agreed to permit American construction companies to bid on Japanese public works projects, and agreed to a phased opening of its market for beef and oranges.[33]

Because each Japanese concession has engendered domestic political conflict, the implementation of liberalization has often been slow. In 1988, the American rice producer's lobby demanded liberalization of Japanese rice imports. The Japanese Ministry of Agriculture responded by accelerating a long-term program to rationalize rice production. Quite predictably, LDP support among farmers dropped sharply in recent by-elections and prefectural elections. The pace of liberalization in general and agricultural liberalization in particular may be affected by the Recruit scandal and the Uno affair. As the Recruit scandal and Uno affair eroded general support for the LDP, the political significance of the farm bloc and other import-competing interests within the LDP increased. A senior LDP official in charge of farm policy indicated that the social damage done by liberalization and rationalization of Japanese farming may outweigh the economic benefits.[34] The case of liberalization of rice imports provides both an example of partially successful bilateral bargaining and a clear warning on the consequences of domestic weakness for implementation of import liberalization.

The success of American tacit bilateralism is underappreciated. During the 1980s, Japan implemented at least seven sets of market-opening measures. While any given round of specific Japanese-American negotiations resulted in only limited liberalization of the Japanese market, American tacit bilateralism taken in the aggregate

---

[33] *Asia Yearbook 1988* (Hongkong: Far Eastern Economic Review, 1988), 155; and *Asia Yearbook 1989* (Hongkong: Far Eastern Economic Review, 1989), 144.

[34] Charles Smith, "Rice Bowl Politics: LDP may Scrap Rice Reform to Hold Farm Vote," *Far Eastern Economic Review* 29 (June 1989): 25–26.

has reduced Japanese barriers to imports substantially.[35] However, incremental improvements in market access may fall below thresholds of perception within the United States. Most American legislators do not recognize that cumulative Japanese concessions have been substantial. The specificity that Japanese negotiators require to win domestic battles over liberalization may be inconsistent with the simplicity that American negotiators require to stave off protectionist sentiment within the United States.

The Trade Act of 1988: Super 301 and the Schumer Amendment

If Japanese concessions have been substantial yet have not been recognized within the United States, then Japanese-American bilateral trade imbalances have been both substantial and visible. As a consequence, the United States moved from tacit toward explicit bilateralism. In 1988, Congress responded to the deteriorating American trade balance and rising Japanese investments in the United States by requiring American trade negotiators to pursue a strategy of loose bilateral reciprocity. The Super 301 provisions of the Trade Act of 1988 compelled the executive to develop an "enemies list" of nations engaging in unfair trade practices and to enter into negotiations to eradicate unfair trade practices. Super 301 also compelled the executive to impose penalties on listed nations if negotiations failed. Under the Trade Act of 1988, the executive branch retained discretion in defining unfair trade practices and in adding nations to the enemies list, as amendments to treat the existence of significant bilateral imbalances on trade account as evidence of unfair trading practices were narrowly defeated. The Trade Act of 1988 also mandated financial market reciprocity. The Primary Dealers Act, or Schumer Amendment, set forth reciprocal national treatment as a standard for granting market access in financial services. That is, Japanese firms would be allowed to operate on an equal footing with American firms in the American market if American firms are allowed to operate on an equal footing with Japanese firms in the Japanese market. Proponents of Super 301 and the Schumer Amendment contended that reciprocity would improve American access to Japanese markets for goods and services—that reliance on bilateral reciprocity would yield greater openness. Opponents of Super 301 and the Schumer Amendment contended that reliance on bilateral reciprocity would

---

[35] For a list of Japanese concessions, see Maswood, *Japan and Protection*, chapter 5, "Trade Imbalance and Import Promotion."

spark trade wars and reduce openness. How did these two reciprocity provisions of the 1988 Trade Act fare in practice?

First, the United States and Japan continued to negotiate sector specific market access. In 1989, the U.S. Trade Representative composed a list of nations to be singled out for ostensibly unfair trading practices. Japan was included on the list. An American trade negotiator described the strategy as "enlisting Fujitsu and Mitsubishi to reduce the disproportionate influence of citrus growers, rice farmers, and beef producers."[36] He contends a strategy of bilateral reciprocity, not multilateral negotiations over general levels of protection under the GATT, has been and will continue to be the principal force for Japanese import liberalization.[37] Under the conventional first track, Japan ultimately reduced effective levels of protection facing products for which the United States was a principal supplier, including processed forest products, supercomputers, and cellular telephones. The United States provided assurances of continuing Japanese access to the American market by promising to treat U.S.-Japan trade questions outside of the framework of Super 301. As in the RTAA negotiations of the late 1930s and the MOSS negotiations of the early 1980s, economic discrimination served as a force for economic liberalization. American trade negotiators invoked explicit threats of unfavorable treatment under Super 301, then pointed to the possibility of far more severe legislative action in the event that negotiations failed. Like the RTAA and MOSS strategies, the conventional track of trade negotiations mobilized Japanese export-oriented sectors in the struggle against protection. This more or less conventional negotiating strategy succeeded in reducing both conventional and unconventional barriers to imports. Japan agreed to import processed forest products instead of unprocessed logs, permitting principal

---

[36] Telephone interview with anonymous staff member, Office of the U.S. Trade Representative, February 1989.

[37] These observations are reinforced by the comments of a village elder in a Japanese citrus producing region in May 1985. The elder pointed to the age distribution of the villagers and noted with some pride that all of the young adults born in the village were working for export-oriented corporations in the cities. Over the long term, he suggested, agricultural import liberalization was inevitable. The elder was intimately familiar with the status of American trade bills—far more knowledgeable than American graduate students in schools of public policy. He predicted that the United States would adopt a policy of conditional reciprocity and that the LDP would respond by abandoning the villagers to preserve the international market shares of the corporations that employed their sons and daughters. He noted somewhat sadly that all planning by the local agricultural cooperative was premised on the assumption that visible and invisible barriers to American citrus would be eradicated in the next few years. Interview with Hirata Yoshitomo, Heta, Yamaguchi-Ken, May 1985. Hirata is the local leader of the LDP.

suppliers in America to capture more of the value added. Japan agreed to adopt the Motorola standard for cellular telephones over competing standards proposed by Japanese companies, providing Motorola with lead time to establish a position in an expanding Japanese market. Japan agreed to purchase a Cray supercomputer, albeit at a time when Japanese corporations were on the verge of achieving parity with Cray. As in the MOSS talks, Japan made piecemeal concessions of varying significance. As in the MOSS talks, piecemeal concessions may have fallen below the threshold of recognition within the American polity. As in the MOSS talks, piecemeal concessions did not have perceptible effects on bilateral current account imbalances.

However, if bilateralism is to be an effective force for liberalization in Japanese-American trade relations, then the United States must in fact grant market access in exchange for market access. The notion of targeting unfair trade practices is not, in and of itself, objectionable, but the tone and content of debate over the 1988 Trade Bill suggests that there is substantial risk that the United States will restrict market access even as Japan liberalizes.[38] To counter this risk, the theory of discriminatory bargaining presented in this book suggests that Japanese concessions should be designed to preference American exporters explicitly and clearly. If Japanese access to the American market hinges on increasing American exports to the Japanese market, then Japanese liberalization should be structured to favor American exporters. Yet Japanese concessions have been formally nondiscriminatory. Reductions in tariffs, quotas, and certification standards ostensibly benefit all exporters covered by MFN. The Japanese problem reduces to the following. If third parties compete effectively with American products in Japan, then two possibilities arise. American exporters may cut back on their lobbying against American restrictions on Japanese imports. Alternately, American pressure for formal preferencing of American products may increase. To forestall both possibilities, the Japanese government has liberalized in areas of American advantage and has administered liberalization to preference American producers.

Traditionally, Japan has pursued *less* discriminatory import policies than other advanced industrial societies. In fact, Japanese import policy is becoming more discriminatory as it becomes more liberal. The United States is not the only efficient producer of any product that

---

[38] For an explicit discussion of how problems of recognition and control can reduce the efficiency of strategies of reciprocity, see George Downs, David Rocke, and Randolph Siverson, "Cooperation and Arms Control," in *Cooperation under Anarchy,* ed. Kenneth A. Oye (Princeton, N.J.: Princeton University Press, 1986).

has been liberalized through bilateral Japanese-American negotiations. South East Asian rice producers, European telecommunications manufacturers, Canadian foresters, Argentine gaucheros, and Spanish tanners are all competitive with their American counterparts. Yet the American share of Japanese purchases of these products has been disproportionately high. Consider one example. Under American pressure, Japan liberalized Nippon Telephone and Telegraph procurement policies during the 1980s. The American share of foreign sales to NTT varied between 80 percent and 90 percent—well in excess of the American share of telecommunications exports to non-Japanese markets.[39] Furthermore, Japanese patterns of foreign investment in anticipation of liberalization center on the United States.

Second, the Trade Act of 1988 mandated negotiations over access to markets for financial services. The effects of the Schumer Amendment in financial services were comparable to the effects of Super 301 on other elements of trade. Thomas Bayard and Kimberly Elliott of the Institute of International Economics provide a clear account of the success of the Schumer Amendment.[40] Prior to passage of the Schumer Amendment, Japanese-American negotiations over financial market liberalization and market access were largely unsuccessful. The Japanese government had responded positively to some American complaints by permitting American banks to acquire securities branches and to manage trust funds, but had not permitted foreign firms to participate in underwriting government bonds or to become members of the Toyko Stock Exchange. These Japanese restrictions on operations of American firms contrasted with American treatment of Nomura Securities and Daiwa Securities. In 1986, the New York Federal Reserve Bank had licensed Nomura, Daiwa, and other Japanese firms to serve as primary dealers in American government securities. In 1987, Representative Schumer introduced a bill to prohibit the FED from designating foreign firms as primary dealers in American securities if their home governments denied American firms equal access to their home security markets. In a visit

[39] Maswood, *Japan and Protection*, 112.

[40] Thomas Bayard and Kimberly Elliott, "Reciprocity in Financial Services: The Schumer Amendment and the Second Banking Directive" (Washington, D.C.: Institute of International Economics, 1990). Unpublished paper delivered to the American Economics Association Annual Convention, December 1990. Although Bayard and Elliott find that the Schumer Amendment was effective, they oppose reliance on bilateral reciprocity. They maintain that the potential costs of spiraling commercial and financial conflict more than offset the potential benefits of modest discriminatory liberalization. The inclusion of the Bayard-Elliott case study on Schumer should not be taken as an endorsement by Bayard and Elliott of the argument developed in this chapter.

to Toyko, Congressman Schumer argued that bilateral reciprocity would strengthen the hand of Japanese supporters of financial liberalization. In fact, Bayard and Elliott report that the Ministry of Finance Securities Bureau and the large Japanese securities firms supported the proposed change. They state:

> The congressional delegation's visit, the Schumer Amendment per se, and more generally the House of Representatives' passage of a trade bill replete with tough reciprocity provisions appears to have shaken the Japanese financial community. High level officials from Nomura and Daiwa, which were targets of the Schumer bill, publically called for a switch to a government bond auction and expanded membership for foreigners on the Toyko stock exchange. In April and May of 1987, the Ministry of Finance announced the introduction of a limited auction for 20 percent of the 10 year bond issue and the Stock Exchange announced plans to expand its membership and consider additional foreign applications.[41]

As in the case of Super 301, the executive branch opposed bilateral reciprocity while using the threat of legislation to secure concessions. In the summer of 1987, Treasury Assistant Secretary David Mulford repeatedly warned Japanese firms of the importance of Japanese financial liberalization and called on Japanese firms with international financial operations to strongly support commercial and financial openness.[42]

The Structural Impediments Initiative

Although Super 301 and the Schumer Amendment yielded the Japanese concessions described above, American trade deficits did not fall quickly. Between 1980 and 1989, the bilateral American deficit with Japan deteriorated from $11 billion to $56 billion and the aggregate American trade deficit rose.[43] In fact, it is unclear whether

[41] Bayard and Elliott, "Reciprocity in Financial Services," 20–21.

[42] Between 1987 and 1990, the executive branch position evolved toward support for bilateral reciprocity on financial services. In a reversal of position, the U.S. Treasury designated Japan, South Korea, Taiwan, and several Latin American countries as violating precepts of equality of national treatment. In effect, the Treasury threatened to support mirror image reciprocity provisions in the Fair Trade in Financial Services Act unless major foreign financial service markets were opened to American firms on an equality of national treatment basis. Susumu Awanohara, "Tit for Tat: US Set to Harden Policy on Asian Financial Markets," *Far Eastern Economic Review* 27 (December 1990).

[43] The American imbalance with Japan was not atypical. Between 1980 and 1989, the American trade balance with major clusters of trading partners deteriorated: bal-

Japanese concessions fell above thresholds of perception for the American public in general or for American legislators in particular. If American trade performance did not improve, then Congress would pass a far more restrictive trade bill. U.S. Trade Representative Carla Hills and Japanese trade negotiator Koji Watanabe devised a strategy to deflect protectionist pressure within the United States and to augment forces for liberalization within Japan. During 1989–90, the United States and Japan negotiated over an unconventional array of nominally *domestic* practices with *indirect* effects on import and export performance. In July 1989, the agenda of Japanese-American bilateral negotiations moved beyond import barriers and export subsidies. The Structural Impediments Initiative (SII) rested on the proposition that eradication of traditional barriers to imports could *not* eliminate trade imbalances. The SII focused on altering *domestic* practices to influence demand for imports and capacity for exports. Recall Aesop's fable of the ant and the grasshopper. Under SII, the ant agreed to emulate the grasshopper even as the grasshopper agreed to emulate the ant. To raise imports, Japan agreed to raise consumption levels, discourage savings, and spend 430 trillion yen on public works. To increase marginal propensity to import, Japan agreed to eliminate laws favoring small domestically oriented retailers, specifically by revising the Large Retail Store Law. Conversely, Japanese negotiators offered observations on the external implications of domestic American practices. To decrease American imports, lower American consumption levels by raising savings and investment and by lowering American fiscal deficits. To increase American export potential, improve American education, adopt the metric system, and restructure tax laws to favor long-term rather than short-term investment strategies. The Bush administration agreed to support "tax revenue increases," to urge Congress to enact the Savings and Economic Growth Act of 1990, and to ease antitrust regulations on joint production, and to improve education and worker training programs.[44] By negotiating over ostensible structural impediments to trade, the United States and Japan departed from the old agenda in two critical respects. The focus of negotiations shifted toward what had been viewed as domestic issues even as the benefits of adjust-

---

ances with Europe fell from a $20 billion surplus to a $2 billion deficit; balances with Canada fell from a $1 billion surplus to a $10 billion deficit; balances with the Asian Newly Industrializing Countries fell from a $4 billion deficit to a $20 billion deficit; and balances with Latin America fell from a $2 billion surplus to a $10 billion deficit.

[44] Japanese Ambassador Michio Mizoguchi offered a wry characterization of SII as singularly appropriate for an "Age of Meddling." Panel discussion, J.A.C.L. Panel on U.S.-Japan Relations, San Diego, California, June 1990.

ments in domestic economic policies would be diffused across trading partners and could not be focused narrowly on either the United States or Japan. In effect, the externalities associated with changes in domestic economic policies would have the characteristics of public goods.[45]

The Japanese-American case provides illustrations of the potentials and pitfalls of bilateralism. On the one hand, discriminatory bargaining has reduced restrictions on products and restrictive practices that are not governed by the GATT. As this case has shown, tacit bilateralism has mobilized export-oriented sectors against import-competing interests within both Japan and the United States. On balance, economic discrimination has yielded economic liberalization. On the other hand, American proponents of bilateralism are pushing to limit Japanese access to the American market for failing to liberalize enough. The excruciating incrementalism of Japanese liberalization and the real or feigned inability of American legislators to recognize piecemeal liberalization are also rooted in domestic political structures. There is always a risk that irritation and misunderstanding will develop into a trade war. Finally, Japanese-American trade relations point ahead to the importance of monetary and financial factors as determinants of trade flows. During the 1980s, the sharp appreciation and depreciation of the dollar relative to the yen affected Japanese-American trade far more significantly than did bilateral discussions of trade.

BILATERAL LIBERALIZATION AND CANADIAN-AMERICAN TRADE

In January 1988, the United States and Canada signed a bilateral agreement to create a free trade zone between the world's largest

[45] The United States and Japan negotiated over financial questions that were substantively unrelated to bilateral trade conflict. American Treasury Secretary Nicholas Brady had devised a plan to contain the chronic Third World debt crisis through debt relief. Japanese participation was a necessary, though not sufficient, condition for success of the Brady Plan. Like their European counterparts, Japanese banks were partners in syndicated loans. Even more significantly, credit rich Japanese banks were important potential sources of fresh lending and were the most important potential purchasers of discounted debt. In June 1990, as the United States and Japan were negotiating over market access and structural impediments to trade, the Japan Center for International Finance announced that Japanese banks would not lend new money to any country that accepted debt reduction under the Brady Plan. Tomomitsu described Brady as an American initiative financed by Japanese money and stated that the Ministry of Finance and private Japanese banks would "continue to reject suggestions" to provide new money under the Brady Plan.

trading partners.[46] The Free Trade Agreement (FTA) calls for removal of all tariffs and many NTBs imposed by both countries on each other's products over a period of ten years. This section suggests that the discriminatory content of the agreement was instrumental in mobilizing domestic support, particularly within Canada, for liberalization.

Although the agreement does not call for elimination of all barriers to Canadian-American trade, its provisions will substantially reduce effective levels of protection. The bilateral agreement abolishes all tariffs on Canadian and American products except duties on some agricultural goods and cultural products. It lowers nontariff barriers. It opens up most government contracts to competitive bidding from suppliers in Canada and the United States. It eliminates some other restrictions, including Canadian duty remission subsides on American automobiles and (most) American regulations limiting imports of Canadian oil and natural gas. It exempts Canadian and American products from GATT Article 19 "safeguard actions" unless the partner's imports are "contributing importantly" to the serious injury.

Each of these provisions is also discriminatory. As Canadian-American liberalization proceeds, the products of third countries will face higher differential levels of protection than at present. These reductions in tariffs, regulatory restrictions, safeguard actions, and government procurement codes are not to be passed on to third parties. Because the agreement does not impose uniform Canadian and American barriers to imports from third countries, the agreement specifies domestic content eligibility requirements to prevent third parties from reexporting within the free trade zone. On other issues, the discriminatory content of the Canadian-American bilateral is less clear. Disputes over Fair Trade including allegations of dumping and unfair production subsidies are relegated to a complex dispute settlements procedure that will be fully defined as disputes arise.[47]

What role did discrimination play in fostering liberalization be-

---

[46] The 1988 Canadian-American bilateral was foreshadowed by a 1985 U.S.-Israel Free Trade Area Agreement. For a comprehensive evaluation of the U.S.-Israel agreement, see Howard F. Rosen, "The US-Israel Free Trade Area Agreement: How Well Is It Working and What Have We Learned?" in *Free Trade Areas and US Trade Policy*, ed. Jeffrey J. Schott (Washington, D.C.: Institute of International Economics, 1989).

[47] This summary is drawn from William Diebold, "The New Bilateralism?" in *Bilateralism, Multilateralism and Canada in U.S. Trade Policy*, ed. William Diebold (Cambridge: Ballinger, 1988), 132–45; Jeffrey J. Schott and Murray G. Smith, eds., *The Canada-United States Free Trade Agreement: The Global Impact* (Washington, D.C.: Institute for International Economics, 1988); and Jeffrey J. Schott, "More Free Trade Areas?" in *Free Trade Areas and U.S. Trade Policy*, ed. Jeffrey Schott (Washington, D.C.: Institute of International Economics, 1989), 6.

tween the United States and Canada? Consider the context of bilateral negotiations. Multilateral liberalization under the Uruguay Round of GATT negotiations had been stalled. By narrowing participation in trade liberalization to the United States and Canada, bilateral negotiations circumvented the deadlocks of the Uruguay Round. Furthermore, piecemeal efforts at Canadian-American liberalization on a sectoral basis were failing. As had happened so often in the past, import-oriented sectors and regions within both the United States and Canada organized to defend protection more effectively than export-oriented sectors and regions organized to oppose protection. By broadening the agenda of trade discussions between the United States and Canada, comprehensive bilateral negotiations circumvented the sectoral deadlocks of narrower negotiations.

From the perspective of the Conservative government, a free trade zone provided solutions to two problems. The agreement secured access to the American market during a time of increasing American reliance on NTBs. Before implementation of the bilateral agreement, the U.S. market accounted for 80 percent of all Canadian exports. During bilateral negotiations, the United States had restricted Canadian exports in a series of unfair trade actions. Given Canadian export dependency on the United States and the American tilt toward protection, Canada assigned a high priority to guaranteeing market access to the United States. Less obviously, the agreement provided an external solution to an internal problem. As Gilbert Winham observes, Prime Minister Mulroney acted to implement the recommendations of the MacDonald Royal Commission on the Economy to deregulate the domestic Canadian economy by moving toward free trade. By eliminating barriers to imports, a free trade zone would create a more competitive economic environment for Canadian producers and the Canadian government. This harsher environment would select for efficient private producers and for deregulatory government policies.[48] Liberalization, not discriminatory liberalization, was the key to Mulroney's long-term strategy.

Yet without discrimination it is unlikely that Canada would have embraced liberalization. Although Prime Minister Mulroney saw virtue in a more competitive environment, import-competing sectors do not. The 1988 Canadian national elections were a referendum on the United States-Canada bilateral. The discriminatory aspects of the bilateral agreement broadened and deepened Conservative party sup-

---

[48] Gilbert Winham, "Why Canada Acted," in Diebold, *Bilateralism, Multilateralism and Canada in U.S. Trade Policy*, 44. Mulroney's view on the possible effects of external economic liberalization on the political feasibility of internal deregulation and efficiency may be also be held by Ronald Reagan and Mikhail Gorbachev.

port.[49] Discriminatory liberalization was an easier sell than nondiscriminatory liberalization for two reasons. First, discrimination provided export-oriented interests with a clear stake in fighting for import liberalization—improved access to real markets. By *not* passing on the benefits reductions in tariffs and NTBs to other trading partners, the bilateral agreement gave export-oriented interests a small but measurable advantage over exporters from third countries. Without this preference, the benefits to Canadian manufacturing would have been eroded by competition from the East Asia Newly Industrializing Countries and Japan. Second, discrimination limited the scope of domestic dislocations that would be suffered by import-competing sectors. If the Canadian market were opened to all producers rather than American producers alone, the costs to be borne by import-competing sectors and regions would have been far more substantial. In strictly economic terms, the discriminatory openness is inferior to nondiscriminatory openness. However, liberalization without discrimination was politically unattainable.

The broader international implications of the Canadian-American bilateral are not yet clear. The bilateral may not violate the letter of the GATT. Under Article 24, customs unions and free trade areas are deemed to be consistent with the GATT if the parties notify the GATT, if the parties do not raise barriers facing third countries, and if "substantially all" merchandise trade between the parties is covered. Canada and the United States notified GATT signatories and the agreement does not raise or lower barriers facing third countries. Because the GATT coverage requirement does not apply to sectors unregulated by the GATT, the exclusion of agriculture from the bilateral is permissible. However, the exclusion of "cultural industries" may comprise a technical violation of the coverage requirement. It is unlikely that either of the principal non-American suppliers of culture to Canada—Great Britain and France—will challenge the agreement as a whole because of this limitation on coverage. By and large, the Canadian-American bilateral appears to comply with the requirements of the GATT.

Although in compliance with the GATT, the Canadian-American bilateral poses a serious threat to the GATT. Neither Canada nor the United States entered negotiations to displace the GATT. As Gilbert Winham has observed: 'The reality of Canada's trade is *bilateral*, and the initiation of a bilateral negotiation simply had the potential to ad-

[49] See Ian Whan Tung, "Canadian-American Trade Relations," unpublished thesis, Department of Politics, Princeton University, 1989.

dress more Canadian issues than did a multilateral negotiation."[50] This description of Canada's motives could apply to any participant in any of the minor or major bilateral and regional trade negotiations taking place today. A pragmatic interest in improving market access remains the principal force for liberalization and discrimination in contemporary trade. The very success of bilateral negotiations in liberalizing the world's largest trading relationship may threaten the GATT by providing a powerful example of the benefits of economic discrimination.

The broader international effects of the bilateral are not limited to the power of example. Like the 1938 Canadian-American bilateral, the 1988 bilateral is designed to exclude third parties from the benefits of liberalization. Although the 1988 FTA does not include rate differentiations based on the weight of cows, reductions in nontariff barriers were structured to benefit Canadians without necessarily conferring benefits on Mexicans. The elimination of regulations that had restricted imports of Canadian petroleum and natural gas will not substantially benefit PEMEX. Export-oriented Mexican sectors are already pushing for bilateral discussions with the United States. As in the 1930s, third parties are likely to respond to their exclusion by initiating bilateral negotiations of their own.

REGIONAL LIBERALIZATION AND THE SINGLE INTEGRATED MARKET PROPOSAL

In 1987, the members of the European Community agreed to form a Single Integrated Market by 1992. The proposal is both liberalizing and discriminatory. It would eliminate most restrictions on flows of goods, services, labor, and capital within the European Community. If implemented, the proposal will create the world's largest market. The proposal is also discriminatory. As Figure 7.1 showed, European Community members rely substantially on nontariff barriers to trade in both agriculture and manufactures. If the European Community leaves external barriers at current levels, the gap between external and internal barriers will widen significantly.[51] Why did the members of the European Community move toward regional openness? And what are the implications of an economically integrated Europe for the global political economy?

[50] Winham, "Why Canada Acted," in Diebold, *Bilateralism, Multilateralism, and Canada in U.S. Trade Policy*, 51.

[51] To form a single market, members of the community must scrap individual national trade barriers and formulate a common external trade policy. This negotiating process is discussed below.

As Wayne Sandholtz and John Zysman suggest, the European turn toward regional liberalism may be a direct response to Japan and the East Asian Dragons and to the formation of a North American trading bloc. In their view, large captive domestic and regional markets provide a platform for effective competition in global markets. Old-fashioned economies of scale and new-fangled learning curve effects may be exploited more effectively within a single vast European market than within smaller national markets.[52] Their argument is correct and consequential. But size may confer even greater benefits in the contemporary trade environment.

In a world of negotiated market access, the large may have an additional advantage over the small. The weakness of the nondiscriminatory GATT system and the trend toward reliance on discriminatory trading practices provide a political incentive for formation of a single market.[53] In the postwar world where access to markets was negotiated on a nondiscriminatory multilateral basis, small- and medium-sized nations free rode on liberalization achieved by bargaining among the large. In a corrupt civil society where access to markets is negotiated on a bilateral basis, market size may affect the terms of access. As in the 1930s, the large and the wealthy are better positioned to secure commercial preferences than the small and the poor. A principal international economic advantage conferred on an integrated Europe is derived from potentially greater effectiveness in political negotiation.

To realize these economic and political advantages of size, the single market proposal must move from paper to reality.[54] Extra-Euro-

---

[52] See Wayne Sandholtz and John Zysman, "1992: Recasting the European Bargain," *World Politics* 42 no. 1 (October 1989).

[53] The relationship between market size and ability to negotiate market access in bilateralized international economic environments does not deny the role of other factors in determining economic performance. For example, domestic political structures may permit or impede adjustment to changing international economic circumstances. As Peter Katzenstein suggests, small democratic corporatist states outperformed larger nations such as the United States and Great Britain during the 1960s and 1970s. The economic performance of an integrated Europe will hinge on its ability to mold its external environment through negotiation and to respond to uncontrollable environmental changes. Both of these factors will be influenced strongly by the evolution of Europe-wide political institutions, a process beyond the bounds of this study. See Peter J. Katzenstein, *Small States in World Markets: Industrial Policy in Europe* (Ithaca, N.Y.: Cornell University Press, 1985).

[54] At the time of this writing, it is not clear whether the agreement will be implemented. The very comprehensiveness of the agreement has generated substantial internal opposition. For example, German trade unions are mobilizing to defend their position against what they see as a two-edged threat of labor imports and capital exports. Trade unions throughout the higher wage northern tier countries may be ex-

pean Community (EC) protection may be a requisite of intra-EC liberalization. The specifics of ongoing negotiations over the
implementation of the single market proposal are mind numbing.
Removal of internal nontariff barriers to trade is intrinsically difficult. Germany and Britain are wrangling over safety certification
standards for manufactures. At present, only 2 percent of EC government contracts are filled by firms in other EC countries, yet little
progress has been made in eliminating restrictive government procurement codes. In financial services and insurance, substantial differences in national regulations are unlikely to be eliminated by the
European Commission.[55] The EC's external trade policies will be affected by how these internal issues are resolved. Differential treatment of non-EC nations is certain to be a requisite of agreement on
these issues within Europe.

The EC's external trade policy remains largely undefined. The
June 1988 European Summit in Hanover took one small step toward
defining an external trade policy for an integrated Europe. The Hanover Summit communique declared: "The internal market should
not close in on itself. In conformity with the provisions of the GATT,
the Community should be open to third countries and must negotiate
with those countries where necessary to ensure access to their market
for Community exports. It will seek to preserve the balance of advantages accorded, while respecting the identity of the internal market
of the Community."[56] The generality of the Hanover communique
contrasts with the specificity of the external trade policy agenda. To
form a single market, European nations must reconcile their extraordinarily diverse national trade policies. The members of the EC currently rely on approximately 700 different national quantitative restrictions on imports. As Figure 7.1 showed, there is substantial
variation across EC members in the comprehensiveness of explicit
NTBs on manufactured goods and on agricultural products. German
liberalism on agricultural products must be reconciled with French
protection. Danish liberalism on manufactured products must be reconciled with French protection. Consider the example of national
quotas on the market share of Japanese automobiles. France (3%),
Italy (0%), and Britain (11%) restrict Japanese imports severely, while

---

pected to follow suit. Because the principal sources of opposition to the single market
are defined in terms of class rather than sector, the attractions of improved access to
the markets of Southern Europe may be less effective than corresponding incentives
in the Canadian-American case. The agreement on an integrated market will be implemented only if management and capital either prevail over or buy off labor.

[55] "1992 Under Construction: A Survey," *Economist* (July 8–14, 1989): S-12, 15, 16.
[56] Ibid., S-6.

Germany offers substantial market access. It is not clear whether the community policy on Japanese automobiles will lean toward German or Italian policies.

Developing an external policy on more subtle forms of nontariff protection including government procurement codes, certification standards, and regulation of insurance and financial services will be even more difficult. Again, it is not clear whether community external policies will lean toward the most restrictive or the least restrictive. Finally, the European nations have varied substantially in their propensity to rely on safeguard actions, dumping charges, and export subsidy accusations as a means of protecting. Standards for judging that a price difference reflects dumping or a subsidy or that an increase in imports is doing substantial injury to a domestic sector are intrinsically obscure. Once again, it is not clear whether community practices will lean toward the most restrictive or the least restrictive. In fact, it is not clear whether national trade policies on some of these issues will be effectively displaced by a common European policy.

Consider European efforts to reduce effective internal barriers to trade in financial services. The EC's 1990 Second Banking Directive contains two key provisions. First, the Second Banking Directive establishes a communitywide regulatory standard for licensing and certification of credit institutions. If an institution can satisfy common capital requirements, restrictions on participation in nonfinancial activities, limitations on activities, and accounting procedures, then an institution is licensed to operate throughout the European Community.[57] The Second Banking Directive effectively replaces national requirements for licensing with European standards for licensing. As such, it comprises an almost pure example of regional liberalization. Second, the directive also discriminates between European financial companies and foreign financial companies. Foreign access to the lucrative European financial services market is contingent on European access to foreign markets. As Joel Trachtman observes, the Second Banking Directive proposes two versions of reciprocity. Article 9(4) sets forth a minimal standard of de facto equality of national treatment. If European firms are not permitted to operate on an equal footing with foreign firms in foreign markets, then the EC will deny licenses to foreign firms to operate within Europe. Article 9(3) sets forth a more restrictive "effective equality of market access standard."

---

[57] Second Council Directive of December 15, 1989 on the Coordination of Laws, Regulations and Administrative Provisions Relating to the Taking Up and Pursuit of the Business of Credit Institutions and Amending Directive 77/780/EEC, 32 O.J. EUR. COMM. NO. L 386.

If European firms are not granted effective market access comparable to that provided by the community, then the EC must enter into
negotiations with foreign nations to secure equality of market access.
Both the de facto "equality of national treatment" standard of 9(4)
and the "negotiate equality of access" requirement of 9(3) are inherently ambiguous.[58] As in more traditional areas of trade, the EC's external strategy on trade in financial services remains undefined. External forces are likely to determine foreign access to the European
financial services market.

How have major financial nations responded to the European policy? Consider the response of the United States. As in Japanese-
American cases discussed earlier, the Congress has played a leading
role in pushing European-American relations toward narrow rather
than broad conceptions of reciprocity. Days after the EC passed the
Second Banking Directive, Senators Riegle and Garn introduced the
Fair Trade in Financial Services Act of 1990. The Riegle-Garn Bill
sets forth equality of national treatment as the standard for granting
foreign firms access to the American financial services market.[59] The
steps in the dance between the executive and legislative branches are
by now quite familiar. Treasury Undersecretary David Mulford tes-
tified against reciprocity in financial services, arguing that: "The U.S.
objection to even limited reciprocity has been the risk that reciprocity
will be used and that retaliation would follow. The impact could be
devastating to confidence in world financial markets and established
patterns of monetary and capital flows."[60] At the same time, the
American Treasury relied on threats of congressional action to secure a temperate interpretation of Article 9(3) and (4) from the EC.
In effect, by threatening European financial firms' access to the
American market, the Riegle-Garn Bill may mobilize internationally
oriented European financial firms in defense of generous definitions
of the de facto national treatment standard.

If theories of endogenous protection may be applied to the EC as
a whole, it seems likely that the external trade policy of the EC will

[58] Joel P. Trachtman, "Recent Initiatives in International Financial Regulation and
Goals of Consistency, Effectiveness, Competiveness, and Cooperation." Unpublished
working paper, Fletcher School of Law and Diplomacy, 1991, 24–26.

[59] Ibid., 40–42.

[60] Testimony before the Task Force on the International Competitiveness of U.S.
Financial Institutions, House Committee on Banking, Finance, and Urban Affairs,
February 28, 1990. As cited in Thomas Bayard and Kimberly Elliott, "Reciprocity in
Financial Services: The Schumer Amendment and the Second Banking Directive"
(Washington, D.C.: Institute of International Economics, 1990). Unpublished paper
delivered to the American Economics Association Annual Convention, Washington,
D.C., December 1990.

be biased toward protection. The interest of import-competing sectors (within and across nations) in securing protection are concentrated, while the interests of export-oriented sectors and consumers in resisting protectionism are relatively diffuse. Furthermore, the mindnumbing specificity and opaqueness of nontariff barriers may accentuate this bias. The mechanisms of protection and the processes through which protection is secured cannot be even understood without sustained attention and technical information. European actors that are not directly affected by subtle forms of protection are unlikely to be attentive, interested, or active.[61] As a consequence, European external trade policies may well be biased toward protection.

In each of the earlier trade examples, external bilateral bargaining helped offset domestic biases toward protection. In the European Community case, the common external trade policy is likely to be affected by the character of the international commercial environment. The rise of bilateralism beyond Europe's borders may well have liberalizing consequences on Europe. The Hanover Communique noted that the principle of equality of market access would play a significant role in the external trade policy of the community. That principle is a two-edged sword. European exporters are likely to find that their access to the North American and Japanese markets is contingent on North American and Japanese access to the European market.[62] The external liberalism promised by the Hanover Communique is most likely to be realized if major trading nations outside of Europe rely on explicitly discriminatory negotiating strategies.

Conclusions on Discrimination and Liberalization in Trade

In the OECD Export Credit Agreement, Japanese-American tacit bilateralism, Canadian-American explicit bilateralism, and European regionalism cases, discrimination reduced or promised to reduce barriers to movements of goods and services across international boundaries. In fact, these cases are among the most significant examples of economic liberalization during the past decade.[63] All were achieved through discriminatory bilateral or regional strategies.

[61] I suspect that most readers of this book will reach this point without reading the paragraphs describing NTBs. If my suspicion is correct, a European bias toward protection is even more likely.

[62] The expectation that Europe will be open internally but somewhat closed externally has already triggered substantial direct investment by North American and Japanese corporations.

[63] For additional cases of liberalizing reciprocity, see Carolyn Rhodes, "Reciprocity in Trade: The Utility of a Bargaining Strategy," *International Organization* 43, no. 2

Through what mechanisms did discrimination have liberalizing effects? First, by providing export-oriented sectors with a narrow interest in campaigns against protection of import-competing sectors, international discriminatory threats partially offset domestic biases toward protection. This effect of discrimination on openness is evident in each of the cases taken independently. Second, by creating incentives for excluded third parties to barter over market access, these discriminatory agreements may have contributed to the spread of liberalization beyond the parties to bilateral and regional agreements. This effect of discrimination on systemic openness only becomes clear after considering the cases serially.

These conclusions on the effects of economic discrimination on economic openness must be slightly qualified. Although discrimination always has trade diverting effects, it does not always have trade increasing effects. In the OMA quota cases, gains for Indonesia and China came at the expense of third parties. Bilateral negotiations did not increase or decrease the overall effective levels of protection of the Indonesians, the British, the Chinese, or the Americans.

Taken together, this study of commercial practices in the 1980s supports at least one unhedged conclusion. The formal debate over the relative virtues of discriminatory and nondiscriminatory approaches to the management of contemporary trade has been mooted by events. Like it or not, contemporary commercial practice is marked by increasing bilateralism and regionalism.

(Spring 1989). Rhodes concludes that "coercion elicited cooperative responses from trading partners" in the U.S.-EC carbon steel dispute of 1981–82, the U.S.-Japan auto dispute of 1980–81, the U.S.-Canada automobile dispute of 1963–65, and the U.S.-EC wheat flour dispute of 1980–present. Her analysis rests on traditional unitary rational actor assumptions and excludes by definition the effects of international bargaining processes on correction of domestic biases that are at the core of this argument.

Chapter Eight

THE POLITICS OF DEBT AND DEFICITS

FINANCIAL AND MACROECONOMIC RELATIONS IN THE 1980s

IN CONTEMPORARY financial and macroeconomic affairs, multilateral negotiations created the impression of successful crisis management, while unresolved fundamental problems reinforced movement toward regionalism and bilateralism. In financial affairs, a slow motion default was masked by rounds of rescheduling agreements and by the Baker and Brady Plans. International financial cooperation helped insulate financial centers from the crisis in the periphery. However, developing country debt–export ratios doubled while new private lending remained negligible.[1] I suggest that movement toward preferential repayment and refinancing is likely and may be a requisite of North-South financial reconstruction.

On international macroeconomic issues, economic summitry sustained an illusion of management in a period of wholesale monetary turbulence and in so doing may well have staved off more serious monetary disorder. Yet nations have not succeeded in managing externalities associated with macroeconomic policies. The public character of macroeconomic externalities and uncertainty over the signs and magnitudes of international effects create fundamental problems in this area. As a consequence, nations seeking monetary stability in a period of exchange rate volatility have turned toward regionalism. The emergence of nascent dollar, ECU, and yen blocs is a response to the failure of macroeconomic coordination.

THE DEVELOPING COUNTRY DEBT CRISIS

Both commercial and financial externalities can be diverted from country to country. In trade, nations have relied on bilateralism and regionalism to barter market access for market access while affirming devotion to the GATT principle of nondiscrimination. However, in

[1] See Jeffrey Sachs, "Introduction" and Paul Krugman, "Private Capital Flows to Problem Debtors," in *Developing Country Debt and Economic Performance: The International Financial System*, ed. Jeffrey Sachs (Chicago: University of Chicago Press, 1989).

financial affairs, creditors have respected cross default clauses and debtors have not accorded preferential treatment to some creditors at the expense of others. Why has discrimination been far less pronounced in contemporary finance than in trade? How has the absence of economic discrimination affected the quality of international responses to the chronic Third World debt crisis?

Financial externalities are intrinsically privatizable. By selectively servicing loans, debtors can shift the costs of default from one creditor to another. By promising to preference some loans at the expense of others, debtors may play creditors off against each other. As a consequence, creditors commonly discourage the privatization of debt servicing. Domestic bankruptcy law limits the ability of debtors to reward or punish individual creditors and cross default clauses in international loan agreements stipulate that default against one creditor is a default against all. These nondiscriminatory financial norms were constructed to serve the interests of creditors.

During normal times, these distinctions are of little consequence. If debt burdens are low and default seems unlikely, financial practices will be in accord with nondiscriminatory financial norms. During periods of crisis, discriminatory financial practices threaten the stability of multilateral financial orders. Nondiscriminatory rules and multilateral cooperation may collapse quickly if borrowers or lenders turn toward discrimination. During periods of reconstruction, adherence to nondiscriminatory norms may inhibit new lending. By exchanging preferential debt servicing for preferential access to fresh credits, lenders and borrowers may restore flows of funds, albeit on a discriminatory basis.

During the 1980s, multilateral financial negotiations among bankers, between bankers and creditors, and among creditor governments created the impression of successful crisis management, but unresolved problems eroded the basis of multilateral cooperation.[2] Multilateral management insulated financial centers from the crisis in the periphery even as the fundamentals continued to worsen. During the 1980s, developing country debt–export ratios doubled while new private lending remained negligible. As Table 8.1 suggests, developing countries were in a weaker position in 1987 than in 1980. Although the world financial system did not collapse, the foundations of the system weakened.

[2] For comprehensive studies on the origins of the debt crisis and the initial response by private and governmental actors, see Miles Kahler, ed., *The Politics of International Debt* (Ithaca, N.Y.: Cornell University Press, 1984). For a comparative historical study of debt crises, see Albert Fishlow, "Lessons from the Past: Capital Markets During the 19th Century and Interwar Period," *International Organization* (Summer 1985).

TABLE 8.1
Developing Country Debt–Export Ratios

	1980	1981	1982	1983	1984	1985	1986	1987
Africa	92	119	155	171	171	192	239	241
Asia	71	74	87	92	87	101	101	91
Europe	127	133	141	146	144	159	167	168
Middle East	27	34	46	61	71	83	115	110
Latin America	183	210	272	290	273	296	352	341
All LDCs	82	95	119	133	133	150	169	158

Source: International Monetary Fund, *Annual Report 1988* (Washington, D.C., IMF, 1988), 33.

TABLE 8.2
External Flows to All Developing Countries (in billions of dollars)

	1980	1981	1982	1983	1984	1985	1986	1987
Private	75	83	48	24	15	20	3	8
Official	29	37	42	37	37	30	34	34

Source: IMF, *Annual Report 1988*, 31.

Many of the features of the contemporary debt crisis are anticipated by developments during the interwar years. As in the 1930s,
prophecies of financial difficulty were self-fulfilling. Lenders do not
lend to borrowers in difficulty, and debtors that cannot continue to
borrow are borrowers in difficulty.[3] The sharp decline of private
lending to debtor nations and substantial capital flight from debtor
nations to creditor nations are direct consequences of this phenomenon. Private bank lending to the fifteen heavily indebted developing
countries fell from positive $11.1 billion in 1983 to *minus* $1.9 billion
in 1985.[4] Between 1980 and 1987, private flows to developing countries taken in the aggregate dropped steadily. As Table 8.2 indicates,
this decline was not offset by increases in official flows.

As in the 1930s, debtors could not service debt in the absence of
fresh lending without suffering severe economic shocks. When exter-

[3] See Fred Hirsch, "The Bagehot Problem," *Manchester School*, 1977; and Sebastian
Edwards, "Structural Adjustment Policies in Highly Indebted Countries," in Sachs *Developing Country Debt and Economic Performance*, 165 and 173.

[4] Paul Krugman, "Private Capital Flows to Problem Debtors," in Sachs, *Developing
Country Debt and Economic Performance: The International Financial System*, 309.

nal capital flows in, a nation spends more than it produces. When capital flows out, a nation spends less than it produces. Domestic dislocations associated with the collapse of lending were severe. During the 1980s, per capita income in many debtor nations dropped sharply. From 1980 through 1986, Sebastian Edwards reports declines in real per capita GDP of 14 percent in Argentina, 33 percent in Bolivia, 7 percent in Chile, 11 percent in Mexico, 8 percent in Peru, and 21 percent in Venezuela.[5]

As in the 1930s, financial crisis contributed to the adoption of mercantile commercial policies. To service debt in the face of interruptions of fresh capital, debtor nations restricted imports and mounted export drives. Between 1982 and 1986, Argentina licensed imports and imposed a tariff surcharge of 10 percent, Chile imposed import surcharges ranging from 4 percent to 28 percent, hiked all tariffs to 35 percent, then dropped tariffs to 20 percent, Mexico imposed quantitative restrictions on all imports, and Venezuela imposed quantitative restrictions on 70 percent of final consumption goods.

As in the 1930s, financial crisis led to imposition of foreign exchange controls, devaluation of currencies, and adoption of multiple exchange rates. Between 1980 and 1986, Sebastian Edwards reports substantial real annual devaluations by Argentina (301%), Brazil (195%), Chile (40%), Mexico (82%), Nigeria (19%), Peru (111%), the Philippines (24%), and Venezuela (17%). To service debt while suppressing imports, Venezuela, Mexico, and Chile and other nations adopted multiple exchange rates that differentiated between foreign debt repayments and imports.[6] However, other phenomena characteristic of earlier financial crises did not materialize in the 1980s. During the 1930s, perceptions of financial weakness spread from debtors to lenders, as nonperforming loans cast doubt on the solvency of lenders. During the 1980s, successive rescheduling agreements that rolled interest into principal, modest infusions of official capital, and the existence of depositor insurance on banks insulated financial centers from developments in the periphery. What Benjamin Cohen has termed "the evolutionist" approach to debt management staved off wholesale collapse by transferring burdens of adjustment to debtor states.[7]

The centerpiece of the "evolutionist" approach was the 1985 Baker Plan. It contained three elements. First, commercial banks were to provide $20 billion in new money over three years to the fifteen largest debtors. Second, the World Bank and the Inter-American Devel-

[5] Edwards, "Structural Adjustment Policies," 161.

[6] Ibid., 173–77.

[7] Benjamin J. Cohen, *Developing Country Debt: A Middle Way*, Essays in International Finance 173 (May 1989).

opment Bank were to provide an additional $9 billion in new money
to the fifteen largest debtors over three years, with the United States
supporting a capital increase for the World Bank. Third, Baker proposed earmarking repayments on old loans extended by the IMF for
extremely poor nations with balance of payments difficulties.[8] In effect, the carrot of access to modest fresh funds was to serve as an
inducement to debtor nations to service or at least reschedule debt.

The Baker Plan failed to generate substantial fresh funds from private or official sources. As Table 8.2 showed, private flows of funds
to all the developing countries actually declined during the first year
of the plan, from a low $20 billion in 1985 to $3 billion in 1986. During the first year of the plan, official flows of funds went up by a
modest $4 billion. However, the evolutionary approach succeeded in
staving off collapse. The slow motion default of the 1980s permitted
banks to increase loss reserves and stave off insolvency. The discounted prices for the paper of debtor nations on secondary markets
may be used to place a real value on loan portfolios. Major bank loss
reserves exceed the difference between the face value and real value
of loans. As the major commercial banks increased their loss reserves
in 1987, David Rockefeller wrote: "This transfer of funds—and that
is all it is—has not cost the banks a penny. It does not reduce the
obligations of the debtor nations, nor will it diminish the efforts by
the banks to recover all the interest and principal represented by
their current loans."[9] On balance, coordination among governments,
among central banks, and among commercial banks created a valu-
able illusion of management. Because panic was averted, the multilateral financial system as a whole did not collapse.

But the holding operation at the center did not address fundamentals in the periphery. To a substantial degree, creditors were able to
preserve the multilateral financial system by shifting burdens onto
debtors. As debtor governments became less willing to impose austerity on debtor populaces and announced that they would not be able
to meet their international financial obligations, lenders rolled more
interest into principal.[10] As official credits from the IMF approached
exhaustion, the role of lender of last resort and enforcer of condi-
tionality was handed off to the World Bank.[11] As official credits from
the World Bank approached exhaustion, the role of lender of last

[8] *Economist*, October 12, 1985, 75.

[9] Quoted in Benjamin J. Cohen, *Developing-Country Debt: A Middle Way*, Essays in International Finance 173 (May 1989).

[10] On "unilateral" rescheduling, see Alexis Rieffel, *The Role of the Paris Club in Managing Debt Problems*, Essays in International Finance 161 (December 1985).

[11] Richard E. Feinberg, "The Changing Relationship between the World Bank and
the IMF," *International Organization* 42, no. 3 (Summer 1988).

resort passed back to the governments of the major creditor nations. These actions altered the balance between private and public creditor exposure without reducing the stock of debt.

Through debate or by default, the stock of debt will be reduced. In March 1989, Treasury Secretary Nicholas Brady publicly advocated debt relief on a multilateral nondiscriminatory basis. His plan called on creditor governments and banks to share financial responsibility for writing off a portion of the debt. Although the United States and Japan have pledged credits to the Brady plan, the banks have been unwilling to forgive or forget. The total funds committed to date are insufficient to effect the Brady program. In fact, a piecemeal program of debt relief had been under way for a year at the time the Brady plan was announced. Many of the techniques discussed below are legitimated by the Brady proposal.

Negotiations between individual creditors and debtors have spawned a variety of techniques for restructuring outstanding debt in ways that may reduce the real obligations of debtor states. *Debt buybacks* permit countries to repurchase their debt at a discount using funds obtained from official or private sources. For example, in 1987 Bolivia repurchased $400 million of its bank debt at about eleven cents per dollar of face value—the price of Bolivian paper on the secondary markets at the time the agreement was negotiated. The Bolivians used funds donated to a special IMF voluntary contribution account to finance the repurchase of debt. *Debt conversions* permit countries to swap financial obligations for equity, other financial obligations, or development rights to rain forest. The extent of debt relief granted hinges on the terms of the conversion. For example, in 1987 Mexico offered banks an opportunity to exchange medium-term debt for Mexican bonds collateralized by the U.S. Treasury. Bidding by banks established the rate of conversion at $3.7 billion in existing bank debt for $2.6 billion in collateralized bonds. In July 1989, Mexico negotiated further debt relief in an agreement with commercial banks. Banks are exchanging debt for Mexican bonds secured by IMF and World Bank guarantees. The discount that Mexico accepted in the 1989 agreement was *less* than the 60 percent discount on Mexican debt prevailing in secondary markets.[12] However, the conversion will reduce Mexican debt payments from $12 billion to $10 billion per year.

It is at this juncture that financial discrimination by debtor states is

[12] Mexico may have accepted these somewhat unfavorable terms not so much to improve its access to future bank credits, but to attract direct investment, stem Mexican capital flight, and improve general relations with the United States.

likely to materialize. The complexity of debt conversion schemes facilitates de facto discrimination by debtors. These innovative financial instruments are foreshadowed by developments in the 1930s. Chapter Six discussed German repurchases of heavily discounted bonds on secondary markets in the middle 1930s. In preparation for his repurchasing campaign, Dr. Schacht issued statements that depressed the price of bonds held by small American creditors while taking care to reassure British banks. The combination of this subtle form of discrimination and repurchasing permitted Schacht to service British loans and to acquire access to fresh credits from Britain. There is no indication that Bolivia or Mexico has followed Schacht's example by deliberately depressing the price of its debt before repurchasing or conversion or by developing strategies to discriminate between creditors.

Debt concentration has already affected trading patterns as major creditor nations tacitly preferenced imports from major debtors. The early stages of the Third World debt crisis were managed, in part, through linkages to trade. The United States, Japan, and Western Europe offered de facto preferences for imports from debtors. The United States administers its nominally nondiscriminatory trade policy to favor exports from Latin America, Western European nations accept an increasingly disproportionate share of exports from Africa, and Japanese liberalization tends to favor exports from the United States. To measure movement toward trade concentration, I computed Relative Acceptance Indices for these dyads. Relative Acceptance Indices for Latin American exports to the United States, African exports to the European Community, and American exports to Japan were all reasonably high in the 1960s and 1970s. In the early 1980s, the Relative Acceptance Indices on each of these dyads rose. Concentration of debt has been reflected, albeit weakly, in concentration of trade.[13]

However, this modest trend toward bilateralism and regionalism in trade has not spilled back into finance. Management of the Third World debt crisis has regionalized as the United States, Europe, and Japan have managed rescheduling problems in Latin America, Africa, and Asia respectively. But to date, creditors have respected

[13] The Relative Acceptance Index is based on the division of observed levels of trade by expected levels of trade. Following the logic of the Chi Squared, the *expected* level of trade between any pair of nations is calculated from marginals by multiplying exporter and importer shares of world trade. My calculations are based on IMF Direction of Trade Data for alternate years between 1961 through 1983. For definitions of the Relative Acceptance Index, see Richard I. Savage and Karl W. Deutsch, "A Statistical Model of the Gross Analysis of Transaction Flows," *Economica* 28 (1960).

cross-default clauses while debtors have refrained from preferential servicing. The absence of substantial financial discrimination has preserved the North-North financial system, but may have had the effect of retarding restoration of the North-South financial system. The northern governments have offered minimal fresh official credits and private lenders have proved unwilling to reenter Third World markets because the costs and risks associated with these acts are private while the benefits are diffused evenly across trading partners and creditors. Yet because neither debt forgiveness nor fresh lending has materialized, debt–export ratios continue to mount as interest is rolled into principal. At some point, a shock will bring down the facade. The logic of discriminatory political exchange suggests that when the multilateral financial order collapses, lending and trade will be restored along bilateral and regional lines.

MACROECONOMIC COORDINATION

The macroeconomic policies of one country affect inflation, employment, and growth in other countries. If these international spillover effects are strong, nations may enjoy lower inflation, higher employment, and stronger growth by coordinating their domestic fiscal and monetary policies. Under the gold exchange standard of the 1920s and the postwar Bretton Woods system, macroeconomic coordination reduced to determining who would expand and who would contract to preserve fixed exchange rates. Under the floating exchange rate systems of the 1930s and in the post-Bretton Woods era, the problem of coordinating national macroeconomic policies emerged as an issue in its own right. By permitting exchange rates to vary, nations eliminated one constraint on bargaining over monetary and fiscal externalities. In theory, nations freed themselves from the problem of exchange rate management to focus on the more fundamental goal of improving collective macroeconomic performance by managing international macroeconomic spillover effects.

In practice, nations have generally failed in their efforts to manage macroeconomic externalities. During the late 1970s and 1980s, the United States encouraged Japan and West Germany to adopt more expansive policies, while Japan and West Germany encouraged the United States to pursue a less expansive fiscal policy. At best, the record is mixed. Neither ad hoc preparatory negotiations prior to the Seven Power economic summits nor more institutionalized discussions under the auspices of the International Monetary Fund significantly affected the macroeconomic policies of major economic powers. Two familiar problems have impeded management of macroeconomic spillover effects throughout the 1980s.

First, macroeconomic spillover effects have the properties of public goods. The international benefits or costs associated with national fiscal or monetary policies are diffused relatively evenly across a large number of countries. All share more or less equally in the benefits associated with adjustments in macroeconomic policy. None can be excluded from the benefits. But the costs associated with inducing change in another nation's domestic macroeconomic policies are largely private—offering concessions on nonmacroeconomic issues and making adjustments to one's own macroeconomic policies. As a consequence, countervailing international pressure to induce nations to take account of macroeconomic spillover effects is likely to be underprovided. The ineffectiveness of macroeconomic coordination is not surprising. The failure of contemporary efforts to coordinate national macroeconomic policies, discussed hereafter, follows logically from the largely public characteristics of macroeconomic policy externalities.

Second, the management of macroeconomic externalities is also complicated by uncertainty. The magnitude and even the signs of the effects of one nation's macroeconomic policies on other nations' macroeconomic performance are not well understood. From an economic perspective, uncertainty reduces welfare gains that could be realized through coordination. Jeffrey Frankel goes so far as to argue that macroeconomic coordination under conditions of uncertainty may reduce, rather than increase, collective welfare.[14] From a political perspective, uncertainty reduces the ability of nations to engage in macroeconomic coordination. Negotiating and implementing agreements is at best difficult when the parties to negotiation may reasonably hold markedly different views on the effects of policies on outcomes.

Coordination by Political Bargaining: The London and Bonn Accords

The 1978 Bonn Accords are commonly regarded as an example of successful international macroeconomic coordination. The terms of the deal were straightforward. West Germany adopted expansive measures that the United States had long sought. In turn, the United States adopted measures to reduce oil imports that Germany had been pressing on the United States. Richard Cooper observes: "Of

[14] Jeffrey A. Frankel, *Obstacles to International Macroeconomic Policy Coordination*, Princeton Studies in International Finance, no. 64 (December 1988).

the various attempts at macroeconomic coordination, the Bonn economic summit of 1978 stands out for the range and specificity of the commitments and for the follow-through."[15] Robert Putnam and Nicholas Bayne note that international agreement helped President Carter and Chancellor Schmidt to build domestic support for energy reform and macroeconomic expansion. They conclude: "In historical perspective, the Bonn accords represent a rare and perhaps even unique example of international coordination of economic policies. Mutually supportive decisions were taken that probably would not have been possible otherwise."[16] This interpretation of the 1977 London and 1978 Bonn summits is less sanguine. The expectation of future negotiations over energy and macroeconomic issues at Bonn may have caused an eight-month delay in adoption of expansionary German policies.

The London and Bonn Accords rested on the assumption that coordinated reflation would yield higher rates of growth with lower rates of inflation than would uncoordinated national macroeconomic policies.[17] As Putnam and Bayne note:

> By allowing the weaker economies to benefit from expanding export markets, the three stronger economies would serve as "locomotives" for global recovery. International Keynesian analysis indicated that this coordinated fiscal stimulus would have a more significant multiplier effect than could be accomplished by any single government, acting alone. At the same time, this programme would reduce the substantial and growing payments imbalances among the Western economies—in particular, by shrinking the surpluses of Japan and Germany—and would thus relax the balance of payments constraint on economic policies within the deficit countries, as well as contribute to exchange rate stability.[18]

Substantive disagreements over the probable macroeconomic consequences of macroeconomic actions complicated negotiations over coordination. West German models projected higher growth rates for given levels of stimulation and higher inflation rates for given growth rates than did American models. Although the economic powers

[15] Richard N. Cooper, "International Cooperation in Public Health as a Prologue to Macroeconomic Cooperation," p. 179, in Richard Cooper et al., *Can Nations Agree: Issues in International Economic Cooperation* (Washington, D.C.: Brookings, 1989).

[16] Robert D. Putnam and Nicholas Bayne, *Hanging Together: The Seven-Power Summits* (Cambridge: Harvard University Press, 1984), 96.

[17] For analysis of Carter administration macroeconomic coordination initiatives, see Robert O. Keohane, "Economic Relations Among the Advanced Industrial Countries," in *Eagle Entangled: US Foreign Policy in a Complex World*, eds. Kenneth A. Oye, Robert J. Lieber, and Donald Rothchild (New York: Longman, 1979).

[18] Putnam and Bayne, *Hanging Together*, 68–69.

could not agree on the relative virtues of their models, the three strongest economic powers managed to agree on targets for real 1977 growth prior to the London Summit.[19]

At the time and in retrospect, it is not clear whether the London agreement merely ratified or actually raised growth targets. However, it is clear that all three nations missed the targets to which they had committed. As Table 8.3 suggests, real economic growth fell well short of projections. Only four months after the London summit, it was clear that modest German and Japanese fiscal and monetary measures would not push 1977 growth rates up to promised levels.

Neither Germany nor Japan was willing to adopt more expansionary policies to meet the London obligations. Japan's reluctance to expand followed from a stubbornly high inflation rate. Japanese inflation had fallen from 24.5 percent in 1974 to 9.3 percent in 1976 and then leveled off at 8.1 percent in 1977. Reflation risked reigniting Japanese inflation. By contrast, West German growth *and* inflation were low. A preoccupation with international externalities associated with domestic macroeconomic policies should not obscure the obvious. German inflation had fallen gradually from 7.0 percent in 1974 to 3.7 percent in 1977 even as German unemployment had held steady at around 3.6 percent. Germany seemed to have a narrow na-

TABLE 8.3
London Summit Targets and Macroeconomic Performance

	London Target	GNP Growth		Inflation		Balance/GNP	
		1977	1978	1977	1978	1977	1978
United States	6.0	4.7	5.3	6.5	7.6	−0.7	−0.7
Germany	5.0	2.7	3.3	3.7	2.7	0.8	1.4
Japan	6.7	5.3	5.2	8.1	3.8	1.6	1.7

Source: London growth targets are from Putnam and Bayne, *Hanging Together*, 75. Figures on 1977 and 1978 actual growth (real growth in GNP), inflation (change in consumer price index), and current account balance divided by GNP are from *OECD Economic Outlook* 45 (June 1989): 172, 182, 191.

[19] The agreement on growth targets was conducted in parallel with discussions over unrelated issues. The conflict over nuclear exports policies was particularly hot. President Carter had restricted uranium exports to Western Europe as part of his campaign against German and French sales of reprocessing technology to Brazil and Pakistan. At the London Summit, Carter accepted establishment of an international study group on nuclear export issues. As Putnam and Bayne observe, "the procedural compromise allowed both sides to back away from a useless confrontation." Putnam and Bayne, *Hanging Together*, 78.

tional interest in reflation. Putnam and Bayne note that in early 1978, Schmidt's closest economic advisors argued that stimulation would yield higher growth without raising inflation and note that Schmidt shared their views. They observe that Schmidt did not reflate in late 1977 and early 1978 to buy time to build a stronger domestic coalition in favor of reflation. They also note in passing that Schmidt held out in order to extract "energy restraint from the Americans and concessions on trade policy from the British and French."[20] If this final element of Putnam and Bayne's interpretation is correct, then Chancellor Schmidt engaged in macroeconomic extortion. By refraining from reflation under conditions of low growth and low inflation, Schmidt was imposing costs on himself as well as others.

The Bonn Summit agenda was defined by the international commercial and monetary effects of German macroeconomic extortion and of the less willful failure of the Japanese to meet growth targets. As Table 8.3 has shown, German and Japanese current account surpluses increased while the American current account deficit did not improve. Exchange rates responded quite predictably to current account balances. Between 1977 and 1978, the yen appreciated from 268.5 to 210.4 and the deutsche mark appreciated from 2.322 to 2.009 against the dollar. Preparatory negotiations leading up to the 1978 Bonn Summit centered on two sets of issues. The United States asked Germany to stimulate the sluggish West German economy and thereby alleviate pressure on the dollar. Japan and Germany asked the United States to reduce American oil imports to alleviate one important source of pressure on crossrates and to reduce global inflation.

The outcome of the Bonn Summit is commonly regarded as the strongest example to date of successful macroeconomic coordination. The Schmidt government agreed "to propose to legislative bodies additional and quantitatively substantive measures up to one per cent of GNP, designed to achieve a significant strengthening of demand and a higher rate of growth." The Carter administration promised to adopt a program of oil price deregulation that would "result in oil import savings of approximately 2.5 million barrels per day by 1985."[21] Should the Bonn Accord be treated as a rare example of successful macroeconomic coordination?

At best, the Bonn Accords may have permitted governments to take actions that they could not have undertaken in the absence of an agreement. As Putnam has suggested, the international bargain con-

[20] Putnam and Bayne, *Hanging Together*, 87.
[21] Putnam and Bayne, *Hanging Together*, 92–93.

summated at Bonn clearly helped Schmidt and Carter build domestic support for their preferred policies.[22] The point is important but the strength of this effect is unclear. Eight years after the Bonn Summit, I asked Former Treasury Secretary Michael Blumenthal if the Accord had affected American or German policies. He responded:

> On the American side, to be frank, the effects of the agreement were limited. It may have made it a little easier for us to do what we were planning to do, with or without the Germans. Four years after the summit, I asked Helmut Schmidt if international coordination had actually made a difference. He said that the agreement made it possible to move a little sooner. He laughed and said maybe one or two months sooner. I'm not sure that it made a difference.[23]

At worst, the Bonn Accord may be likened to an arms control agreement eliminating weapons systems that would not have been built had negotiations not been contemplated.[24] The prospect of the Bonn negotiations strengthened the domestic German coalition against expansion that the Bonn Accord ultimately weakened. In Germany, unconditional opponents of expansion were joined by a chancellor seeking leverage over American energy policy. If Schmidt refrained from reflating to extract energy concessions from the United States, then German expansion was delayed at a time when expansion was seen as desirable.[25] If American "concessions" on energy were actions the United States would have taken in the absence of German pressure, then the costs of slower West German growth were not offset by any palpable benefits. The *expectation* of negotiations at Bonn may account for the *deferral* of German expansion between September 1987 and July 1978.

The two succeeding summits had less malign effects on macroeconomic performance. In retrospect, the 1979 Tokyo and 1980 Venice summits appear to have ratified national macroeconomic policies

[22] See Robert D. Putnam and C. Randall Henning, "The Bonn Summit of 1978: A Case Study in Coordination," pp. 20–97, in Richard Cooper et al., *Can Nations Agree? Issues in International Economic Cooperation* (Washington, D.C.: Brookings, 1989).

[23] Panel Discussion on "Macroeconomics, the Dollar, and World Trade," Michael Blumenthal, William Branson, and Kenneth Oye, Princeton, N. J., April 12, 1986.

[24] The expectation of arms control negotiations can lead to the acceleration of weapons procurement programs. As unconditional supporters of weapons systems are joined by those who want weapons as bargaining chips for the negotiating table, coalitions supporting marginal weapon systems can strengthen. If an arms control agreement is negotiated, proponents of weapons-as-bargaining chips withdraw support and marginal weapons systems are scrapped.

[25] In fact, German expansion following the Bonn Accords proved to be procyclical. It accentuated the inflationary effects of the (unanticipated) second oil crisis.

without affecting national policies at all. The second energy shock had increased inflation rates in all of the advanced industrial nations, and governments were inclined to pursue restrictive fiscal and monetary policies to bring down inflation rates irrespective of the policies of others. The communiques of the Tokyo and Venice summits merely described and endorsed restrictive macroeconomic policies. Because national preferences were in harmony, international bargaining had little role to play in coordinating national macroeconomic policies.

Coordination by Economic Markets: Benign Neglect 1981–85

During the first half of the 1980s, macroeconomic externalities were managed by economic markets rather than by political negotiations. The Reagan administration entered office with a simple recipe for global macroeconomic management: develop domestic fiscal and monetary policies without regard to international spillover effects and let private international capital markets cope with the international externalities. In an address to the September 1981 annual meeting of the IMF and World Bank, President Reagan declared, "The most important contribution any country can make to world development is to pursue sound economic policies at home." The administration explicitly rejected macroeconomic coordination and exchange rate intervention in favor of benign neglect. The administration recognized that divergent national fiscal and monetary policies would affect international capital movements and exchange rates. It assumed that the invisible hand of private markets would yield more efficient international outcomes than the visible hand of government-to-government negotiations.[26]

During 1981–1982, the leaders of other advanced industrial countries objected less to the concept of benign neglect per se than to the effects of fiscal expansion and monetary restraint on their economies *and* the economy of the United States. During this period, private international capital markets "coordinated" national macroeconomic policies by raising interest rates and slowing growth throughout the advanced industrial economies of the West.

[26] For a defense of the "domesticist" approach to international economic management, see Henry Nau, "Where Reaganomics Works," *Foreign Policy* 57 (Winter 1984–85). For critical appraisals of benign neglect, see Kenneth A. Oye, "Constrained Confidence and the Evolution of Reagan Foreign Policy" and Benjamin Cohen, "Economic Relations Among Advanced Industrial Nations," in *Eagle Resurgent? The Reagan Era in United States Foreign Policy*, eds. Kenneth A. Oye, Robert J. Lieber, and Donald Rothchild (Boston: Little Brown, 1987).

During 1982–1985, the Reagan administration retained its aversion to explicit macroeconomic coordination and monetary intervention and continued to pursue an expansionary fiscal policy, while the Federal Reserve eased American monetary policy. During this period, international markets for goods and capital spread the benefits of lower American interest rates and robust growth throughout the West.

BENIGN NEGLECT WITH TIGHT MONEY: 1981–82

The experiment with macroeconomic management by economic markets was contaminated from the start by the Reagan administration's conception of sound domestic policy. Consider the macroeconomic policies of the early Reagan years. Reaganomics with the Laffer curve promised tax reductions without revenue reductions, rapid growth without inflation, and higher absolute levels of spending on investment, defense, and consumption. Tax cuts did not increase revenues, military spending increases were not offset by domestic spending cuts, and the federal budget deficit rose from an average of 1.8 percent of GNP during the 1970s to an average of 4.3 percent of GNP during the first term of the Reagan administration.

Even as rising budget deficits stimulated aggregate demand, Federal Reserve Chairman Paul Volcker restrained expansion of money and credit to wring inflation out of the economy. The combination of fiscal expansion and monetary restraint forced American interest rates up.[27] The real discount rate, defined as the nominal rate minus inflation, rose from − 1.7 percent in 1980 to 3.0 percent in 1981. The real prime rate rose from 1.8 percent in 1980 to 8.5 percent in 1981. Volcker's restrictive monetary program succeeded in slashing American inflation even as it threw the United States into the deepest recession since the 1930s.

American interest rates rose far more rapidly than interest rates in Western Europe and Japan. International differentials in real interest rates had predictable effects on private capital movements and exchange rates. Japanese, Western European, and Third World cap-

[27] More precisely, financial markets acted on the *expectation* that budgetary deficits would increase and that the unorthodox combination of fiscal expansion and monetary restraint would force interest rates up in the future. Real interest rates rose after tax cuts and defense spending increases had been announced but before deficits had materialized. As William Branson has argued, these dramatic increases in real interest rates reflected the capacity of financial markets to bring the future into the present. See William H. Branson, "Causes of Appreciation and Volatility of the Dollar," in *The U.S. Dollar—Recent Developments, Outlook, and Policy Options* (Kansas City: Federal Reserve Bank of Kansas City, 1985).

ital flowed into the United States even as American capital stayed at home.[28] Taken together, net inflows of capital permitted the United States to spend 3 percent more than it produced. These capital movements were of historic dimensions. Figure 8.1 charts U.S. net capital inflows in the years 1946 to 1989 as a percentage of U.S. GNP. Two features stand out. To the left we find capital movements associated with the Marshall Plan and American postwar assistance to occupied Japan. To the right we find the Marshall Plan in reverse—massive capital inflows to the United States from Japan and Western Europe.

As net capital inflows continued, the dollar appreciated steadily against most major currencies. As Table 8.4 shows, the major Euro-

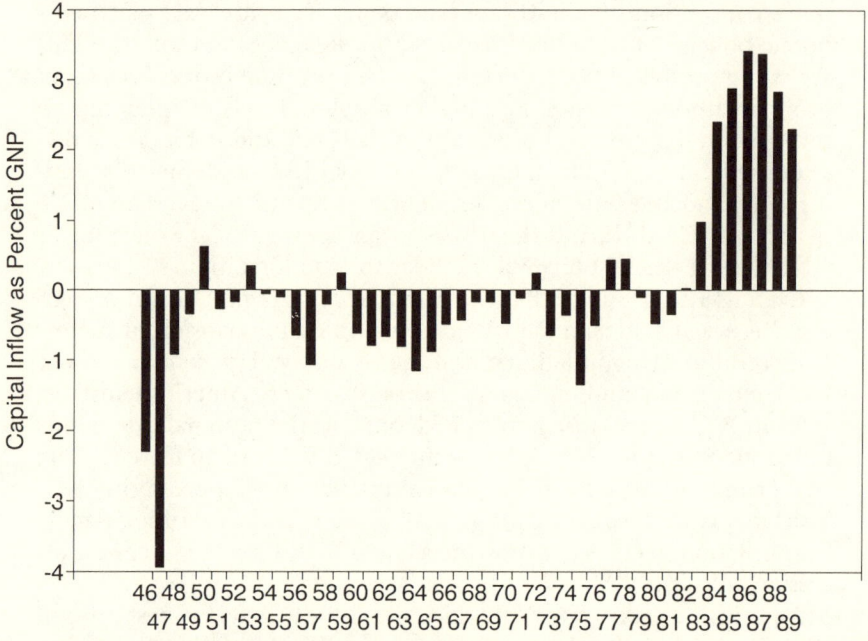

Fig. 8.1.   U.S. Capital Inflows 1946–1989

[28] The rise in real interest rates also contributed to American capital imports through a second less obvious channel. Third World debtors had borrowed heavily from Western banks in the 1970s and in 1980–82. The interest rate on these loans was typically defined in terms of a spread over nominal interest rates. As interest rates rose sharply, initially in the United States and then in other Western advanced industrial countries, the debt servicing burdens of borrowers in the Third World rose substantially. Banks responded to the resulting debt crisis by reducing their exposure in Third World nations. After 1982, new loans to developing nations virtually ceased even as some existing debt was serviced. See Jeffrey Sachs, "Introduction," in *Developing Country Debt and Economic Performance*, ed. Jeffrey Sachs (Chicago: University of Chicago Press, 1989), 9.

pean currencies dropped sharply relative to the dollar while the yen depreciated modestly. The American combination of fiscal expansion and monetary restraint created dilemmas for governments in Europe and Japan. Simply allowing their currencies to depreciate risked reigniting inflation. However, slowing monetary growth or reducing fiscal stimuli to support their currencies risked raising levels of unemployment and lowering rates of growth. Furthermore, as American interest rates increased, interest rates and unemployment in Western Europe and Japan also rose.

During 1981–1982, private international capital markets "coordinated" national macroeconomic policies by raising interest rates and slowing growth throughout the advanced industrial economies of the West. Western European governments repeatedly directed the attention of the Reagan administration to these negative macroeconomic spillover effects. As early as 1981, during preparatory discussions for the Ottawa summit, François Mitterrand denounced American interest rates as "intolerable" and Helmut Schmidt declared that American macroeconomic policies had cursed Germany with "the highest real interest rates since the birth of Christ."[29] In 1982, Chancellor Howe told the House of Commons that "it is important that our country and other countries help to make plain to the United States our concern over the level of their prospective budget deficit and its implications for interest rates around the world."[30] In the first two years of the Reagan administration, virtually every advanced industrial nation condemned American macroeconomic policies.

However, during the early 1980s, no advanced industrial nation offered material incentives to encourage the United States to depart from its unorthodox mix of fiscal expansion and monetary restraint.

TABLE 8.4
Exchange Rates with U.S. Dollar 1980–1985

	1980	1981	1982	1983	1984	1985
Yen	226.0	220.6	249.1	237.5	237.6	238.6
DM	1.817	2.259	2.427	2.553	2.846	2.944
Franc	4.226	5.434	6.572	7.621	8.739	8.984
Pound	0.430	0.498	0.573	0.660	0.752	0.799

Source: OECD Economic Outlook 45 (June 1989): 192.

[29] Putnam and Bayne, Hanging Together, 156.
[30] Putnam and Bayne, Hanging Together, 158.

At the 1981 Ottawa and 1982 Versailles summits, the Europeans and Japanese joined in denouncing American macroeconomic policy to varying degrees. The advanced industrial societies explained how their macroeconomic choices were contingent on American macroeconomic actions. But no individual or collective effort to induce the Reagan administration to take account of the international externalities associated with its domestic macroeconomic policies materialized. The intrinsically public character of international macroeconomic spillover effects encouraged free riding. More significantly, Reagan administration macroeconomic policy was designed to be nonnegotiable. The Reagan administration's attachment to its chosen policy mix and its explicitly stated aversion to notions of macroeconomic coordination and monetary intervention suggested that even substantial concerted action to influence the United States would fail.

BENIGN NEGLECT WITH EASY MONEY: 1982–85

Between the Versailles summit of 1982 and the Plaza meetings of 1985, macroeconomic spillover effects continued to be managed or mismanaged largely by market forces. The Reagan administration retained its aversion to macroeconomic coordination and exchange rate intervention. However, the substance of domestic American macroeconomic policy changed. The Congress and the president continued to pursue an expansive fiscal policy, but the Federal Reserve Board moved from a restrictive to expansive monetary policy.

The Federal Reserve Board decision accorded well with the interests of the Western Europeans and Japanese. As American interest rates fell, interest rates throughout international capital markets also declined. As the American economy recovered, growth rates throughout the West increased. The economic conditions and economic choices confronting governments in other advanced industrial countries were materially and substantially improved by the American action. In effect, a surging American economy served as a locomotive pulling weaker economies out of recession. During 1982–1985, private international capital markets "coordinated" national macroeconomic policies by lowering interest rates and ending recession throughout the advanced industrial economies of the West.

Like most macroeconomic actions, the easing of American monetary policy in 1982 was a response to narrowly domestic concerns. During 1981–1982, the American economy plunged into the deepest recession of the postwar period. By July 1982, the recession appeared to threaten the stability of the American banking system. The combination of recession and high interest rates had squeezed borrowers in the United States and in the Third World alike. The threat of defaults at home and abroad threatened the solvency of American banks. During 1980–1982, American inflation rates had fallen by half. Annual increases in the consumer price index had moved from 13.5 percent in 1980 to 6.1 percent in 1982, largely in response to Volcker's restrictive monetary policies, and the risk of reigniting inflation seemed small. The Federal Reserve Board responded to the looming risk of domestic bank failures by easing money supply and lowering interest rates.

If the Federal Reserve Board decision to ease American money policy had coincided with the Versailles meetings only two weeks before, political economists would now study the Versailles Summit as an example of successful macroeconomic coordination. If the decision had coincided with the IMF annual meeting two months later, political economists would now study the Versailles Summit as an example of the significance of international regimes. If the decision had been reached as part of bilateral discussions between the United States and Germany, I must confess that I would probably be treating it as a rare example of the effectiveness of *ad hoc* bargaining over macroeconomic issues. In fact, international political negotiations had virtually no role in the 1982 Federal Reserve Board decision or in any other major fiscal or monetary decisions until the Plaza Accords of 1985.

The uncoordinated domestic macroeconomic policies pursued in the period 1982–1985 served collective Western interests reasonably well. Continuing American fiscal stimulation taken in conjunction with expansionary domestic monetary policies in the United States, Western Europe, and Japan yielded reasonably substantial growth with fairly modest inflation. By the standards of the 1970s and early 1980s, this outcome appeared acceptable.

However, the system had a puzzling flaw. As American trade deficits and Japanese and German trade surpluses grew larger, orthodox theories of exchange rate determination suggested that the demand for dollars should fall and the demand for yen and deutsche marks should rise. Yet the dollar continued to appreciate relative to the yen and Deutsche mark. Capital continued to flow into the United States and the dollar continued to rise even as the American trade deficit deteriorated. This economic phenomenon created two problems.

The first problem centered on the risks of a free fall of the dollar. It was clear at the time that the fundamentals—in particular the American trade deficit—would not sustain a strong dollar over the long term. By 1984, the question was not "will the dollar fall" but "when will the dollar fall, and how rapidly will it fall." Foreign exchange traders answered "not tomorrow" and "slowly enough to permit me to liquidate my positions." Because all foreign exchange traders had a narrow interest in moving out of dollars as quickly as possible once a major realignment began, monetary authorities feared that any realignment might develop into a major monetary panic. Short-term capital inflows had played a significant role in the appreciation of the dollar in 1982–1984 and short-term capital outflows could bring about a "hard landing" of the dollar.

The second problem centered on trade. Within the United States, the strong dollar harmed producers while benefiting consumers. By increasing the price of American products relative to the price of foreign products, a rising dollar hurt both export-oriented *and* import-competing sectors within the United States. As American exports fell and American imports increased, agriculture and manufacturing suffered from substantial structural dislocation. Export-oriented interests lobbied for a lower dollar and for bilateral commercial reciprocity to improve their access to foreign markets. Import-competing interests filed for relief under existing trade law and lobbied for increased levels of protection. By late 1984, charges of "yen fixing" and calls for protection were poisoning bilateral relations with Japan. The modest appreciation of the yen in early 1985 did not reduce these political pressures. In the spring of 1985, a resolution attacking Japan for unfair trade practices passed in the House and the Senate with virtually no opposition.

Within Japan, the strong dollar and weak yen had provided substantial benefits for export-oriented manufacturing and for import-competing agriculture at the expense of Japanese consumers. Provided that access to the American market appeared secure, yen appreciation had little appeal to two of the LDP's principal constituencies. The strength of protectionist sentiment within the United States forced export-oriented Japanese manufacturers to choose between accepting appreciation of the yen or risking attenuation of access to the American market. While both choices would entail some loss of market shares, a high yen strategy would permit Japanese firms to offset losses of exports with increased direct investment.

Coordination by Political Bargaining Again: Plaza, Louvre, and Beyond

The Reagan administration's policy of relying on private markets to manage exchange rates was patently unsuited to addressing these problems. Between 1985 and 1988, the visible hand of intergovernmental negotiation displaced the invisible hand of the market. Throughout most of this period, virtually all advanced industrial nations exerted pressure on the United States to adopt less expansive fiscal policies. The United States exerted pressure on Japan and West Germany to adopt more restrictive monetary and more expansive fiscal policies. Implicit cross-issue linkages to trade played a significant role in negotiations over fiscal and monetary affairs. While the externalities associated with macroeconomic policies are public, the benefits of market access may be diverted from country to country at will. Tacit threats of discrimination in commerce contributed to macroeconomic coordination and financial liberalization.

EXCHANGE RATE INTERVENTION: THE 1985 PLAZA ACCORDS

In September 1985, Group of Five finance ministers reached agreement on the Plaza Accords. They announced their intention of intervening in foreign exchange markets to depress the value of the dollar. Specifically, the Group of Five committed to "lean with the wind" by dumping dollars into weak markets. The communique and press briefings did not disclose target rates, national commitments of exchange reserves to intervention, or the planned duration of intervention. By cloaking the specific plans for intervention in secrecy, the ministers hoped to maximize the impact of intervention.

Through masterful detective work, Yoichi Funabashi of the *Asahi Shimbun* pieced together an account of the covert discussions behind the Plaza Accords. This discussion is based largely on his account.[31] David Mulford, Assistant Secretary of the Treasury for International Affairs, prepared a detailed blueprint for intervention. His blueprint was slightly amended and accepted at the Plaza.[32] The parties agreed to aim for a 10 to 12 percent depreciation of the dollar in the near term. Over a period of six weeks, the parties committed to a maximum of $18 billion, with the United States contributing 30 percent, Japan 30 percent, Germany 25 percent, France 10 percent, and the United Kingdom 5 percent.[33] Finally, the parties accepted domestic macroeconomic commitments. The domestic macroeconomic aspects and international monetary aspects of the secret Plaza Accords were

[31] This paragraph is based on Yoichi Funabashi, *Managing the Dollar: From the Plaza to the Louvre* (Washington, D.C.: Institute of International Economics, 1988), 16–18.

[32] Funabashi notes that the statement was so sensitive that Mulford collected all drafts at the conclusion of the preparatory meeting on September 15. Mulford was well accustomed to manipulating exchange rates in total secrecy. As an advisor to the Saudi Arabian Monetary Authority during the late 1970s, Mulford had responsibility for placing annual Saudi surpluses that were substantially larger than the *total* foreign exchange reserves eventually deployed under the Plaza intervention plan. Interview with David Mulford, April 1982, Princeton, N.J.

[33] The Germans and French insisted that their 25 percent and 10 percent national shares be treated as a collective EMS share of 35 percent.

not entirely consistent. The United States pledged to adopt a less expansive fiscal policy by reducing the budget deficit by 1 percent in fiscal year 1986 and by making further significant reductions in the future. A less expansive fiscal policy might alleviate pressure on American interest rates, reduce capital inflows, and thereby depress the value of the dollar. However, slackening American demand might trim American imports, reduce the American current account deficit, and thereby cause the dollar to appreciate. Japan agreed to cut its budget deficits (reducing demand) and to enlarge consumer and credit markets (stimulating demand). Finally, West Germany agreed to reduce government spending and to cut taxes, but did not specify whether spending cuts would offset tax reductions. The effects of these offsetting macroeconomic policies on markets for foreign exchange were at best unclear.

In the six weeks after Plaza, monetary authorities intervened with around $10 billion. The United States sold $3.2 billion, West Germany, Japan, Britain, and France sold $5 billion, and Canada, Italy, Sweden, Belgium, and the Netherlands sold $2 billion.[34] To place these figures in context, the American current account deficit in 1985 was $115 billion, the Japanese surplus was $49 billion, and the West German surplus was $16 billion.[35] Intervention in foreign exchange markets is a notoriously ineffective instrument for influencing exchange rates, and the magnitude of intervention was fairly modest. As Table 8.5 shows, the dollar fell sharply immediately after the accord was announced, recovered slightly, and then depreciated steadily for three years.

TABLE 8.5
Exchange Rates with U.S. Dollar 1985–1989

	1985	1986	1987	1988	1989
Yen	238.6	168.5	144.6	128.2	142.0
DM	2.944	2.172	1.797	1.756	1.920
Franc	8.984	6.927	6.009	5.956	6.520
Pound	0.799	0.682	0.612	0.562	0.630

Source: Figures for 1985–88 are annual averages from OECD Economic Outlook 45 (June 1989): 192. Figures for 1989 are July 8 exchange rates from Economist.

[34] Koichi Hamada and Hugh T. Patrick, "Japan and the International Monetary Regime," in The Political Economy of Japan: The Changing International Context, eds. Takashi Inoguchi and Daniel Okimoto (Stanford: Stanford University Press, 1988), 121–23.
[35] OECD Economic Outlook (June 1989): 190.

The steady fall in the value of the dollar was caused by more than "leaning with the wind." Immediately after Plaza, both Japan and Germany raised real interest rates while intervening in foreign exchange markets. Monetary authorities in the two largest surplus countries did not fully sterilize the interventions. By maintaining restrictive monetary policies and allowing interest rates to rise, monetary authorities in Germany and Japan narrowed real interest rate differentials with the United States.

MACROECONOMIC COORDINATION:
BILATERAL AND MULTILATERAL BARGAINING 1985–88

The Plaza Accords helped bring about a massive realignment in exchange rates without triggering a monetary crisis. Given the volatility of international capital markets and the risk of headlong flight from the dollar, G-5 success in avoiding wholesale monetary panic must be viewed as a major accomplishment. However, the Plaza realignments did not succeed in alleviating commercial tensions even as the value of the dollar dropped well below the Plaza medium-term target range. Current account imbalances continued to rise and protectionist sentiment continued to grow despite depreciation of the dollar and appreciation of the yen and Deutsche mark. During the late 1980s, the governments of the G-5 turned back toward macroeconomic coordination to reduce current account imbalances, to stave off rising protectionist sentiment, and to stabilize the value of the dollar.

Orthodox trade theory predicts that real exchange rate depreciation should reduce a nation's trade deficit, albeit with a lag. The 1985 Plaza Accords facilitated substantial exchange rate realignments but exchange rate realignments did not reduce current account imbalances.[36] Table 8.6 presents G-5 current account imbalances between 1984 and 1988. In late 1985 and early 1986, the simple lags embodied in the J-Curve of orthodox trade theory appeared to explain the unresponsiveness of current account imbalances to changes in exchange rates. The American current account deficit continued to increase as the dollar fell. The Japanese and West German current account surpluses continued to increase as the yen and deutsche mark rose. Only the French and British current account moved as orthodox theory would predict. By the middle of 1986, the J-Curve no

[36] Even as the dollar depreciated relative to other currencies, American trade deficits/capital inflows continued. To offset the effects of exchange rate appreciation on competitiveness and to capitalize on low real prices for American assets, European and Japanese corporations and institutional investors responded to these developments by purchasing real assets in the United States.

TABLE 8.6
Current Balances 1984–1988 (in billions of dollars)

	1984	1985	1986	1987	1988
United States	− 107.1	− 115.1	− 138.8	− 154.0	− 135.3
Japan	35.0	49.2	85.9	87.0	79.6
Federal Republic of Germany	9.8	16.4	39.2	45.1	48.5
France	− .8	− .4	− 3.0	− 4.1	− 3.8
United Kingdom	2.8	4.3	.2	− 4.8	− 26.1

Source: OECD Economic Outlook 45 (June 1989): 190.

longer provided an adequate explanation of growing imbalances on trade account.

Between 1986 and 1988, governments in all of the advanced industrial countries acknowledged that exchange rate policy alone would not reduce current account imbalances. However, no consensus existed on who should bear the burdens of adjustment to bring current account imbalances down or on what form adjustments should take. Both the usual struggle over the distribution of burdens of adjustment and unusual uncertainty over the effects of domestic policies on current balances impeded macroeconomic coordination during this period.

First, each government struggled to induce others to make the needed adjustments in domestic fiscal and monetary policy and to avoid making adjustments itself. Japan urged the United States to adopt a less expansive fiscal policy to improve the American current account balance without depreciating the dollar further. The West Germans urged Japan to adopt expansive measures and the United States to cut the budget deficit. The United States favored further appreciation in the yen and deutsche mark and urged West Germany and Japan to adopt expansive domestic macroeconomic policies. These distributional conflicts are reflected directly in the scarcity of specific substantive commitments in agreements negotiated during this period. One finds specific procedural commitments to exchange information and to consult along with vague substantive commitments to exercise restraint or to expand in support of commonly accepted goals.

Second, the governments did not agree on how some domestic macroeconomic measures would affect balances on current account. An expansive fiscal policy appears to have consistently positive international spillover effects by raising income and increasing demand for other nation's exports. However, the effects of monetary expansion on current account balances are less clear. Monetary policy has offsetting effects on the current account. Monetary expansion raises domestic income levels and thereby increases demand for imports. It also depreciates currencies and thereby retards imports and stimulates exports. In his survey of eleven major econometric models, Jeffrey Frankel notes that three models suggest that German and Japanese monetary expansion would *increase* American current account deficits as exchange rate effects outweigh income effects while eight predict the opposite. Three models predict that American monetary expansion would *decrease* the American current account deficit while eight predict the opposite.[37]

Real uncertainty over the effects of monetary expansion on current account balances may be reflected in oscillations in American policy. In 1985, Treasury Secretary Baker pressured Japan and West Germany to adopt restrictive monetary policies to reduce current account surpluses via the exchange rate effect. In 1986, Baker pressured Japan and West Germany to adopt expansive monetary policies to reduce their current account surpluses via the income effect. Quite understandably, the Japanese and the West Germans were reluctant to enter into binding commitments on domestic monetary policy. At the 1986 Tokyo Summit, Japan and West Germany suggested that rising American budget deficits—not Japanese or West German monetary policy—might be a more productive focus for discussion on the sources of current account imbalances. However, the G-7 heads of state did agree to establish a system of economic indicators to monitor their economic performance and to "make the best effort to reach an understanding" on appropriate remedial measures if indicators turned bad.[38]

In February 1987, the finance ministers and central bank governors of the United States, Japan, West Germany, France, Britain, and Canada completed the Louvre Accords. Exchange rate management was to be complemented by macroeconomic coordination. Surplus countries agreed to follow policies that strengthened domestic demand and reduced external surpluses. Deficit countries agreed to encourage steady, low inflation growth while reducing their domestic imbalances and external deficits; the accords did not specify the means or the magnitude of deficit country stimulation or surplus country expansion. The signatories also agreed to stabilize exchange

[37] Jeffrey A. Frankel, *Obstacles to International Macroeconomic Coordination*, Princeton Studies in International Finance 64 (December 1988): 18–19.

[38] Funabashi, *Managing the Dollar*, 131–37.

rates at around then current levels; the accords did not specify how stabilization was to be achieved. Although the signatories agreed to consult with each other if exchange rates moved outside of a target band, the Louvre Accords did not define what policy adjustments would be made.[39]

At the June 1987 Venice Economic Summit, the heads of the major advanced industrial nations agreed to strengthen the "indicators" approach to macroeconomic coordination. They promised to develop medium-term macroeconomic goals and projections and to evaluate economic trends in light of performance indicators. In the final communique, the signatories promised to "develop objectives and projections that are mutually consistent" and to "use performance indicators to review and assess current economic trends and to determine whether there are significant deviations from an intended course that require consideration of remedial actions." At subsequent meetings of the Group of Seven in 1987 and 1988, finance ministers and central bank governors reaffirmed the desirability of promoting exchange rate stability and reducing external imbalances, without committing to specific means to these ends, and added a commodity price index to the list of indicators. The June 1988 Toronto Summit was if anything even less substantive. The heads of state agreed to consider international dimensions of their policies and strongly endorsed the addition of a commodity price index to the set of indicators.[40]

Responding to Failures of Macroeconomic Coordination

Macroeconomic coordination in the late 1980s may be fairly characterized as a kinder and gentler version of benign neglect. The United States and other advanced industrial nations professed concern for macroeconomic spillover effects and set up elaborate systems of indicators and cross-consultation, but did little to internalize international macroeconomic policy externalities. In fact, the international spillover effects of Reagan administration domestic fiscal and monetary policies were the focus of international macroeconomic negotiations throughout the 1980s. From the Ottawa Summit in 1981 to the Toronto Summit in 1988, other advanced industrial nations repeatedly challenged the assumptions on which Reagan policies were based and drew attention to the international consequences of American actions. Yet countervailing pressure on the United States to alter its macroeconomic policies was quite limited. Because the international spillover effects from American macroeconomic policies were

[39] See Funabashi, *Managing the Dollar.*
[40] International Monetary Fund, *Annual Report 1988,* 5–6.

diffused relatively evenly across the other advanced industrial nations, material foreign inducements and threats were underprovided. What are the consequences of this pattern of failure to coordinate macroeconomic policies?

Consider a pessimistic view. The accumulation of dollar denominated claims in the face of continuing American trade deficits may create a crisis of confidence in the dollar. Like participants in Ponzi schemes and stock manias, holders of dollars must assume that others will continue to act as if the dollar will not fall. Over the medium term, capital inflows may accentuate the inherent instability of current dollar-centered international monetary arrangements. Continuing capital inflows increase exchange rate volatility and foster monetary compartmentalization. The principal nations of Western Europe founded the European Monetary System to insulate their economies from violent fluctuations in the value of the dollar during the late 1970s. The rise of the dollar in 1981–84 and the fall of the dollar in 1985–86 accentuated this preexisting tendency toward formation of regional currency blocs. As in the 1930s, nations may continue to turn to regional arrangements to accommodate divergent tastes for expansion and deflation between blocs while affording some measure of exchange rate stability within each bloc.

Consider an optimistic view. The problems that were not addressed in the bilateral and multilateral negotiations summarized above have slowly improved. The dollar stabilized at close to the Louvre Accord rates, the American trade deficit narrowed in 1988–89, and trade tensions associated with current account imbalances declined. First, the depreciation of the dollar relative to other currencies ultimately narrowed the American trade deficit. The surplus on capital account by definition mirrors the deficit on trade account. As the American trade deficit fell, net capital inflows necessarily declined. Second, as capital flows to the United States continued, the stock of foreign capital in the United States rose. Foreign capital stock in the United States generated earnings—interest on bank deposits and bonds, stock dividends, rents on real estate, and profits of subsidiaries. As earnings were reinvested and repatriated, *net* capital inflows fell. In effect, international markets for goods and capital may have slowly managed problems that could not be addressed through explicit political negotiation.

Conclusion

Why is the political economy of hypocrisy so characteristic of the 1980s? Hypocrisy is endemic in political systems in transition. When fixed rules do not coincide with shifting interests, rules tend to be violated before they are formally disavowed. The global economy is very much in transition. As Robert Gilpin has observed, the economic rise of Japan and the Dragons of the Pacific Basin and the prospective consolidation of Europe into a single market with a single currency signal the end of American hegemonic management.[41] The United States can no longer manage international economic relations through the open hand of economic largesse, the mailed fist of economic coercion, or the velvet glove of international economic institutions. Yet no alternative mode of international economic management has been established.

The recession of American economic power exposed a conflict between the postwar *anciens regimes* and bilateralism and regionalism. As long as the postwar rules served American interests, the tension between rules based management and ad hoc bargaining remained inconsequential. In fact, in the early postwar period, the United States used and tolerated highly discriminatory economic policies to construct the liberal multilateral order.[42] However, the relative decline of the United States has created a disjunction between the rules that the United States established and American interests. As American relative economic strength has declined, first in manufacturing and now in finance, the United States found that it must choose between sustaining the multilateral order that it created or defending American interests through bilateral and regional means.[43]

The current practice of professing respect for nondiscrimination while discriminating is not likely to persist. As discrimination becomes more common, the pace of discriminatory bargaining tends to accelerate. Like factories and laundries struggling over divertible externalities, nations bargaining over contemporary commercial and financial issues will find that early deals tend to be more advantageous

---

[41] See Robert Gilpin, *The Political Economy of International Relations* (Princeton, N.J.: Princeton University Press, 1987).

[42] On commercial discrimination, see Otto Hieronymi, *Economic Discrimination Against the United States in Western Europe 1945–1958: Dollar Shortage and the Rise of Regionalism* (Geneva: Librairie Droz, 1973); and Gardner Patterson, *Discrimination in International Trade: The Policy Issues 1945–1965* (Princeton, N.J.: Princeton University Press, 1966). On the use of financial instruments to shape the monetary order, see Richard Gardner, *Sterling-Dollar Diplomacy in Current Perspective* (New York: Columbia University Press, 1980). On security motivations for construction of the postwar order and for tolerating discrimination against the United States, see Robert Pollard, *Economic Security and the Origins of the Cold War* (New York: Columbia University Press, 1985).

[43] As the following cases suggest, the size of the American market confers on the United States substantial leverage in current and future discriminatory negotiations. As Susan Strange and the more recent counter-declinists have observed, the United States remains both very wealthy and very large.

than late deals. Each nation has an incentive to negotiate quickly if the existing order appears unstable. In financial and commercial affairs, when multilateral structures malfunction, the conversion to discriminatory bilateral and regional management can be almost discontinuous. Over the long term, the tension between adherence to nondiscriminatory rules and reliance on discriminatory bargaining is likely to be resolved in favor of bilateralism and regionalism.

PART V

Conclusion

Chapter Nine

THE PERILS OF IMPRECISE ANALOGY

COMPARISONS BETWEEN THE 1930s
AND THE 1980s

ANALOGIES BETWEEN the 1930s and the 1980s loom large in contemporary debates on foreign economic policy. If economic discrimination accelerated movement toward economic closure during the 1930s, then conditional reciprocity, preferential debt servicing and lending, and regionalization of monetary relations may lead toward closure of the contemporary economic order.[1] If the remnants of the postwar regimes were responsible for the continuing openness of global economic relations in the 1980s, then a turn toward discriminatory policies may shatter the last ragged line of defense against closure. By contrast, this study suggests that discrimination was a force for liberalization during both periods.

This chapter begins by examining *similarities* between the 1930s and 1980s. It reviews the theories introduced in the first half of this book and searches for regularities across the overtly discriminatory 1930s and the covertly discriminatory 1980s. It should be noted at the outset that the close fit between "predictions" and "evidence" cannot be taken as an independent confirmation of the theory of ad hoc bargaining. Because the theory and (post hoc) evidence developed together, this study should not be viewed as an independent test of my ideas on unrestricted bargaining. Nonetheless, the history of bilateralism and regionalism in both periods suggests that inherently discriminatory bargaining strategies can serve as a significant force for reducing barriers to goods and capital.

This chapter concludes by examining *differences* between the 1930s and 1980s. In so doing, it reinforces the case for optimism on the survival of an open economic order with or without greater economic discrimination. It argues that contemporary analogies to the experience of the 1930s are based on two fundamental fallacies. First, ana-

[1] At a conference of policy makers and academics on the trade bill held in Washington, D.C., during October 1987, I counted six references to the 1930s in one hour of discussion among policy makers. For an example of commentary on the American unfair trade practices target list, see *Economist* 312, no. 7608 (24–30 June 1989).

lysts often unconsciously transpose their preferences onto the decision makers of the period, and in so doing misinterpret the effects of international political process. Second, analysts unconsciously transfer modern economic knowledge onto decision makers of the period, and in so doing downplay the role that extraordinarily inappropriate domestic economic policies played in intensifying the depression. If we project modern preferences and beliefs into the past, we develop invalid analogies between the past and the present—analogies that grossly understate the strength of forces for openness in contemporary international economic relations.

REGULARITIES

Public, private, and divertable international policy externalities should elicit markedly different responses from rational actors. These properties of externalities are intrinsic attributes of issues. Macroeconomic policies give rise to public externalities. The effects of domestic fiscal and monetary policy are diffused across many nations. Generators of macroeconomic externalities have little control over the international distribution of benefits and costs. The effects of commercial and financial policies may be diverted from nation to nation or diffused across many nations at will. Generators of commercial and financial spillover effects face a choice between discrimination and nondiscrimination. If the efficiency of unrestricted bargaining is in fact influenced by the characteristics of policy externalities, then regularities in the management of public macroeconomic externalities and in the management of divertable commercial and financial externalities should carry across both periods.

Managing Public Externalities

If externalities are public, decentralized political processes are likely to underproduce countervailing inducements and threats. Structural inequality and preexisting institutionalized rules may mitigate tendencies toward inefficiency. My findings on macroeconomic coordination in the 1930s and 1980s are even more pessimistic than the theoretical chapters suggest. During both periods, nations did not take account of the international consequences of their macroeconomic actions.

Consider examples of apparent conspicuous failures. In the fall of 1931, the British government acted on the belief that parity between sterling and gold could not be preserved without deflating the British economy. Britain was unwilling to adopt restrictive fiscal and monetary policies to save the sterling-gold parity, and proceeded to suspend convertibility between sterling and gold. The British suspension of convertibility outraged nations that remained on the gold standard, but gold standard nations proceeded to adjust to British monetary policy rather than to try to eliminate the externality at the source. In 1933, the Roosevelt administration acted on the belief that gold purchasing and price raising would stimulate domestic economic activity. These domestic policies were clearly inconsistent with exchange rate stabilization. When the United States permitted the dollar to depreciate, other nations voiced indignation but did nothing to organize countervailing inducements or threats. In 1981–82, the Reagan administration acted on the belief that fiscal expansion and monetary orthodoxy would eliminate inflation and stimulate growth. As the dollar appreciated and as interests rates at home and abroad rose, other nations expressed dissatisfaction with American policies but did nothing to induce change in American policy. In each case, the public nature of policy externalities was an impediment to the organization of countervailing inducements and threats. However, it is not clear that the outcomes in these cases were pareto inefficient. Given the overvaluation of sterling, given Roosevelt's commitment to domestic price raising through gold purchasing, and given Reagan's commitment to fiscal expansion and monetary orthodoxy, the perceived costs imposed on other nations did not outweigh the perceived benefits for the generators of the externalities. From the perspective of the actors involved, no mutual interest in macroeconomic coordination existed.

Examples of "successful" monetary and macroeconomic coordination in both periods ratified actions that would have served national interests in the absence of coordination. The 1936 Tripartite Stabilization Agreement confirmed American, French, and British monetary policies and imposed no concrete restrictions on their actions. The 1978 Bonn Summit ratified German expansion and American energy decontrol; both Germany and the United States would have taken these actions without agreement. The 1985 Plaza Accords ratified national decisions to dump dollars when the dollar was overvalued, while the 1987 Louvre Accords ratified decisions to buy dollars when the dollar was undervalued. When nations took macroeconomic actions that conferred benefits on others, they did so because they believed that those actions would provide direct benefits to themselves.

In short, *no* mode of international management had substantial effects on macroeconomic externalities in either period. Unilateralism predominated in both the failures and the successes. Although the packaging has varied, benign neglect is a constant in international macroeconomic affairs. Roosevelt's "bombshell" message to the London Economic Conference in 1933 and Reagan's public affirmation of a policy of "benign neglect" in 1981–82 explicitly confirmed that macroeconomic policies would not take account of international spillover effects. The language of the 1936 Tripartite Stabilization Agreement, the 1978 Bonn Accords, the 1985 Plaza Accords, and the 1987 Louvre Accords explicitly suggested that national macroeconomic policies should take account of international ramifications. The principal difference between the failures and successes was rhetorical.

Managing Divertable Externalities

If externalities are divertable, the tension between management by bargaining and management by rules will be acute. The relative merits of these modes of management will hinge on extrinsic considerations. If preexisting rules limit generation of externalities and control free riding, then nondiscriminatory collectivist approaches to externalities management should be retained. However, as is commonly the case, when Grotian approaches are unsuccessful in managing policy externalities, then continuing respect for the principle of nondiscrimination will impede rather than facilitate realization of mutual interests through economic discrimination and political exchange. This tension between reliance on discriminatory bargaining and institutionalized rules is evident in both the 1930s and the 1980s.

ECONOMIC DISCRIMINATION AND INTERNATIONAL REGIMES IN THE 1930s

In the first phase of the depression, economic powers chose paths to domestic recovery that could not be reconciled with existing international economic regimes. During 1930 and 1931, central decision makers in the United States and France believed that domestic reflation required defense of exchange rates and import restrictions. Neither government considered jeopardizing domestic employment by liberalizing commercial policy. During the summer of 1931, banks in New York, London, and Paris believed that their solvency rested on controlling foreign exposure. These banks were unwilling to extend fresh credits to debtor nations in Central Europe and thereby ended the multilateral clearing system. If national preferences are treated as sovereign, the economist's first best world of commercial openness, financial stability, and monetary convertibility simply could not be sustained in the face of the great contraction. During the first phase of the depression, adherence to secondary norms proscribing privatization and discrimination may well have contributed to the under-production of countervailing political pressure. The American non-discriminatory tariff increases of 1930 elicited widespread indignation, but other nations did not back up their words with contingent action to bring down general American rates. The failure of London, Paris, and New York to extend sufficient fresh credits to contain the Central European financial crisis of 1931 shattered the multilateral clearing system and imposed costs on all creditors and debtors.

In the second phase of economic disintegration, discriminatory commercial and financial practices spread rapidly throughout the global political economy. With the wholesale dissolution of primary norms, the old regimes no longer provided access to markets, monetary stability, or distress credits. The disintegration of the public international economic order raised barriers to economic exchange but eliminated barriers to bilateral and regional bargaining. A strong tendency toward use of discriminatory economic policy followed as nations utilized what potential economic leverage they possessed to secure access to markets, a degree of monetary stability, and access to distress credits. The effects and effectiveness of bilateral and regional discrimination varied significantly from issue to issue. Financial discrimination took place against a backdrop of extraordinarily low levels of international financial activity. The spread of preferential debt servicing may have contributed to the restoration of international financial activity by building individual lender confidence in individual borrowers. Commercial discrimination took place against a backdrop of low, but significant, international commercial activity. Political exchange functioned largely to redistribute and compartmentalize trade without necessarily increasing systemic openness. The regionalization of international monetary relations took place against a backdrop of wildly fluctuating exchange rates. Given divergent tastes on the appropriate rate of domestic monetary expansion, the emergence of blocs of states with similar monetary tastes may well have muted international exchange rate instability. The process of decentralized political bargaining tended to coalesce around preexisting blocs. The French and British used bilateral political bargaining to attract additional states to their core empires, and the Germans expanded their zone of economic and political influence in Central Europe.

In the third phase of the depression, the management of divertable policy externalities was driven by liberalizing shifts in national economic preferences. Idiosyncratic factors including the evolution of economic beliefs, the rise of employment and price levels, and the emergence of the German security threat affected national tastes for protection. More centrally, the wholesale bilateralism, regionalism, and imperialism of the preceding period altered national preferences. By mobilizing export-oriented sectors against import-competing sectors, particularly within the United States, pervasive international economic discrimination offset domestic biases toward protection. In 1934, the United States shifted from unconditional protection to discriminatory liberalization. Under the Reciprocal Trade Agreements Program, the United States exchanged market access for market access on a conditional basis. American bilateral back-scratching with Latin American and Caribbean nations, Canada, and Great Britain was trade expanding as well as trade diverting.

ECONOMIC DISCRIMINATION AND INTERNATIONAL REGIMES IN THE 1980s

Both commercial and financial externalities can be diverted from country to country. In trade, nations have relied on bilateralism and regionalism to barter market access for market access while affirming devotion to the GATT principle of nondiscrimination. However, in financial affairs, creditors have respected cross default clauses and debtors have not accorded preferential treatment to some creditors at the expense of others. Why has discrimination been far less pronounced in contemporary finance than in trade? How has the incidence of economic discrimination affected the efficiency of commercial and financial management?

In commercial affairs during the 1980s, economic discrimination has been an important force for liberalization. Under the GATT multilateral negotiations of the 1950s through 1970s, tariff levels on manufactured products had fallen to record lows. However, the collectivist GATT approach had failed to open agriculture, and nontariff barriers were actually rising. As in the 1930s, bilateral and regional negotiations were a response to areas of weakness in existing regimes. The exchange of preferential market access for preferential market access was central to Japanese-American bilateral liberalization, the Canadian-American Free Trade Agreement, and the European Community Single Integrated Market Proposal. Discriminatory targetting of export credits was central to negotiation of the OECD credit subsidy agreement. In fact, all cases of substantial economic liberalization during the past decade were achieved through discriminatory bilateral or regional bargaining.

Economic discrimination contributed to economic openness through two channels. First, by providing export-oriented sectors with a narrow interest in campaigning against protection of import-competing sectors, international discriminatory threats partially offset domestic biases toward protection. This effect of discrimination on openness is evident in each of the cases taken independently. Second, by creating incentives for excluded third parties to barter over market access, these discriminatory agreements may have contributed to the spread of liberalization beyond the parties to bilateral and regional agreements. This effect of discrimination on systemic openness only becomes clear after considering the cases serially.

These conclusions on the effects of economic discrimination on commercial openness are only slightly qualified. In the OMA quota cases, gains for Indonesia and China came at the expense of third parties. Bilateral negotiations did not increase or decrease the overall effective levels of protection of the Indonesians, the British, the Chinese, or the Americans. Although discrimination always has trade diverting effects, it does not always have trade increasing effects.

Economic discrimination did not play a significant role in international financial affairs during the 1980s. Once again, discussion of the merits or demerits of economic discrimination must begin with analysis of the effectiveness of institutionalized rules. In financial affairs, serial rescheduling agreements that rolled interest into principal, modest infusions of official capital, and the existence of depositor insurance on banks insulated financial centers from developments in the periphery. The international financial regime preserved the system as a whole by transferring burdens of adjustment to debtor states. The success of the collectivist response obviated the need for discriminatory bilateral bargaining.

However, the international financial regime has not restored fresh flows of funds and debt service export ratios have continued to rise. These weaknesses of the collectivist response to date may well encourage financial discrimination by debtor states. The complexity of debt conversion schemes facilitates de facto discrimination by debtors even as the deteriorating position of debtors serves as a spur to move toward bilateral strategies. To date, major debtors have not deliberately depressed the price of debt before repurchasing or developed strategies to preference some creditor nations at the expense of others. However, unless the international financial regime increases flows of funds and secures substantial debt relief, debtors are likely to move toward explicitly discriminatory strategies.

Qualifications and Extensions

The general case for discriminatory bargaining in the presence of divertable externalities rested on the assumption that discrimination would facilitate single-issue and cross-issue political exchange. Discrimination may facilitate extortion as well as exchange. In fact, extortion seems to have been used infrequently in the cases treated in the studies of the 1930s and 1980s. This judgment is slightly hedged. Scholars and policy makers have incomplete information on national preferences. Because the categorization of an action as extortion requires access to preferences, ambiguous cases exist. In fact, all of the cases that are possible candidates for extortion involved the issuance of threats that were not clearly averse to national interests. Argentina blocked the accounts of British creditors and companies and secured leverage over the British in anticipation of the Roca-Runciman negotiations. But Argentina also had a clear interest in reserving foreign exchange during their payments crisis. France imposed an unusually restrictive set of quotas that France then doled out to secure access to the markets of others. But these actions also served France's perceived interest in shielding its domestic economy from global deflation. Finally, during the contemporary period, Helmut Schmidt may have deferred macroeconomic expansion to extort American energy deregulation. But as Putnam and Bayne observe, the Bonn Agreement may have been necessary to formation of a domestic coalition behind West German economic expansion. The ambiguity of these cases suggests that the Coasian's failure to consider blackmailing may not seriously undercut their conclusions on the effectiveness of political exchange.

The consequences of economic actions extended across traditional issue boundaries, but international political processes appeared to be largely issue structural. In the 1930s, unconditional protectionism reduced debtor nation export earnings and contributed to the collapse of international financial relations. The Central European financial crisis altered preferences for holding sterling and thereby contributed to the collapse of the unstable sterling-gold parity. The departure of sterling and the dollar from gold undermined the commercial position of the gold bloc nations, and thereby contributed to a wave of new protectionism in trade. In the 1980s, the appreciation of the dollar in 1981–82 increased current account imbalances and contributed to the growth of protectionist sentiment in trade. Because Third World debt was dollar denominated, the rise of the dollar increased effective debt burdens substantially. As Third World debtors sought to expand exports and reduce imports to service debt, they increased levels of protection and imposed exchange controls.

These and other substantive connections between issues were commonly recognized in memoranda, speeches, and the financial press in both the 1930s and the 1980s. Yet neither regimes nor ad hoc bargaining managed to take account of these cross-issue externalities in either period. The functional organization of regimes and national economic bureaucracies clearly discourages formation of cross-issue linkages. The scarcity of ad hoc cross issue linkages is harder to explain. In some cases, the public nature of externalities associated with pivotal macroeconomic decisions discouraged formation of cross-issue linkages. In other cases, the sheer economic and political complexity of assembling packages of positions on multiple issues may have served as an impediment to political exchange. In any event, neither institutionalized rules nor discriminatory bargaining appear capable of managing cross-issue policy externalities.

ON THE PERILS OF IMPRECISE ANALOGY

Contemporary interpretations of international political economy during the 1930s project features of the present onto the past, and paradoxically contribute to an exaggerated view of the likelihood of imminent economic disintegration. Even as discriminatory bargaining comes to displace rules based management, two important and underrecognized differences between the periods should be kept in mind. Our conception of the effects of international process on outcomes during the 1930s is based on two fundamental fallacies.

Transposing Preferences and Mischaracterizing Political Process

The vast majority of academics and policy makers in advanced industrial states hold liberal-neomercantile images of international commercial, financial, and monetary relations and see the transcendence of dilemmas of collective action as the central problem in contemporary international political economy. Even those that espouse protection generally take care to assert that adoption of their programs would not trigger a slide toward double defection. Proponents of domestic content legislation in the United States and members of the Cambridge School in Great Britain proclaim the benefits of mutual openness over mutual closure even as they advocate mercantilist policies.[2]

The discipline of international political economy has contributed to the promotion of an imprecise analogy by transposing the preference structures of the 1980s onto interpretations of international economic disintegration during the 1930s. The central problem during the first phase of international economic disintegration during the

[2] Of course, liberal-neomercantile preferences are not *universally* held. Andre Grjebine and Jean Annais of France and Wolfgang Hager of the West German Social Democratic Party (SPD) appear to espouse protection even if such a policy were to trigger a slide toward mutual defection.

1930s was that there were no dilemmas of collective action to transcend. Key actors in each instance preferred to countenance destruction of the ancien economic regimes rather than risk what they saw as certain domestic economic immiseration by conforming to the primary norms of the regimes.

By assuming that actors during the 1930s shared mutual interests in maintaining the old regimes, contemporary international political economists have reached incorrect conclusions as to the effects of bilateralism and regionalism on the extent of economic closure. If one begins with the presumption that national interests are best served by maintaining an open international commercial and financial system and by stabilizing exchange rates, then discriminatory political exchange appears to impede realization of mutual interests. If one begins with the presumption that movement toward commercial and financial closure and devaluation of currencies relative to gold served the perceived interests of key actors, then discriminatory political exchange facilitates internalization of some, but not all, of the external costs associated with the departure from liberalism. Discrimination and political exchange were consequences, and not causes, of collapse of primary norms. As the international economic system closed, discrimination and political exchange may well have comprised a politically and economically second best alternative to the unrealizable economically first best world of openness and nondiscrimination.

Transposing Knowledge and Mislocating Mismanagement

My interpretation of the causes of international economic disintegration during the 1930s focused on the international response to contraction and devoted relatively little attention to the effects of international economic and political processes on the intensity of contraction. I treated contraction as a largely exogenous event because the fundamental causes of contraction appear to lie largely below and beyond the level of international politics.

First, the depression was intensified by inappropriate *domestic* policies that fostered neither national nor international recovery. With the benefit of fifty years of hindsight and economic wisdom, imperfect though our understanding of macroeconomics may be, it appears that changes in domestic economic policies could have moderated the depression in 1930 and 1931. Keynesians point to the error of striving to balance budgets in the face of a downward spiral of aggregate demand, and note that recovery followed from the inability of governments to follow their declaratory fiscal policies. Monetarists point to the error of adhering to a restrictive monetary policy even as withdrawals of funds from banks, conversions of currency into gold, bank failures, and the collapse of credit sharply reduced money supply. Recovery in the United States followed from changes in monetary policy and banking regulations implemented during the early days of the Roosevelt administration. If the Keynesian interpretation is correct, then a stimulative fiscal policy could have contained the recession in America in 1930. Such a policy was neither encouraged nor discouraged by existing international economic arrangements, and had a stimulative fiscal policy been adopted, the international spiral of falling aggregate demand might have been contained. If the monetarist interpretation is correct, then expansion of the money supply could have contained the recession in 1930. Although President Hoover believed that a loose money policy would have undermined international monetary stability, such a policy would have eased the Central European financial crisis of 1931 and alleviated pressure on the sterling-dollar rate. Under either interpretation, proper domestic and international policy would have been synonymous. The American failure to adopt a stimulative fiscal or expansive monetary policy in 1930 is the key to explaining domestic and international contraction. This failure is a product of what we see with hindsight as economic ignorance, not as a consequence of international political process.

Second, the depression was exacerbated by the intrinsic fragility of the international monetary and financial systems that evolved during the 1920s. The domestic economic policies excoriated above imposed substantial stresses on the gold exchange standard and the two cycles of international finance. To venture into the realm of the counterfactual, a benign hegemon committed to international leadership but believing in the fiscal and monetary orthodoxy of the period would not have forestalled collapse. In retrospect, the central policy errors appear to fall more into the category of "beggar thyself and thy neighbor" than "help thyself and beggar thy neighbor." The transposition of contemporary economic knowledge leads to the mislocation of mismanagement.

Although differences in macroeconomic circumstance, economic ideology, and the structure of international economic relations undercut the validity of the analogy between the 1930s and the 1980s, the difficult problem of managing externalities during the present may be rendered somewhat more tractable by the continuing hold of the inappropriate analogy. The single most consequential difference between the periods is the existence of the analogy between the periods. The specter of disastrous disintegration of the international economic system brought about by the mindless and short-sighted pursuit of narrow national interests provides a powerful spur to multilateral cooperation. The fable of the 1930s may be spurious. The moral is not.

BIBLIOGRAPHY

JOURNAL ARTICLES, BOOK CHAPTERS, AND PAPERS

Alt, James, and Barry Eichengreen. "Simultaneous and Overlapping Games." Paper presented at the NBER Conference on Political Economy of International Macroeconomic Coordination, Andover, Mass., November 6–7, 1987.

Axelrod, Robert. "Comment on How Should the United States Respond to Other Countries' Trade Policies?" In *U.S. Trade Politics in a Changing World Economy*, edited by Robert M. Stern. (Cambridge: MIT Press, 1987).

———. "The Emergence of Cooperation Among Egotists." *American Political Science Review* 75 (June 1981).

Barbone, Luca. "Import Barriers: An Analysis of Time-Series Cross-Section Data," *OECD Economic Studies* no. 11 (Autumn 1988).

Bayard, Thomas O., and Kimberly Ann Elliott. "Reciprocity and Retaliation in Financial Services: The Shumer Amendment and the Second Banking Directive." Paper presented to the American Economics Association Annual Convention, Washington, D.C., January 1991.

Branson, William H. "Causes of Appreciation and Volatility of the Dollar." In *The U.S. Dollar—Recent Developments, Outlook, and Policy Options* (Kansas City: Federal Reserve Bank of Kansas City, 1985).

Brown, E. Cary. "Fiscal Policy in the 'Thirties,' a Reappraisal." *American Economic Review* 46 (December 1946).

Coase, Ronald. "The Problem of Social Cost." *Journal of Law and Economics* 3 (Autumn 1960).

Conybeare, John A. C. "International Organizations and the Theory of Property Rights." *International Organization* 34 (Summer 1980).

Cooper, Richard N. "International Cooperation in Public Health as a Prologue to Macroeconomic Cooperation." In *Can Nations Agree: Issues in International Economic Cooperation*, edited by Cooper et al. (Washington, D.C.: Brookings, 1989).

Deardorff, Alan V., and Robert M. Stern. "Current Issues in Trade Policy: An Overview." In *U.S. Trade Policies in a Changing World Economy*, edited by Robert M. Stern. (Cambridge: MIT Press, 1987).

Diebold, William. "The New Bilateralism?" In *Bilateralism, Multilateralism and Canada in U.S. Trade Policy*, edited by William Diebold. (Cambridge: Ballinger, 1988).

Downs, George, David Rocke, and Randolph Siverson. "Cooperation and Arms Races." In *Cooperation under Anarchy*, edited by Kenneth A. Oye. (Princeton, N.J.: Princeton University Press, 1986).

Edwards, Sebastian. "Structural Adjustment Policies in Highly Indebted Countries." In *Developing Country Debt and Economic Performance*, edited by Jeffrey Sachs. (Chicago: University of Chicago Press, 1989).

Eichengreen, Barry. "Protection, Real Wage Assistance, and Employment." International Financial Discussion Paper no. 150, Washington, D.C.: Federal Reserve Board of Governors, 1979.

Feinberg, Richard E. "The Changing Relationship between the World Bank and the IMF." International Organization 42, no. 3 (Summer 1988).

Finlayson, Jock A., and Mark W. Zacher. "The GATT and the Regulation of Trade Barriers: Regime Dynamics and Functions." In International Regimes, edited by Stephen D. Krasner. (Ithaca, N.Y.: Cornell University Press, 1983).

Fishlow, Albert. "Lessons from the Past: Capital Markets During the 19th Century and Interwar Period." International Organization 39 (Summer 1985).

George, Alexander. "The Operational Code: A Neglected Approach to the Study of Political Leaders and Decision-making." International Studies Quarterly 13 (June 1969).

Gowa, Joanne. "Rational Hegemons, Excludable Goods, and Small Groups: An Epitaph for Hegemonic Stability Theory?" World Politics 61, no. 3 (April 1989).

Haas, Ernst. "Why Collaborate? Issue Linkage and International Regimes." World Politics 32 (April 1980).

Hamada, Koichi, and Hugh T. Patrick. "Japan and the International Monetary Regime," in The Political Economy of Japan: The Changing International Context, edited by Takashi Inoguchi and Daniel Okimoto (Stanford: Stanford University Press, 1988).

Hirsch, Fred. "The Bagehot Problem." Manchester School, 1977.

Holsti, Ole. "The Operational Code Approach to the Study of Political Leaders: John Foster Dulles' Philosophical and Instrumental Beliefs." Canadian Journal of Political Science 3 (March 1970).

Howson, Susan. "The Management of Sterling." Journal of Economic History 40 (March 1980).

Jervis, Robert. "Cooperation Under the Security Dilemma." World Politics 30 (January 1978).

Keohane, Robert O. "Demand for International Regimes." International Organization 65 (Spring 1982).

———. "The Theory of Hegemonic Stability and Changes in International Regimes, 1967–1977." In Change in the International System, edited by Ole Holsti, Randolph Siverson, and Alexander George. (Boulder, Colo.: Westview, 1980).

Kindleberger, Charles P. "Dominance and Leadership in the International Economy: Exploitation, Public Goods, and Free Rides." International Studies Quarterly 25 (June 1981).

Krasner, Stephen D. "Are Bureaucracies Important?" Foreign Policy 7 (Summer 1972).

———. "States Power and the Structure of Foreign Trades." World Politics 28 (April 1976).

———. "The Tokyo Round: Particularistic Interests and Prospects for Stability in the Global Trading System." *International Studies Quarterly* 23 (December 1979).

Krugman, Paul. "Private Capital Flows to Problem Debtors." In *Developing Country Debt and Economic Performance: The International Financial System*, edited by Jeffrey Sachs. (Chicago: University of Chicago Press, 1989).

Magee, Stephen P., and Leslie Young. "Endogenous Protection in the United States, 1900–1984." In *U.S. Trade Policies in a Changing World Economy*, edited by Robert M. Stern. (Cambridge: MIT Press, 1987).

Marwell, G., and R. Ames. "Experiments on the Provision of Public Goods: Resources, Interests, Group Size, and the Free Rider Problem." *American Journal of Sociology* 84 (1979).

———. "Experiments on the Provision of Public Goods: Provision Points, Stakes, Experience, and the Free Rider Problem." *American Journal of Sociology* 85 (1980).

McKeown, Timothy. "Hegemonic Stability Theory and 19th Century Tariff Levels in Europe, Group Size, and the Free Rider Problem." *International Organization* 37 (Winter 1983).

———. "Tariffs and Hegemonic Stability." *International Organization* 37 (Winter 1983).

Moravcsik, Andrew M. "Disciplining Trade Finance: The OECD Export Credit Agreement." *International Organization* 43 (Winter 1989).

Nau, Henry. "Where Reaganomics Works." *Foreign Policy* 57 (Winter 1984–85).

Nichols, Jeannette P. "Roosevelt's Monetary Diplomacy, 1933." *American Historical Review* 55 (January 1951).

Nozick, Robert. "Coercion." In *Philosophy, Science, and Method: Essays in Honor of Ernest Nagel*, edited by Sidney Morgenbesser, Patrick Suppes, and Morton White. (New York: St. Martins, 1969).

Okimoto, Daniel I. "Political Inclusivity: The Domestic Structure of Trade." In *The Political Economy of Japan: The Changing International Context*, edited by Takashi Inoguchi and Daniel I. Okimoto. (Stanford: Stanford University Press, 1988).

Olson, Mancur, and Richard Zeckhauser. "An Economic Theory of Alliances." *Review of Economics and Statistics* 48 (August 1966).

Oye, Kenneth A. "Constrained Confidence and the Evolution of Reagan Foreign Policy." In *Eagle Resurgent? The Reagan Era in American Foreign Policy*, edited by Kenneth A. Oye, Robert Lieber, and Donald Rothchild. (Boston: Little Brown, 1987).

———. "The Domain of Choice: International Constraints and Carter Administration Foreign Policy." In *Eagle Entangled: United States Foreign Policy in a Complex World*, edited by Kenneth A. Oye, Donald Rothchild, and Robert Lieber. (New York and London: Longman, 1979).

———. "Explaining Cooperation under Anarchy." In *Cooperation under Anarchy*, edited by Kenneth A. Oye. (Princeton, N.J.: Princeton University Press, 1986).

———. "On Underprovision of Compensation: Some Implications of Incomplete Information and Fragmented Actors." APSA Conventional Panel 26-2, September 3, 1988.

Putnam, Robert D., and C. Randall Henning. "The Bonn Summit of 1978: A Case Study in Coordination." In *Can Nations Agree? Issues in International Economic Cooperation*, edited by Richard Cooper et al. (Washington, D.C.: Brookings, 1989).

———. "Diplomacy and Domestic Politics: The Logic of Two-Level Games." *International Organization* 42, no. 3 (Summer 1988).

Rhodes, Carolyn. "Reciprocity in Trade: The Utility of a Bargaining Strategy." *International Organization* 43 no. 2 (Spring 1989).

Rosen, Howard F. "The US-Israel Free Trade Area Agreement: How Well Is It Working and What Have We Learned?" In *Free Trade Areas and US Trade Policy*, edited by Jeffrey J. Schott. (Washington, D.C.: Institute of International Economics, 1989).

Ruggie, John Gerard. "International Regimes, Transactions, and Change: Embedded Liberalism in the Postwar Economic Order." In *International Regimes*, edited by Stephen D. Krasner. (Ithaca, N.Y.: Cornell University Press, 1983).

Sachs, Jeffrey. "Introduction." In *Developing Country Debt and Economic Performance: The International Financial System*, edited by Jeffrey Sachs. (Chicago: University of Chicago Press, 1989).

Sandholtz, Wayne, and John Zysman. "1992: Recasting the European Bargain." *World Politics* 42, no. 1 (October 1989).

Savage, Richard I., and Karl W. Deutsch. "A Statistical Model of the Gross Analysis of Transaction Flows." *Economica* 28 (1960).

Schank, Roger. "Conceptualization Underlying Natural Language." In *Computer Models of Thought and Language*, edited by Kenneth Colby and Roger Schank. (San Francisco: W. H. Freeman, 1973).

Sebenius, James. "Negotiation Arithmetic." *International Organization* 37 (Spring 1983).

Sen, Amartya. "Behavior and the Concept of Preference." *Economica* 40 (August 1973).

Snidal, Duncan. "The Limits of Hegemonic Stability Theory." *International Organization* 39 (Autumn 1985).

Stassen, Glenn H. "Senatorial Responses to Secretaries Acheson and Dulles." *World Politics* 25 (October 1972).

Stein, Arthur. "The Politics of Linkage." *World Politics* 33 (October 1980).

Strange, Susan. "The Management of Surplus Capacity: Or How Does Theory Stand Up to Protectionism 1970s Style?" *International Organization* 33 (Summer 1979).

Sugden, Robert. "Reciprocity: The Supply of Public Goods through Voluntary Contributions." *Economic Journal* 94 (December 1984).

Tollison, Robert D., and Thomas D. Willett. "An Economic Theory of Mutually Advantageous Issue Linkage in International Negotiations." *International Organization* 33 (Autumn 1979).

Williams, David, "The 1931 Financial Crisis." *Yorkshire Bulletin of Economic and Social Research* (15 November 1963a).

Winham, Gilbert. "Why Canada Acted." In *Bilateralism, Multilateralism, and Canada in U.S. Trade Policy*, edited by William Diebold. (Cambridge: Ballinger, 1988).

Books and Monographs

Aggarwal, Vinod K. *Liberal Protectionism: The International Politics of Organized Textile Trade.* Berkeley: University of California Press, 1985.

Angell, James W. *Financial Foreign Policy of the United States.* New York: Council on Foreign Relations, 1933.

Axelrod, Robert. *The Evolution of Cooperation.* Ann Arbor, Mich.: Institute of Public Policy Studies, 1982.

————, ed. *Structure of Decision: The Cognitive Maps of Political Elites.* Princeton, N.J.: Princeton University Press, 1976.

Robert E. Baldwin. *The Political Economy of U.S. Import Policy.* Cambridge: MIT Press, 1985.

Beckett, Grace. *The Reciprocal Trade Agreements Program.* New York: Columbia University Press, 1941.

Bidwell, Percy W. *The Invisible Tariff: A Study of the Control of Imports into the United States.* New York: Council on Foreign Relations, 1939.

————. *Tariff Policy of the United States: A Study of Recent Experience.* New York: Council on Foreign Relations, 1933.

Brown, William Adams Jr. *The International Gold Standard Reinterpreted 1914–1934.* 2 vols. New York: National Bureau of Economic Research, 1940.

Carr, Edward Hallett. *The Twenty Years Crisis, 1919–1939.* New York: Harper & Row, 1964.

Child, Frank. *The Theory and Practice of Exchange Controls.* The Hague: Nijhoff, 1958.

Clarke, Stephen V.O. *Central Bank Cooperation: 1924–31.* New York: Federal Reserve Bank of New York, 1967.

————. *Exchange Rate Stabilization in the Mid-1930s: Negotiating the Tripartite Agreement.* Princeton Studies in International Finance, no. 41. Princeton, N.J.: International Finance Section, 1977.

————. *The Reconstruction of the International Monetary System: The Attempts of 1922 and 1933.* Princeton Studies in International Finance, no. 33. Princeton, N.J.: International Finance Section, 1973.

Clay, Henry. *Lord Norman.* London: Macmillan, 1957.

Cline, William R. *Reciprocity: A New Approach to World Trade Policy.* Washington, D.C.: Institute of International Economics, 1982.

Cohen, Benjamin J. *Developing Country Debt: A Middle Way.* Essays in International Finance, no. 173, May 1989.

Colby, Kenneth, and Roger Schank. *Computer Models of Thought and Language.* San Francisco: W. H. Freeman, 1973.

Condliffe, J. B. *The Reconstruction of World Trade.* New York: W. W. Norton & Co., 1940.

Conybeare, John A. C. *Trade Wars: The Theory and Practice of International Commercial Rivalry.* New York: Columbia University Press, 1987.

Culbertson, William S. *Reciprocity: A National Policy for Foreign Trade.* New York: Whittlesey House, 1937.

Dallek, Robert. *Franklin D. Roosevelt and American Foreign Policy, 1932–1945.* New York: Oxford University Press, 1979.

Davis, Joseph S. *The World Between the Wars, 1919–1939: An Economist's View.* Baltimore, Md.: Johns Hopkins University Press, 1975.

Destler, I. M., John S. Odell, and Kimberly Ann Elliott. *Anti-Protection: Changing Forces in United States Trade Politics.* Washington, D.C.: Institute of International Economics, 1987.

Diebold, William, ed. *Bilateralism, Multilateralism and Canada in U.S. Trade Policy.* Cambridge: Ballinger, 1988.

Drummond, Ian M. *British Economic Policy and the Empire, 1919–1939.* London: Allen and Unwin, 1972.

———. *The Floating Pound and the Sterling Area.* Cambridge: Cambridge University Press, 1981.

———. *London, Washington, and the Management of the Franc, 1936–39.* Princeton Studies in International Finance, no. 45. Princeton: International Finance Section, 1979.

Drummond, Ian M., and Norman Hillmer. *Negotiating Freer Trade: The United Kingdom, the United States, Canada, and the Trade Agreements of 1938.* Waterloo, Ont.: Wilfrid Laurier University Press, 1989.

Dulles, Eleanor Lansing. *The Bank for International Settlements at Work.* New York: Macmillan, 1932.

Economic Consequences of the League: The World Economic Conference. London: Europa Publishing Company, 1934.

Einzig, Paul. *The Bank for International Settlements.* London: Macmillan, 1930.

Eichengreen, Barry. *Behind the Scenes of International Finance.* London: Macmillan, 1931.

Eichengreen, Barry, and Alec Cairncross. *Sterling in Decline.* Oxford: Oxford University Press, 1984.

Ellis, Howard S. *Exchange Control in Central Europe.* Cambridge: Harvard University Press, 1941.

Feis, Herbert. *1933: Characters in Crisis.* Boston: Little, Brown & Co., 1966.

Fetter, Frank Whitson. *The New Deal and Tariff Policy.* Public Policy Pamphlet no. 7. Chicago: University of Chicago Press, 1933.

Feinberg, Richard E. *Subsidizing Success: The Export-Import Bank in the U.S. Economy.* Cambridge: Cambridge University Press, 1982.

Frankel, Jeffrey A. *Obstacles to International Macroeconomic Policy Coordination.* Princeton Studies in International Finance, no. 64, December 1988.

Frolich, Norman, Joe A. Oppenheimer, and Oran R. Young. *Political Leadership and Collective Goods.* Princeton, N.J.: Princeton University Press, 1971.

Friedman, Milton, and Anna Jacobson Schwartz. *From New Deal Banking Reform to World War II Inflation.* Princeton, N.J.: Princeton University Press, 1980.

————. *The Great Contraction: 1929–1933*. Princeton, N.J.: Princeton University Press, 1965.

Funabashi, Yoichi. *Managing the Dollar: From the Plaza to the Louvre*. Washington, D.C.: Institute of International Economics, 1988.

Fusfeld, Daniel R. *The Economic Thought of Franklin D. Roosevelt and the Origins of the New Deal*. New York: Columbia University Press, 1956.

Gamson, William A., and Andre Modigliani. *Untangling the Cold War*. Boston: Little, Brown & Co., 1971.

Gardner, Lloyd C. *Economic Aspects of New Deal Diplomacy*. Boston: Beacon Press, 1964.

Gardner, Richard. *Sterling-Dollar Diplomacy in Current Perspective*. New York: Columbia University Press, 1980.

Gayer, Arthur D., and Carl T. Schmidt, ed. *American Economic Foreign Policy: Postwar History, Analysis, and Interpretation*. United States Memorandum, no. 6. New York: American Coordinating Committee for International Studies, 1939.

Gerould, James Thayer, and Laura Shearer Turnbull. *Interallied Debts and Revision of the Debt Settlements*. New York: H. W. Wilson, 1928.

Gilbert, Milton. *Currency Depreciation 1929–1935*. Philadelphia: University of Pennsylvania Press, 1939.

Gilpin, Robert. *U.S. Power and the Multinational Corporation*. New York: Basic Books, 1975.

————. *War & Change in World Politics*. Cambridge: Cambridge University Press, 1981.

Gordon, Margaret S. *Barriers to World Trade: A Study of Recent Commercial Policy*. New York: Macmillan, 1941.

Gourevitch, Peter. *Politics in Hard Times: Comparative Responses to International Economic Crises*. Ithaca, N.Y.: Cornell University Press, 1986.

Graham, Frank D., and Charles R. Whittlesey. *Golden Avalanche*. Princeton, N.J.: Princeton University Press, 1939.

Guillebaud, C. W. *The Economic Recovery of Germany: From 1933 to the Incorporation of Austria in March 1938*. London: Macmillan, 1939.

Haberler, Gottfried. *Prosperity and Depression: A Theoretical Analysis of Cyclical Movements*. Lake Success: United Nations, 1946.

————. *The World Economy, Money, and the Great Depression 1919–1939*. Washington, D.C.: American Enterprise Institute, 1976.

Hardin, Russell. *Collective Action*. Baltimore, Md.: Johns Hopkins University Press, 1982

Harris, C.R.S. *Germany's Foreign Indebtedness*. London: Oxford University Press, 1935.

Hawley, Ellis W. *The New Deal and the Problem of Monopoly: A Study in Economic Ambivalence*. Princeton, N.J.: Princeton University Press, 1966.

Heilperin, Michael A. *The Trades of Nations*. New York: Alfred A. Knopf, 1947.

Heuser, Heinrich. *Control of International Trade*. London: George Routledge & Sons, 1939.

Hieronymi, Otto. *Economic Discrimination Against the United States in Western Europe 1945–1958: Dollar Shortage and the Rise of Regionalism.* Geneva: Librairie Droz, 1973.

Hirschman, Albert O. *National Power and the Structure of Foreign Trade.* Berkeley: University of California Press, 1969.

Hirst, Francis W. *Wall Street and Lombard Street: The Stock Exchange Slump of 1929 and the Trades Depression of 1930.* New York: Macmillan, 1931.

Hodson, H. V. *Slump and Recovery 1929–1937: A Survey of World Economic Affairs.* London: Oxford University Press, 1938.

Holsti, Ole, Randolph Siverson, and Alexander George. *Change in the International System.* Boulder, Colo.: Westview, 1980.

Hoover, Herbert. *The Memoirs of Herbert Hoover: The Great Depression 1929–1941.* New York: Macmillan, 1952.

———. *The State Papers and Other Public Writings of Herbert Hoover.* 2 vols. Garden City, N.Y.: Doubleday, Doran & Company, 1934.

Inoguchi, Takashi, and Daniel I. Okimoto, eds. *The Political Economy of Japan: The Changing International Context.* Stanford: Stanford University Press, 1988.

International Monetary Fund, *Annual Report 1988.* Washington, D.C.: IMF, 1988.

Jervis, Robert. *Perception and Misperception in International Politics.* Princeton, N.J.: Princeton University Press, 1976.

Jones, Joseph M. *Tariff Retaliation: Repercussions of the Hawley-Smoot Bill.* Philadelphia: University of Pennsylvania Press, 1934.

Kahler, Miles, ed. *The Politics of International Debt.* Ithaca, N.Y.: Cornell University Press, 1984.

Katzenstein, Peter J. *Small States in World Markets: Industrial Policy in Europe.* Ithaca, N.Y.: Cornell University Press, 1985.

Kreider, Carl. *The Anglo-American Trade Agreement: A Study of British and American Commercial Policies, 1934–1939.* Princeton, N.J.: Princeton University Press, 1943.

Kindleberger, Charles P. *Power and Money: The Economics of International Politics and the Politics of International Economics.* New York: Basic Books, 1970.

———. *The World in Depression: 1929–1939.* Berkeley: University of California Press, 1973. Revised and expanded edition 1986.

Keohane, Robert O. *After Hegemony: Cooperation and Discord in the World Economy.* Princeton, N.J.: Princeton University Press, 1984.

Keohane, Robert O., and Joseph S. Nye. *Power and Interdependence: World Politics in Transition.* Boston: Little, Brown, & Co., 1977.

Krasner, Stephen D. *Defending the National Interest: Raw Materials Investments and U.S. Foreign Policy.* Princeton, N.J.: Princeton University Press, 1978.

———, ed. *International Regimes.* Ithaca, N.Y.: Cornell University Press, 1983.

Kunz, Diane. *Battle for Britain's Gold Standard in 1931.* London: Croom-Helm, 1987.

Lasswell, Harold D., and Abraham Kaplan. *Power and Society: A Framework for Political Inquiry.* New Haven, Conn.: Yale University Press, 1950.

Leith-Ross, Frederick. *Money Talks: Fifty Years of International Finance.* London: Hutchinson, 1968.

Lekachman, Robert. *The Age of Keynes.* New York: McGraw-Hill, 1966.

League of Nations. *Balances of Payments 1930.* Geneva: League of Nations, 1932. Also reports for 1931, 1932, 1933, 1934, 1935, and 1936.

———. *Commercial Banks: 1925–1933.* Geneva: League of Nations, 1934.

———. *The Courses and Phases of the World Depression.* Geneva: League of Nations, 1931.

———. *International Currency Experience: Lessons of the Interwar Period.* Geneva: League of Nations, 1944.

———. *International Trade Statistics 1930.* Geneva: League of Nations, 1932.

———. *Review of World Trade 1930.* Geneva: League of Nations, 1931. Also reviews for 1931, 1932, 1933, 1934, 1935, and 1936.

———. *World Economic Survey 1931–32.* Geneva: League of Nations, 1932. Also surveys for 1932–33, 1933–34, and 1934–35.

———. *World Production and Prices 1925–1933.* Geneva: League of Nations, 1934.

Lieberman, Sima. *The Economic and Political Roots of the New Protectionism.* Totowa, N.J.: Rowman and Littlefield, 1988.

Madden, John T., Marcus Nadler, and Harry C. Sauvain. *America's Experience as a Creditor Nation.* New York: Prentice-Hall, 1937.

Maswood, Syed Javed. *Japan and Protection: The Growth of Protectionist Sentiment and the Japanese Response.* New York: Routledge, 1989.

McGuire, E. B. *The British Tariff System.* London: Methuen & Co., 1939.

Milner, Helen V. *Resisting Protectionism: Global Industries and the Politics of International Trade.* Princeton, N.J.: Princeton University Press, 1988.

Moley, Raymond. *After Seven Years.* New York: Harper & Brothers, 1939.

Morgenbesser, Sidney, Patrick Suppes, and Morton White, eds. *Philosophy, Science, and Method: Essays in Honor of Ernest Nagel.* New York: St. Martins, 1969.

Morton, Walter A. *British Finance 1930–1940.* Madison: The University of Wisconsin Press, 1943.

Mowat, Charles Loch. *Britain Between the Wars: 1918–1940.* Chicago: The University of Chicago Press, 1955.

Myers, William Starr, and Walter H. Newton. *The Hoover Administration: A Documented Narrative.* New York: Charles Scribner's Sons, 1936.

Nogaro, Bertrand. *La Crise Economique dans le Monde et en France.* Paris: Libraire Generale de Droit et de Jurisprudence, 1936.

Olson, Mancur, Jr. *The Logic of Collective Action: Public Goods and the Theory of Groups.* Cambridge: Harvard University Press, 1965.

Oye, Kenneth A., ed. *Cooperation under Anarchy.* Princeton, N.J.: Princeton University Press, 1986.

Oye, Kenneth A., Donald Rothchild, and Robert Lieber, eds. *Eagle Entangled: United States Foreign Policy in a Complex World.* New York and London: Longman, 1979.

Oye, Kenneth A., *Eagle Resurgent? The Reagan Era in American Foreign Policy*. Boston: Little, Brown, & Co., 1987.

Pastor, Robert A. *Congress and the Politics of U.S. Foreign Economic Policy: 1929–1976*. Berkeley: University of California Press, 1980.

Patterson, Gardner. *Discrimination in International Trade: The Policy Issues 1945–1965*. Princeton, N.J.: Princeton University Press, 1966.

Pearson, James Constantine. *The Reciprocal Trade Agreements Program: The Policy of the United States and Its Effectiveness*. Washington, D.C.: Catholic University of America Press, 1942.

Peek, George N. *Why Quit Our Own*. New York: Van Nostrand, 1936.

Pollard, Robert. *Economic Security and the Origins of the Cold War*. New York: Columbia University Press, 1985.

Pomfret, Richard. *Unequal Trade: The Economics of Discriminatory International Trade Policies*. London: Basil Blackwell, 1988.

Putnam, Robert D., and Nicholas Bayne. *Hanging Together: The Seven-Power Summits*. Cambridge: Harvard University Press, 1984.

Richardson, J. Henry. *British Economic Foreign Policy*. New York: Macmillan, 1936.

Rieffel, Alexis. *The Role of the Paris Club in Managing Debt Problems*. Essays in International Finance, no. 161, December 1985.

Robbins, Lionel. *The Great Depression*. London: Macmillan, 1935.

Roosevelt, Franklin D. *Franklin D. Roosevelt and Foreign Affairs*. 3 vols. Cambridge: Belknap Press, 1969.

———. *The Public Papers and Addresses of Franklin D. Roosevelt*. 4 vols. New York: Random House, 1938.

Rowland, Benjamin, ed. *Balance of Power or Hegemony: The Interwar Monetary System*. New York: New York University Press, 1976.

Royal Institute of International Affairs. *The International Gold Problem*. London: Oxford University Press, 1931.

Sachs, Jeffrey, ed. *Developing Country Debt and Economic Performance: The International Financial System*. Chicago: University of Chicago Press, 1989.

Salter, James Arthur. *Memoirs of a Public Servant*. London: Faber and Faber, 1961.

Sandler, Todd M., William Loehr, and Jon T. Cauley. *The Political Economy of Public Goods and International Cooperation*. Monograph Series in World Affairs, vol. 15. Denver, Colo.: University of Denver Graduate School of International Studies, 1978.

Sayers, R. S. *The Bank of England: 1891–1944*. vols. 1, 2, and Appendix. Cambridge: Cambridge University Press, 1976.

Schacht, Hjalmar H. *Confessions of the Old Wizard: The Autobiography of Hjalmar Horace Greeley Schacht*. Westport, Conn.: Greenwood Press, 1974.

Schattschneider, E. E. *Politics, Pressures, and the Tariff: A Study of Free Private Enterprise in Pressure Politics as Shown in the 1929–1930 Revision of the Tariff*. New York: Prentice-Hall, 1935.

Schelling, Thomas C. *Micromotives and Macrobehavior*. New York: W. W. Norton, 1978.

———. *The Strategy of Conflict*. Cambridge: Harvard University Press, 1960.

Schlesinger, Arthur M., Jr. *The Coming of the New Deal*. Boston: Houghton Mifflin, 1959.

———. *The Politics of Upheaval*. Boston: Houghton Mifflin, 1960.

Schott, Jeffrey J., ed. *Free Trade Areas and US Trade Policy*. Washington, D.C.: Institute of International Economics, 1989.

Schott, Jeffrey J., and Murray G. Smith, eds. *The Canada-United States Free Trade Agreement: The Global Impact*. Washington, D.C.: Institute for International Economics, 1988.

Schuker, Stephen. *American Reparations to Germany 1919–33: Implications for the Third-World Debt Crisis*. Princeton Studies in International Finance, no. 61, July 1988.

Simon, Herbert. *The Sciences of the Artificial*. Cambridge: MIT Press, 1969.

Snyder, Glenn H., and Paul Diesing. *Conflict Among Nations: Bargaining, Decision Making and System Structure in International Crises*. Princeton, N.J.: Princeton University Press, 1977.

Stern, Robert M., ed. *U.S. Trade Policies in a Changing World Economy*. Cambridge: MIT Press, 1987.

Tasca, Henry J. *The Reciprocal Trade Policy of the United States: A Study in Trade Philosophy*. Philadelphia: University of Pennsylvania Press, 1938.

Thorbecke, Erik. *The Tendency Towards Regionalization in International Trade 1928–1956*. Hague: Martinus Nijhoff, 1960.

Triffin, Robert. *Gold and the Dollar Crisis*. New Haven, Conn.: Yale University Press, 1961.

Tugwell, Rexford. *In Search of Roosevelt*. Cambridge: Harvard University Press, 1972.

U.S. Congress, House. Committee on Ways and Means. *Hearings on Extension of Reciprocal Trade Agreements Act*. 76th Cong., 3d sess., 1940. 3 vols.

———. *Hearings on Reciprocal Trade Agreements*. 73rd Cong., 2d sess., 1934.

———. *Hearings on Tariff Readjustment—1929*. 70th Cong., 2d sess., 1929. 3 vols.

U.S. Congress. Senate. Committee on Finance. *Hearings on Reciprocal Trade Agreements*. 73rd Cong., 2d sess., 1934.

Waight, Leonard. *The History and Mechanism of the Exchange Equalization Account*. Cambridge: Cambridge University Press, 1939.

Warburg, James P. *The Long Road Home*. Garden City, N.Y.: Doubleday, 1964.

Warren, George F., and Frank A. Pearson. *Gold and Prices*. New York: John Wiley & Sons, 1935.

Warren, Harris Gaylord. *Herbert Hoover and the Great Depression*. New York: Oxford University Press, 1959.

Wee, Herman Van Der. *The Great Depression Revisited: Essays on Economics of the Thirties*. Hague: Martinus Nijhoff, 1972.

Whalley, Richard. *Trade Liberalization Among Major World Trading Areas*. Cambridge: MIT Press, 1985.

Whittlesey, Charles R. *International Monetary Issues*. New York: McGraw-Hill, 1937.

Winham, Gilbert R. *International Trade and the Tokyo Round*. Princeton, N.J.: Princeton University Press, 1985, 60.

Wolfe, Martin. *The French Franc Between the Wars*. New York: Columbia University Press, 1951.

Yeager, Leland B. *International Monetary Relations*. New York: Harper & Row, 1966.

INDEX